DO MORALS MATTER?

JOSEPH S. NYE, JR.

DO MORALS MATTER?

Presidents and Foreign Policy from
FDR to Trump

OXFORD
UNIVERSITY PRESS

OXFORD
UNIVERSITY PRESS

Oxford University Press is a department of the University of Oxford. It furthers
the University's objective of excellence in research, scholarship, and education
by publishing worldwide. Oxford is a registered trade mark of Oxford University
Press in the UK and certain other countries.

Published in the United States of America by Oxford University Press
198 Madison Avenue, New York, NY 10016, United States of America.

First issued as an Oxford University Press paperback 2021

Library of Congress Cataloging-in-Publication Data
Names: Nye, Joseph S., Jr., author.
Title: Do morals matter? : presidents and foreign policy from FDR to Trump /
Joseph S. Nye Jr.
Other titles: Presidents and foreign policy from FDR to Trump
Description: New York, NY : Oxford University Press, 2020.
Identifiers: LCCN 2019012366 | ISBN 9780190935962 (hardback) | ISBN 9780197586297 (paperback) |
ISBN 9780190935979 (updf) | ISBN 9780190935986 (epub)
Subjects: LCSH: United States—Foreign relations—1945-1989—Moral and
ethical aspects. | United States—Foreign relations—1989—Moral and
ethical aspects. | Presidents—Professional ethics—United States. |
Presidents—United States—Decision making. | BISAC: POLITICAL SCIENCE /
International Relations / General. | POLITICAL SCIENCE / Political Freedom
& Security / International Security.
Classification: LCC E744 .N94 2020 | DDC 327.73009/04—dc23
LC record available at https://lccn.loc.gov/2019012366

1 3 5 7 9 8 6 4 2

Printed by LSC Communications, United States of America

A haiku for Molly

We are clay turning
On the potter's wheel of life
Your love centers me

CONTENTS

PREFACE

At dinner with a group of friends, one asked what I had been doing lately. When I said I was writing a book on presidents, ethics, and foreign policy, she quipped: "It must be a very short book." Another added more seriously, "I didn't think ethics played much of a role." That conventional wisdom marks not only dinner discussions, but political analyses as well. An Internet search shows surprisingly few books on how presidents' moral views affected their foreign policies and how that affects our judgments of them.* As Michael Walzer (an important exception to the rule) described American graduate training after 1945, "Moral argument was against the rules of the discipline as it was commonly practiced, although a few writers defended interest as the new morality."[1] A survey of the top three American academic journals on international relations over fifteen years found only four articles on the subject. As one author noted, "Leading scholars . . . do not dedicate serious attention to investigating the influence of moral values on the conduct of nations."[2] It is not a career-enhancing topic for a young scholar, but has long intrigued me as an old practitioner and student of American foreign policy.

The reasons for skepticism seem obvious to many. While historians have written about American exceptionalism and moralism, diplomats and theorists like George Kennan long warned about the bad consequences of the American moralist–legalist tradition.[3] International relations is the

---

* I use "ethics" and "morals" interchangeably to refer to judgments of right and wrong. Ethics are more abstract principles of right conduct, while morals usually refer to more personal judgments that may be based on formal ethics or personal conscience.

realm of anarchy with no world government to provide order. States must provide for their own defense, and when survival is at stake, the ends justify the means. Where there is no meaningful choice there can be no ethics. As philosophers say, "Ought implies can." No one can fault you for not doing the impossible. By this logic, combining ethics and foreign policy is a category mistake, like asking if a knife sounds good rather than whether it cuts well, or whether a broom dances rather than sweeps well. By this logic, in judging a president's foreign policy we should simply ask whether it worked, not also ask whether it was moral.

While this view has some merit, it ducks hard questions by oversimplifying. The absence of world government does not mean the absence of all order. Some foreign policy issues relate to our survival as a nation, but most do not. Since World War II, the United States has been involved in several wars but none were necessary for our survival.[4] And many important foreign policy choices about human rights or climate change or Internet freedom do not involve war at all. Most foreign policy issues involve trade-offs among values that require choices, not application of a rigid formula of "raison d'etat." A cynical French official once told me, "I define good as what is good for the interests of France. Morals are irrelevant." He seemed unaware that his statement itself was a moral judgment. It is tautological or at best trivial to say that all states try to act in their national interest. The important question is how leaders choose to define and pursue that national interest under different circumstances.

What is more, whether we like it or not, Americans constantly make moral judgments about presidents and foreign policy. The advent of the Trump administration has revived interest in what is a moral foreign policy and raised it from a theoretical question to front-page news. For example, after the 2018 killing of Saudi dissident journalist Jamal Khashoggi in the Saudi Arabia consulate in Istanbul, President Trump was criticized for ignoring clear evidence of a brutal crime in order to maintain good relations with the Saudi Crown Prince. Liberals labeled Trump's statement about Khashoggi "remorselessly transactional, heedless of the facts,"[5] while conservatives editorialized that "we are aware of no President, not even such ruthless pragmatists as Richard Nixon or Lyndon Johnson, who would have written a public statement like this without so much as a grace note about America's abiding values and principles."[6] Access to oil, sales of military equipment, and regional stability are national interests, but values and principles that are attractive to others are also national interests. How can they be combined?

Unfortunately, many judgments about ethics and foreign policy are haphazard or poorly thought through, and too much of the current debate focuses on the personality of Donald Trump. As Maggie Haberman, a perceptive long-term reporter once commented to me, "Donald Trump is not unique; he is extreme." Some of his actions are not unprecedented, as we will see as we look at the record of all our presidents since the Second World War. Even more important, Americans are seldom clear about the criteria by which we judge a moral foreign policy. We praise a president like Ronald Reagan for the moral clarity of his statements as though rhetorical good intentions are sufficient in making ethical judgments. However, Woodrow Wilson and George W. Bush showed that good intentions without adequate means to achieve them can lead to ethically bad consequences, such as the failure of Wilson's Treaty of Versailles or Bush's invasion of Iraq. Or we judge a president simply on results. Some observers credit Richard Nixon for ending the Vietnam War, but he sacrificed 21,000 American lives to create a reputational "decent interval" that turned out to be an ephemeral pause on the road to defeat.

Good moral reasoning, as I argue in this book, should be three-dimensional, weighing and balancing the intentions, the means, and the consequences of presidents' decisions. A moral foreign policy is not a matter of intentions versus consequences but must involve both as well as the means that were used. Moreover, good moral reasoning must consider the consequences of general actions such as maintaining an institutional order that encourages moral interests, as well as particular newsworthy actions such as helping a human rights dissident or a persecuted group in another country. And it is important to include the ethical consequences of "nonactions," such as President Truman's willingness to accept stalemate and domestic political punishment during the Korean War rather than follow General MacArthur's recommendation to use nuclear weapons. As

Sherlock Holmes famously noted, we can learn a lot from the dogs that do not bark.

This book is not a history. I make no effort to be complete or to consult all sources in describing the ethical aspects of presidents' foreign policies since World War II. Nor do I attempt to cover the earlier centuries of American foreign policy. What I offer here is an exercise in normative thinking applied to the period since 1945 when the United States has been the most powerful country in the world—sometimes called the era of Pax Americana or the Liberal International Order. Many commentators speculate that this period is coming to an end and that new foreign policies will be necessary to meet the new challenges that I describe in the final chapter. As we debate such policies, ethics will be one part of the arguments that we will use. To pretend that ethics will play no role is as blind as to imagine that the sun will not rise tomorrow. Since we are going to use moral reasoning about foreign policy, we should learn to do it better. The analysis and scorecards developed in this book are modest steps in that direction.

ACKNOWLEDGMENTS

Thousands of people have influenced me over decades of teaching and learning—family, teachers, friends, students, colleagues. No author is an island. I have been truly blessed by the people around me. I have begged, borrowed and stolen ideas from many of them. I am grateful to all, and singling out some is difficult because I cannot hope to remember all my debts. But I must mention my late colleague Stanley Hoffmann, a liberal realist who was a pioneer in thinking about this topic as well as Robert O. Keohane and Graham T. Allison who have tutored me on many hiking and fishing excursions over the years since graduate school.

Others patiently read and commented on parts of the manuscript or talked to me about their experiences and helped to save me from some of my errors, though not all. I cannot rank or thank them properly so I merely list them alphabetically: Amitav Acharya, Nicholas Burns, Peter Feaver, Niall Ferguson, David Gergen, Alan Henrikson, Seth Johnson, Elaine Kamarck, Anne Karalekas, Nancy Koehn, Matt Kohut, Eugene Kogan, Stephen Krasner, Sean Lynn-Jones, Fredrik Logevall, Steven E. Miller, Molly Nye, Meghan O'Sullivan, Roger Porter, Susan Rice, Matthias Risse, David Sanger, Mary Sarotte, Wendy Sherman, Joshua Shifrinson, Kathryn Sikkink, Tony Smith, James Steinberg, Jake Sullivan, Alex Vuving, Calder Walton, David Welch, Arne Westad, Kenneth Winston, Philip Zelikow, Robert Zoellick. I am also grateful to the members of the Applied History Study Group at the Harvard Kennedy School who discussed an early chapter. Some people who spoke to me about recent administrations such as Brent Scowcroft are mentioned in the text or notes, but others wished to remain anonymous and the brief notes reflect their wishes.

I also have institutional debts to the Harvard Kennedy School of Government and its Belfer Center for Science and International Affairs and its Center for Public Leadership, as well as to the Hoover Institution at Stanford University for hosting me while I worked on this book. Rachel Damle helped on footnotes, Lisa MacPhee was an able assistant, and David McBride was a smart editor. But the most important support for any author is emotional, and for that I am deeply grateful to my family, and above all, to Molly who has centered my life.

Joseph S. Nye, Jr.
Lexington, Massachusetts

Introduction
American Moralism

I n his 2017 inaugural address, Donald J. Trump proclaimed that "from this day forward, it's going to be America first. America first . . . We will seek friendship and good will with the nations of the world, but we do so with the understanding that it is the right of all nations to put their own interests first."[1] That seems obvious. Leaders are trustees. We vote for them to protect our interests. But how should they define and represent our interests? How moral do we want our presidents to be in foreign policy? And what would that mean? Do we have duties beyond borders? Can we— indeed, should we—try to make the world a better place?

AMERICAN EXCEPTIONALISM

Americans have long seen our country as morally exceptional. As Theodore Roosevelt put it a century ago, "Our chief usefulness to humanity rests on combining power with high purpose."[2] Based as much on ideas as ethnicity, America has long seen itself as a cause as well as a country. Belief that one's country is exceptional is a common form of nationalist pride. For some Americans, exceptionalism represents chauvinist pride and moral superiority, but for others it simply means patriotism based on shared civic ideals combined with cooperative internationalism.[3] Barack Obama expressed this modest moralism in 2009 when he said, "I believe in American exceptionalism, just as I suspect that the Brits believe in British exceptionalism and the Greeks believe in Greek exceptionalism."[4] But some Americans criticized Obama for the modesty of his claim.

Stanley Hoffmann, a Harvard political scientist who was both French and American, once pointed out that every country likes to think of itself as unique, but France and the United States stand out in their belief that their values are universal. France, however, was limited in its ambitions by the balance of power in Europe and thus could not indulge its pursuit of universal values as much as it wished.[5] In Hoffmann's words, only the United States tried to develop foreign policies that reflect such exceptionalism and also had the leeway of power to do it.

This does not mean that Americans were more moral than other peoples—just ask Mexicans, Cubans, or Filipinos what they think of America's use of war and torture against them in the nineteenth century. But it does mean that many Americans want to believe that we are moral and a force for good in the world. Writing shortly after World War II, Hans Morgenthau, a realist with European roots, complained about this moralism in American foreign policy because it interfered with a clear analysis of power. Such moral sentimentalism, he said, was not limited to the mass public, but "rather the attachment to the advancement of particular moral values reached to the highest levels of the American government even as the United States took on the role of a superpower in the postwar world."[6] Nonetheless, the fact that the United States had a liberal political culture made a huge difference to the nature of the international order that was established after World War II. Dominant powers promote their political values. Today's world would look very different if Hitler had emerged victorious in World War II or if Stalin's Soviet Union had prevailed in the Cold

War. Of the three great ideological narratives of the twentieth century—fascism, communism, and liberalism—only the latter was left standing at its end.

American exceptionalism has several sources. A major strand is the liberal Enlightenment ideas of the founding fathers. We are a nation built on those values. As John F. Kennedy put it, "The 'magic power' on our side is the desire of every person to be free, of every nation to be independent. . . . It is because I believe our system is more in keeping with the fundamentals of human nature that I believe we are ultimately going to be successful."[7] Enlightenment liberalism valued the liberty and rights of the individual and believed such rights were universal, not merely limited to the American republic. And some contemporary political scientists argue that the core reason that the United States is widely viewed as exceptional is because of its intensely liberal character—"an ideological vision of a way of life centered upon freedom, in politics, in economics, and in society."[8]

Right from the start, however, Americans faced contradictions in implementing the values of a liberal ideology, with the inequality of slavery written into our constitution. It took more than a century after the Civil War before Congress passed the 1965 Voting Rights Act, and racism remains a major factor in American politics to this day. Americans have also differed over how to promote liberal values in foreign policy, and racism played a role in American interventions in Mexico, Haiti, and the Philippines.[9] There are different variants of liberal moral energy. For some Americans, it became an excuse for invading other countries and imposing democracy, while for others, it meant the creation of a system of international law and organization that protects domestic liberty by moderating international anarchy.[10]

Another strand of American exceptionalism lies in the religious roots in scripture about being a chosen people and in the Puritan guilt of those who fled Britain in order to worship God in a purer way in a new world. Such high aspirations led to anxieties about whether they were living up to these impossible standards. This strand is less crusading than anxious and inward. Even the founding fathers worried whether their new republic would decline in virtue like the Roman republic.[11] In the nineteenth century,

European visitors as diverse as Alexis de Tocqueville and Charles Dickens noted the American obsession about virtue, progress, and decline. But this moral concern was more inward than outward looking.

Finally, a third source of our exceptionalism arises from America's sheer size and location. Already in the nineteenth century, de Tocqueville noted America's special geographical situation. Protected by two oceans and bordered by weaker neighbors, the United States largely focused on Westward expansion in the nineteenth century, and tried to avoid entanglement in the global balance of power that was centered in Europe. But as the United States became the world's largest economy at the beginning of the twentieth century, it began to think in terms of global power.[12] As we have seen, the largest power has both more leeway and more opportunity to indulge itself, for good and for ill. The largest country also has the incentive and capability to take the lead in the creation of global public goods from which all can benefit and the freedom to define its national interest in broad ways that include such goods as an open international trading system, freedom of the seas and other commons, and development of international institutions. Size creates an important realist basis for American exceptionalism, but puritanism and especially liberalism provide the moral energy. Early in the twentieth century, President Woodrow Wilson made an important effort to combine American liberal values with our new great power status.

WILSONIAN LIBERALISM

Isolationism was our nineteenth-century policy toward the global balance of power. The relatively weak American republic could be imperialistic toward its small neighbors, but had to follow a cautious realist policy toward the global balance of power in Europe. The Monroe Doctrine asserted the separation of the Western Hemisphere from the European balance, but the United States was able to maintain its assertion only because it coincided with British interests and the control of the seas by the Royal Navy.

However, as American power grew, our options increased. An important turning point was in 1917 when Wilson broke with tradition and sent two million Americans to fight in Europe. Like other American leaders early in the twentieth century, Wilson considered himself an idealist.* His idea of an international league for peace started as a European concept, but as a leading American professor and college president, he adapted the European liberal ideas and synthesized them into what he considered a more moral American approach that became a major factor in American foreign policy.

Wilson understood the concept of a balance of power, but he regarded it as immoral because it cut up weak nations like cheeses for the convenience of great powers, as Poland had been divided among Russia, Prussia, and Austria in the eighteenth century. Wilson believed that a league of nations based on a collective security pact against aggressors would be more peaceful and just than the cynical alliances required to balance power. Wilson saw America's mission in World War I not as material aggrandizement but as leading all nations into a new international community organized to achieve right ends.[13] He called the United States an "associate" rather than an ally of the victorious powers. Wilson argued that this was the only kind of peace that would prove acceptable to the American people in the short run and to the moral opinion of the world in the long run.

Where Wilson succeeded was not as a foreign policy leader, but as what we now call a "thought leader." In 1919 when he was idolized both at home and abroad, and again decades later, he became a symbol of a new moral type of international relations. Wilson's ideas for international organization were not implemented by his countrymen for more than two decades. Nonetheless, Wilson strongly affected Franklin Roosevelt and Harry Truman, who launched the liberal international order that prevailed after 1945. Both men considered themselves Wilsonians, and the United Nations, which restricts the grounds on which nations can go to war, is a descendant of Wilson's League of Nations.

---

* Wilson was a liberal idealist, but he did not practice universal human rights. As a Southerner he shared the racial prejudices as well as the prevailing Anglo-Saxon chauvinism of his times, and the American liberal tradition had long accommodated first slavery and then segregation. In addition, Wilson did not hesitate to intervene in Mexico and the Caribbean in response to what he considered their poor governance.

Wilson's liberal internationalist project had two main aims: to tame international anarchy through the erection of binding international law and organization, and to change the other states in the system toward constitutional democracy. He sought a world made safe for democracy.[14] Historian and biographer Arthur Link has argued that in light of the catastrophic events of the 1930s, Wilson's moral vision at Versailles in 1919 was more far-sighted than those of the European leaders Georges Clemenceau or David Lloyd George, who focused on territorial gains. Link called this "the higher realism of Woodrow Wilson." And no less a realist than George Kennan wrote of Wilson in 1991, "I have to correct or modify at this stage of my life, many of the impressions I had about him at an earlier stage. In his vision of the future needs of world society, I now see Wilson as ahead of any other statesman of his time."[15]

Others disagree and believe that the moralistic liberal legacy that Wilson bequeathed has been a trap for American foreign policy. While liberal democracy is the best political system at home, in the realm of international politics, "the belief that all humans have a set of inalienable rights, and that protecting these rights should override other concerns, creates a powerful incentive for liberal states to intervene."[16] Liberalism becomes a source of instability and conflict.[17] Of course, much depends on the definition of liberalism and how it is implemented. But as Henry Kissinger noted, even the ultimate realist Richard Nixon was influenced by Wilson and hung his picture in the White House.[18] Kissinger concluded that "Wilson's ultimate greatness must be measured by the degree to which he rallied the tradition of American Exceptionalism . . . a prophet toward whose vision America has judged itself obliged to aspire."[19]

THE LIBERAL INTERNATIONAL ORDER AFTER 1945

After Wilson sent two million men to fight in Europe and tipped the outcome of the war, it was clear that the United States was not only the world's largest economy, but also crucial to the global balance of power. But when the Senate rejected the Treaty of Versailles and Wilson's League of Nations, the United States failed to act in its new role, and instead continued to behave as a free rider in the provision of global public goods, which Britain could no longer afford to do. In the absence of a global government the world depends on the largest country to provide order and global public goods, and in the nineteenth century the Pax Brittanica contributed security, economic stability, and protection of global commons such as freedom of the seas. After World War I, the United States had replaced Britain as the "indispensable nation" (to use a phrase from the end of the century), but did not see itself that way.

Instead, America returned to normalcy. While the United States took some useful initiatives in the 1920s, public opinion came to see intervention in World War I and efforts to create a world order as a huge mistake. The United States became strongly isolationist, and there was no American led liberal order in the 1930s. The result was an immoral decade of economic depression, a prelude to genocide, and eventually a second world war. While the isolationism of the 1930s was more virulent than usual, it represented a return to the nineteenth-century foreign policy tradition.

American public opinion often oscillates between extroversion and retrenchment.[20] Leaders like Franklin Roosevelt saw the mistakes of 1930s isolationism and began a planning process to create the Bretton Woods international economic institutions in 1944 and the United Nations in 1945. As we shall see in chapter 3, the turning point was Harry Truman's postwar decisions that led to permanent alliances and a continual military presence abroad. When Britain was too weak to support Greece and Turkey in 1947, the United States took its place. We invested heavily in the Marshall Plan in 1948, created NATO in 1949, and led a United Nations coalition that fought in Korea in 1950. In 1960, Dwight Eisenhower signed a new security treaty with Japan.

These actions were part of a realist strategy of containment of Soviet power, but containment was interpreted in various ways. Some foreign policy choices were justified on the basis of containing Communism and others on containing the Soviet Union—witness Truman's support of Communist Yugoslavia. Some decisions had questionable ethical justification, such as overthrow of governments in Guatemala, Iran, and elsewhere. Perhaps most notorious was the intervention in Vietnam—which, as we will see in chapter 4, a series of American presidents justified with a metaphor of dominos falling to Communism, and the ultimate effect on the global balance of power in a bipolar world.

Americans had bitter debates and partisan differences over intervention in developing countries like Vietnam and more recently Iraq, which strongly affected the 1968 and 2006 elections, respectively. But while the ethics of intervention were highly contentious, the issue of a liberal institutional order was much less so. The theologian Reinhold Niebuhr praised the "fortunate vagueness of liberal internationalism," which saved it from ideological rigidity. With victory in the Cold War and the ideological victory of liberalism, Wilsonianism ran the risk of becoming a "hard" ideology of making the world safe *by* democracy rather than *for* democracy. America's "unipolar moment" of unbalanced power raised the risk of hubris. Washington's advocacy for economic globalization, forceful democracy promotion, and American leadership[21] often became an ideological justification for a rigid set of interests. The pursuit of "exalted ends empowers the United States to employ whatever means it deems necessary."[22]

The liberal international order had enjoyed broad support in American foreign policy since World War II, but in the 2016 election Donald Trump discovered the effectiveness of an argument that the alliances and institutions of the post-1945 order had let other peoples benefit to the disadvantage of the United States. His populist appeal rested on far more than foreign policy. The economic dislocations caused by globalization were accentuated by the 2008 Great Recession, and cultural changes related to race, the role of women, and gender identity had polarized the American electorate. Trump successfully linked white resentment over the increasing visibility and influence of racial and ethnic minorities to foreign policy by blaming economic problems on "bad trade deals with countries like Mexico and China and on immigrants competing for jobs."[23]

The current period is not the first time America has seen such populist reactions against a liberal foreign policy.[24] There were antecedents in the 1920s and 1930s.[25] Fifteen million immigrants had come to the United States in the first twenty years of the century, "leaving native Americans with a vague uneasy fear of being overwhelmed from within." In the early 1920s, the Ku Klux Klan had a resurgence and pushed for the National Origins Act of 1924 to "prevent the Nordic race from being swamped," and "preserve the older more homogeneous America they revered." Similarly, Donald Trump's election in 2016 reflected rather than caused the deep racial, ideological, and cultural schisms that had been developing since the 1960s.[26] Some analysts worried that Trump's foreign policies and American retrenchment could result in international disorder similar to the 1930s, but his supporters argued to the contrary that a less generous and tougher US stance would produce greater stability abroad and greater domestic support at home. In any case, Trump's election represented a clear shift away from the Wilsonian tradition.

Some believe that Trump's rise was caused by the failure of liberal elites to reflect the underlying foreign policy preferences of the American people. Stephen Walt, for example, portrays a moralistic foreign policy elite that cares more about liberal values than does the public at large.[27] But this portrait is oversimplified. Of course, there are many strands in American public opinion, and elite groups are generally more interested in foreign policy than the public at large. Since 1974, the Chicago Council on Global Affairs has asked Americans if it were best for the country to take an active part or to stay out of world affairs. Over that period, roughly a third of the public has been consistently isolationist, hearkening back to the nineteenth-century tradition.[28] That number reached 40 percent in 2014, but contrary to popular myth, 2016 was not a high point of post-1945 isolationism. At the time of the election, 64 percent of the American public said they favored active involvement in world affairs and that number rose to 70 percent in the 2018 poll, the highest recorded level since 2002.[29]

Because most Americans do not place a high priority on foreign policy, they tend to be intuitive realists who emphasize security and economic prosperity.[30] Ordinary citizens are concerned primarily about their daily jobs and safety. However, at the same time, the polls also show that while "security from attack and domestic well-being come first ... most Americans also ascribe substantial importance to achieving justice for people abroad and want the United States to pursue altruistic, humanitarian aims internationally." Elites are often more liberal than the general public, but not on all questions. The public is more skeptical on economic issues that affect jobs or committing troops in combat, but the public is more liberal than the elites in their strong support for international organizations, institutions, and agreements.[31] Foreign policy was not the major issue in the 2016 election, and the populist opinion that Donald Trump successfully tapped was not the only strand in foreign policy.

In his inaugural address Trump declared that "we do not seek to impose our way of life on anyone, but rather to let it shine as an example." This "city on the hill" approach has a long pedigree; while it is not purely in the Jeffersonian tradition, it eschews activism.[32] American power is seen as resting more on the "pillar of inspiration" and the soft power of attraction rather than the "pillar of action."[33] The Biblical city-on-the-hill metaphor was used by the seventeenth-century Puritan John Winthrop, who proclaimed "the eyes of all people are upon us." In 1821, John Quincy Adams famously stated that the United States "does not go abroad in search of monsters to destroy. She is the well-wisher to the freedom and independence of all. She is the champion and vindicator only of her own."[34] Trump returned to this theme in December 2017 when he issued his National Security Strategy, which he called "a return to principled realism," stating that "we do not seek to impose our way of life on anyone" but will "celebrate American greatness as a shining example to the world."[35]

There is also a long interventionist strand in American foreign policy. Secretary of State Adams made his statement to fend off political pressures from those who wanted the United States to intervene on behalf of Greek patriots rebelling against Ottoman oppression. Early in the twentieth century, even a self-proclaimed realist like Theodore Roosevelt argued that in extreme cases of abuse of human rights, intervention "may be justifiable and proper."[36] In midcentury, John F. Kennedy called for Americans to ask not only what they could do for their country but for the world, and he sent some 16,000 American military advisors to Vietnam. Since the end of the Cold War, the United States has been involved in seven wars and military interventions, none directly related to great power competition. In 2006, George W. Bush issued a National Security Strategy that was almost the opposite of Trump's, resting on the twin pillars of promoting freedom, justice, and human dignity around the world, and designed to promote a growing global community of democracies.[37] Our history provides quite different answers to what constitutes a moral foreign policy, but Trump rejected both the democratic interventionist and the international institutionalist dimensions of Wilson's liberal legacy.

Critics correctly point out that the American order after 1945 was neither global nor always very liberal.[38] So-called American hegemony left out more than half the world (the Soviet bloc and China) and included a number of illiberal authoritarian states. Defenders argue the liberal international order, albeit imperfect, made the world a better place because it produced an era of unprecedented growth in the world economy, which raised hundreds of millions of people out of poverty and allowed the spread of liberty and democracy.[39] In any event, many analysts believe that the liberal international order is now over with the rise of China, and the rise of nationalistic populism in many countries. Future US presidents will have to make moral choices about foreign policy in a world where the post-1945 Pax Americana and Wilsonian vision have changed. What difference will those moral choices make, and how should we judge what makes a moral foreign policy? Can we construct a scorecard that will allow us to compare presidents in a careful manner? I believe we can, and I turn to that question in the next chapter.

2

What Is a Moral Foreign Policy?

The American debates about values and foreign policy that we just described are part of a broader Western tradition of thinking about morality and foreign policy. Realists who trace their intellectual ancestry to such classic thinkers as Thucydides, Hobbes, and Machiavelli argue that in an anarchic world, foreign policy is largely amoral. Thucydides famously recounts that as the ancient Athenians prepared to slaughter and enslave the people on the island of Melos, they ignored pleas for mercy with the statement that "the powerful do what they will, and the weak suffer what they must."[1] In contrast, European Liberals in the tradition of the Enlightenment philosopher Immanuel Kant argued that basic values are universal and should apply in all circumstances, including foreign policy. Both views have merit, but both are much too simple in suggesting that the moral choices in foreign policy are all or nothing.[2] World politics involves seven and a half billion people in roughly two hundred countries with no world government. Many do not subscribe to Western ethical traditions. However, to admit such complexity does not mean we have to throw up our hands and give up on moral reasoning when we reach the water's edge. So let's start at the beginning.

HOW WE MAKE MORAL JUDGMENTS

We all make moral judgments all the time. Whether we are religious or not, studies have shown that morality is part of our human nature. As the conservative political scientist James Q. Wilson put it, "To say that people have a moral sense is not the same as saying that they are innately good," but "by their nature potentially good."[3] We are a social species and that is how we evolved. Humans are selfish and aggressive, but restraints on conflict and concern for each other were important adaptations that helped our species to become dominant. In the words of social psychologist Jonathan Haidt, moral codes allowed humans "to produce large cooperative groups, tribes, and nations without the glue of kinship . . . Moral reasoning is a skill we humans evolved to further our social agenda—to justify our actions and to defend the teams we belong to." We are hard-wired to have moral impulses though the content of those impulses varies widely.

Humans are selfish, aggressive, and often cruel, but a moral impulse is nearly universal in humans except for those with damage to part of the brain. Different cultures, however, have expressed these moral impulses in different ways, with some codes putting more emphasis on care, harm, and fairness while others put more stress on authority, loyalty, and sanctity.[4] Advances in neuroscience have made it possible to understand the relationship between moral sense and the human brain. Even within our own culture, some of our moral judgments are impulsive and can be traced to one part of the brain; some are more reasoned and depend on another part of the brain. "The decision on how to act is not a single, rational calculation of the sort that moral philosophers have generally assumed is going on, but a conflict between two processes, with one (the emotional) sometimes able to override the other (the utilitarian)."[5] It is a mistake to oppose moral intuition and reasoning.

Both intuition and reason are parts of our moral responses.* Morality involves both conviction and prudence. In expressing this biological moral impulse, our sense of moral obligation draws upon three main social sources: a sense of conscience that can be religiously or individually informed, rules of common morality that society treats as obligations, and codes of professional and personal conduct that define the duties associated with our social roles.[6]

Religion dominates for some, but it does not alone provide a clear guide for moral reasoning. Religious fundamentalists sometimes argue that moral reasoning is superfluous since the answers are written in the scriptures of the Bible or Koran. But even scripture is open to interpretation. According to the writer Garry Wills, the Southern Baptist Jimmy Carter was our most religious president and taught Bible classes all his adult life, including during his White House years. Nonetheless, Wills points out, the religious right rejected him when he was president, and in 2016 the religious right supported Donald Trump, voting "in overwhelming numbers for our arguably least religious president."[7] Abortion and conservative judicial appointments were deemed more important moral issues than nonconsensual groping of women and repeated marital infidelity. As we shall see, the two most openly religious presidents, Jimmy Carter and George W. Bush, had quite difficult ethical scorecards. Moreover, the same scripture can lead to different political interpretations, and scripture sometimes provides very outdated moral advice. For example, Leviticus (18:22) calls homosexuality an abomination, but Leviticus (25:44) also allows slavery if the slaves are purchased from neighboring nations. Apparently, scripture allows Canadians to own Americans—or is it the other way round? Scripture does not tell us how to negotiate with Canadians.

---

* A classic way of illustrating the two aspects of morality is the "trolley car problem." If a runaway trolley is hurtling down a hill and you could throw a switch so it would go down a track that would kill one person rather than another track where it would kill five, many people would reason like utilitarians that the correct moral response would be to throw the switch. But in another example, if you could save five people by pushing a person onto the track to derail the trolley, many people feel intuitively repelled and drop their utilitarian calculation, although the outcome in lives saved is the same in both examples.

Three-Dimensional Moral Reasoning

Given the different cultural backgrounds and religious beliefs of Americans, moral reasoning about foreign policy is often hotly contested, and several popular misconceptions add to the confusion. One, discussed in the preface, is the ultra-realist view that ethics has nothing to contribute because there are no real choices in foreign policy and only one's own country counts—though that of course is a moral choice. Another misconception confuses a president's moral character with his moral consequences, and still another makes judgments based on moral rhetoric rather than results.

As a practical matter, in our daily lives most people make moral judgments along three dimensions: intentions, means, and consequences. Intentions are more than just goals. They include both stated values and personal motives (as in "her motives were well-meaning"). Most people publicly express goals that are noble and worthy, even though their personal motives such as ego and self-interest may subtly corrupt those goals. Moreover, good goals must not only satisfy our values, they also have to pass a feasibility test. Otherwise, the best of intentions can have disastrous moral consequences. They often provide the pavement for the road to hell. Lyndon Johnson may have had good intentions when he sent American troops to Vietnam, but a leader's good intentions are not proof of what is sometimes misleadingly called "moral clarity." Judgments based on good intentions alone are simply one-dimensional ethics. For example, Ari Fleisher, the press secretary for George W. Bush, praised his boss for the "moral clarity" of his intentions, but more than that is needed for a sound moral evaluation of the 2003 invasion of Iraq.[8]

The second important dimension of moral judgment is means. We speak of means as *effective* if they achieve our goals, but *ethical* means also depend upon their quality as well as their efficacy. How do they treat others? Does a president consider the soft power of attraction and the importance of developing the trust of other countries? When it comes to means, leaders must decide how to combine the hard power of inducements and threats, and the soft power of values, culture, and policies that attract people to their goals.[9] As General James Mattis once warned Congress, if you fail to fund the soft power of the State Department, you will have to buy me more bullets.[10] Using hard power when soft power will do, or using soft power alone when hard power is necessary to protect values, raises serious ethical questions about means.

As for consequences, effectiveness is crucial and involves achieving the country's goals, but ethical consequences must also be good not merely for Americans, but for others as well. "America first" must be tempered by what Thomas Jefferson called "a proper consideration for the opinions of mankind." In practice, effectiveness and ethical means are often closely related. George W. Bush may have had good intentions about bringing democracy to Iraq, but the occupation failed because he lacked moral and effective means to do so. A leader who pursues moral but unrealistic goals or uses ineffective means can produce terrible moral consequences at home and abroad. As we shall see in the following cases, presidents with good intentions but weak contextual intelligence and reckless reality-testing sometimes produced bad consequences and ethical failure.[11] Good moral reasoning does not judge presidential choices based on their stated intentions or outcomes alone, but on all three dimensions of intentions, means, and consequences.

DOUBLE STANDARDS AND DIRTY HANDS

Another consideration in the cases that follow is whether we should judge presidents by the same moral standard as ordinary citizens. Historically, leaders often think not. The Bible tells us that when King David lusted after Bathsheba, the wife of one of his army commanders, David sent the commander in the way of certain harm and took Bathsheba. David understood that what he did was wrong, but did not think the moral restrictions applied to him as a king. In the fifteenth century the Borgia Pope Alexander VI presided over a corrupt Vatican and showered favors on his illegitimate children, but argued that was what other popes had done. Similarly, President Nixon argued that "when the president does it, that means it is not illegal,"[12] and President Trump has suggested that he could pardon himself, thus putting himself above the law.[13]

Americans often say that presidents are not above the law. In roles related to legality or acting as a teacher or symbol, Americans believe that presidents should be held to the same moral standards as ordinary people. We tend to draw a distinction between a president's personal and public behavior, but that distinction is changing over time. As we shall see, Jack Kennedy indulged in reckless infidelities in the White House, and in the 1960s, the press chose to ignore them. Three decades later, Bill Clinton was impeached for such behavior (though he was not removed by the Senate). In 2016, Evangelicals supported Trump despite evidence of infidelities.

Sometimes, however, double standards for leaders and ordinary citizens are appropriate. Take the Biblical injunction that "thou shalt not kill." In choosing a spouse or roommate, that commandment ranks high on a list of desired moral values. At the same time, polls show most people would not vote for an absolute pacifist. Presidents are trustees. They have a fiduciary obligation to protect the people who elected them, and under certain circumstances that may involve ordering troops into battle to take lives, however much they abhor it. And nuclear deterrence requires credibility that a president would press the nuclear button. Jimmy Carter noted that "the presidents who have taken our country to war are looked upon as stronger and more able than the ones who tend toward peace. But that doesn't bother me."[14] He prided himself on not using offensive force during his presidency and on curbing the proliferation of nuclear weapons, but he never renounced nuclear deterrence. Sometimes leaders must have "dirty hands," meaning that they must take actions they would otherwise regard as immoral in terms of their personal moral code.[15]

The German theorist Max Weber famously distinguished an ethics of conviction that refuses to tolerate injustice from an ethics of responsibility. In the former case, absolute moral imperatives must not be violated for the sake of good consequences. An ethic of responsibility, however, must focus primarily on the results. When Martin Luther rebelled against a corrupt church and proclaimed, "Here I stand; I can do no other," he was obeying an ethic of conviction. But while Weber respected the role of conviction in core beliefs, he warned against too much purity in politics: "Whoever seeks the salvation of his own soul and the rescue of souls, does not do so by means of politics."[16] Politicians have to compromise between heart and head, combine intuition and prudence, and balance between an ethic of conviction and an ethic of responsibility. In August 2015, in the midst of a huge influx of refugees during the Syrian war, German Chancellor Angela Merkel, the daughter of a Lutheran pastor, took a bravely principled stand on accepting a million refugees, but did it in a way that created consequences that came back to haunt German and European politics by accelerating the rise of the radical right.[17] As admirable as her personal decision may have been, politics and foreign policy are the realm of hard calls, dirty hands, and three-dimensional ethics.

Some Americans live by a fundamentalist ethic based on rules written in the Bible, the Koran, or some other religious text. However, in the philosophical traditions of the eighteenth-century liberal Enlightenment that guided the founding fathers and are still the dominant traditions for many Americans today, ethicists distinguish a rule-based approach associated with thinkers such as Immanuel Kant from a consequentialist approach associated with utilitarians such as Jeremy Bentham and John Stuart Mill. To grasp the difference, ask yourself whether you would torture a terrorist to force him to disclose the location of a ticking time bomb in a crowded city, or kill an innocent person to save a thousand lives. Would it matter if the number were a million?†

People sometimes appeal to a third tradition called "virtue ethics" that can be traced back to Aristotle and the ancient Greeks (or in a non-Western culture, Confucianism). It pays attention to the cultivation of virtuous traits

---

† One can try to reconcile the two positions by including the damage that a decision does to future rules and institutions as a key consequence that must be weighed. In other words, when a utilitarian considers the consequences of her action for the system of rules her act would violate, she may come out in the same place. However, while such rule (or institutional) consequentialism can sometimes lead the utilitarian to the same decision as that advocated by the rule-based deontologist, it cannot always resolve the basic difference between following rules or focusing on consequences. Some tension between the two approaches is insoluble, but since no one can calculate the consequences of all possible options accurately, tried-and-true rules are important and rule-utilitarianism at least attempts to integrate principles and consequences.

of character and emphasizes the morality of the person overall more than the morality of a particular decision. Moral virtues are our dispositions to do what is morally commendable. Character is more than personality. It is the sum of virtues that push a lifetime of decision in certain directions rather than others. People with bad character can sometimes make good decisions, and good character is no guarantee of good action. When someone makes an immoral decision, we often say he or she is acting "out of character." A good leader cultivates virtues and uses experience to develop judgment. "Ethical behavior should not be the outcome of careful and laborious calculation and reflection; it should be immediate, spontaneous, governed by intuition," that "arises from serious attention to the relevant facts, not in place of them."[18] The problem with virtue ethics and intuition, however, is the absence of any larger standards for objective judgment.

In terms of our three-dimensional moral categories of intentions, means, and consequences, virtue ethics places particular emphasis on the first dimension of goals and motives, just as rules-based approaches stress the second aspect of means, and utilitarians focus on consequences. As one philosopher sums up these three main Western traditions: "It is not clear that one must accept only one of these approaches while rejecting the others . . . Even though moral philosophy may often seem a very different enterprise in the hands of Mill, Kant and Aristotle—the one neglecting what the other takes to be of chief importance—we have noticed many common themes and even many shared conclusions among these writers."[19] Though they are complementary, and many presidents intuitively combine them in practice, these important strands of contemporary moral reasoning are often difficult to reconcile in particular cases. As the just war theorist Michael Walzer explains, the tension between rights theory and utilitarianism can never be wholly abolished, and "at the risk of philosophical muddle, we must negotiate the middle ground."[20]

Take Harry Truman's decision to drop the atomic bomb on Hiroshima in an effort to end World War II. In a war where millions of lives had already been lost, Truman was told that he could save hundreds of thousands of American and Japanese lives by avoiding a land invasion of the Japanese home islands.[21] Moreover, the numbers killed at Hiroshima were fewer than those who had been killed in the conventional fire-bombing of Tokyo, and atomic weapons were new and poorly understood. Was Truman's act morally justified? Rules-based theorists would answer that two wrongs do not make a right, and that the deliberate destruction of so many innocent civilians can never be justified. Some consequentialists reply that more lives were saved even though at the cost of many innocent lives. They add that Truman later redeemed himself by refusing to use nuclear weapons when General Douglas MacArthur and others urged him to do so in the Korean War. Even in 1945, after seeing the effects, Truman did not want a third bomb dropped because "he didn't like the idea of killing all those kids."[22] With more time and experience, Truman's character made him reluctant to turn to nuclear weapons again. That taboo or aversion against nuclear use has lasted for nearly seven decades and was important to several presidents, as we shall see. Nuclear weapons raise crucial moral issues for presidents, and our history would look very different if the taboo had not held. When the American Catholic bishops debated the morality of nuclear deterrence during the Reagan administration, they pointed out that ours is the first generation since Genesis with the potential to destroy God's creation, and argued that it could only be temporarily and conditionally acceptable.[23] The debate over the intentions, means, and consequences of nuclear deterrence persists to this day.

Looking back to 1945, however, if Truman had refused to drop the bomb because of his personal moral beliefs, would that have prevented its eventual use in the hands of less scrupulous leaders? And at what price does a leader's concern about personal integrity translate into selfishness and a violation of followers' trust? What were Truman's obligations to the Americans who would have been killed in the invasion of Japan compared to the Japanese citizens who would have been killed by the bomb, or to the Japanese who would have been killed by an invasion and prolonged fighting without the use of the bomb?

Why do we even bother to ask such unanswerable questions? In the words of two top officials who wrestled with these issues when they were responsible for Britain's nuclear weapons, it is because "moral accountability is a central part of what it means to be a human being."[24] There are no easy answers to such problems,[25] and different sources of moral obligation are frequently in tension with each other. As the Oxford philosopher Isaiah Berlin aptly summarized our moral dilemma, since "the ends of men are many, and not all of them are in principle compatible with each other, then the possibility of conflict—and tragedy—can never wholly be eliminated from human life, either personal or social."[26] This is particularly true in the complex domain of foreign policy, where different domestic constituencies—as well as the interests of other peoples—may conflict. As Henry Kissinger once observed, the tough decisions are 51-49, and that is why the leadership "qualities most needed are character and courage."[27] As we examine the cases in this book, we will be interested both in what were good foreign policy decisions, and what were the character and skills to be a good foreign policymaker.[‡]

The Moral Role of Institutions: Reciprocity and Fairness

Many societies have ethical systems that stress impartiality and have an analogue to the Golden Rule: "Do unto others as you would have them do unto you." Your interests and my interests should be treated the same way. The liberal philosopher John Rawls used the wonderful metaphor of an imaginary veil of ignorance about our initial relative positions to illustrate justice as fairness.[28] Act as though you did not know how well off you were. How then would you want people to be treated? However, appealing to an intuitive sense of fairness—treating others as you would want to be treated, not playing favorites, and being sensible to individual needs—does not always provide a solution. For example, Nobel Laureate economist Amartya Sen invites us to imagine a parent with a flute and three children, each of whom wants it. The first child says, "I made it"; the second says, "I am the only one who can play it"; and the third says, "I have no other toys."[29] To whom should you give the flute? Even with a thought experiment about

---

[‡] Going back to the semantics noted in the preface, Mathias Risse points out that the word "ethics" is derived from the Greek word for character, and "morals" comes from the Latin for customs and rules. We are interested here in how both affect foreign policy.

deciding behind an imagined veil of ignorance, the principle of justice as fairness does not solve all cases.

This is where the ethical importance of institutions comes in. In such instances, the parent (or leader) may find it more appropriate to turn to a procedural or institutional solution in which the children learn to bargain with each other or agree on a lottery or upon a neutral figure to judge how time with the flute will be allocated or shared. The parent can also teach or coach the children about sharing, which is a different image of moral leadership as persuasion and education rather than the mere exercise of command. Broadening moral discourse and teaching followers about process and institutions is often one of the most important moral roles that presidents (and parents) play.

In trying to consider ways in which their country can make the world a better place, American presidents have not only to declare good values, but also consider the institutional framework of world politics that makes the achievement of good values more likely. An example is the open rules-based international order that was created after 1945 and that is under threat today. Some aspects of the system were unfair, but better than the alternatives. Institutions do not have to be perfect to play an important role in morality. By creating stable expectations and norms for behavior, they can enhance the prospects for cooperation, reciprocity, and moral concerns. For example, the zero-sum game of prisoner's dilemma imagines that two criminals are arrested for a minor crime, but the police suspect them of a major crime. They offer each prisoner a lighter sentence if he testifies against the other regarding the major crime, but if both succumb to that temptation, they both wind up with long sentences. Each player has a strong incentive to reduce his sentence by undercutting his partner rather than cooperate in silence when the game is played once, but when there is a long series of games, the political scientist Robert Axelrod found that the best strategy was tit-for-tat reciprocity. As he put it, the optimal strategy changes when there is "a long shadow of the future." Institutions help create that long shadow of the future.[30]

Sometimes rigid rules and outdated or unjust institutions become harmful and need to be challenged, as Martin Luther King did with segregation and as Abraham Lincoln did with slavery. But even Lincoln delayed the timing of the Emancipation Proclamation out of concern for border states preserving the institution of the federal union. When leaders consider the consequences of their decisions, they must consider not only the immediate situation but also the impact on institutions and the long shadow of the future. If this is the only time we will play together, I may be tempted to cheat you, but if I know we will be playing together into the indefinite future, I can discover the importance of reciprocity and fairness. One of the most important moral skills of presidents is to design and maintain systems and institutions, not simply to make immediate decisions. But presidents may discover that such a policy involves a long-term vision, which is hard to sell to a public that wants to see more immediate gains.[§]

Lies, Risks, and Misleading Means

What should a president do when his followers focus on the short term or want more immediate gratification? Can he lie to the public?[**] Truth matters in the development of trust in institutions. Sometimes cynics say, "All politicians lie." Indeed they do, and a little introspection leads us to admit that all humans lie from time to time. But the amount and type of lying makes a difference. Too many lies debase the currency of trust. For example, many of Donald Trump's supporters justify his lies on the grounds that it is to be expected of politicians, but the amount and type of lying makes a difference in terms of effects on credibility, trust, and institutions.

Not all lies are born equal. Some are self-serving and others are group-serving. A leader may lie to cover her tracks and avoid embarrassment, or to harm a rival, or for convenience. But in some circumstances, leaders may decide to deceive their followers for what they see as their followers'

[§]   After French President Macron imposed a gasoline tax to reduce carbon emissions that contribute to global climate change, French protesters complained, "You are thinking about the end of the world but we are concerned about the end of the month."

[**]   I do not use gender-neutral language when referring to presidents for obvious historical reasons, but I hope I will have to change that in future editions.

larger or later good. As we shall see, John F. Kennedy misled the public about the role of Turkish missiles in the deal that ended the Cuban missile crisis in 1962,[31] and Franklin Roosevelt lied to the American public about a German attack on an American destroyer. Winston Churchill once argued that particularly in wartime, the truth may be "so precious that she should always be attended by a bodyguard of lies."[32] The political scientist John Mearsheimer admits there can be negative consequences but argues that given the low levels of trust in international relations, "international lying, in other words, is not necessarily misconduct."[33] On the other hand, the Singaporean diplomat Tommy Koh argues that preserving trust is crucial and that in his experience over time, "governments and diplomats with a reputation for veracity tend to enjoy more influence and stature."[34]

Machiavellian deception is often part of a smart strategy, for example, in bargaining to get a deal or even in bringing a group to accept new goals. But deception that is purely self-serving is simply selfish manipulation of others, and over time, others notice and credibility is reduced. Even when motives are not self-serving, presidents should ask about the importance of the goal, the availability of alternative means to achieve that goal, whether the deception can be contained or is likely to spread through precedent or example.[35] In other words, he should think like a "rule utilitarian." Breaking the rule may be convenient but have long-term immoral consequences. The more leaders use deception upon their followers, the more they erode trust, weaken institutions, and create damaging precedents.[36] Roosevelt's lies in 1941 about a German attack on a US destroyer were intended to awaken the American people to the threat from Hitler, but it also set a bad precedent. Lyndon Johnson lied to obtain the Tonkin Bay resolution that contributed to the escalation of the Vietnam War. The danger is that leaders tell themselves they are lying for the good of their followers when they are merely lying for political or personal convenience.

Even if we excuse a lie like Roosevelt's on the grounds that the consequences can sometimes justify the means, we can still make moral judgments about how leaders distribute the risks and costs of their actions. Rash assessments of reality that impose high risks on others can be condemned on moral as well as effectiveness grounds. People who try to climb mountains accept a degree of risk, but a team leader still has to make sure that the followers understand the balance between risk and achievement. It is one thing to pose a grand vision that leads people to the summit; it is another to lead them too close to the edge of a cliff without their knowledge and consent.

How much risk should presidents take on behalf of their followers and how truthful should they be about it? In some circumstances, the public benefits from a president taking a large risk rather than a series of incremental bets, and may later accept that keeping them in the dark was justified for their own sake. For example, after Munich in 1938, FDR bet on eventual war with Hitler, though he was tactically prudent and misleading in explaining his actions to the American public. After the war, Truman took a risk in establishing the Truman doctrine, the Marshall Plan, and NATO to contain Soviet Communism, and he accepted the advice of Senator Arthur Vandenberg that he would have to exaggerate and "scare the hell out of the public" to gain their acceptance. In contrast, Eisenhower spoke boldly about nuclear threats in public but was cautious in practice and placed a series of smaller incremental bets that produced eight years of peace and prosperity during the height of the Cold War. George W. Bush made a big bet on the forced democratization of Iraq that imposed large costs on many people.

Presidents can also be faulted for being too cautious. For example, Zbigniew Brzezinski criticized George H. W. Bush for not taking more risks to accommodate Russia at the end of the Cold War,[37] and Barack Obama was criticized for not taking more risks in 2012 and 2013 to avert the humanitarian disaster of Syria. Clinton was similarly criticized for not acting to stop the genocide in Rwanda in 1994. Answers to such judgments depend heavily on a careful analysis of each situation and a weighing of probabilities and expected values of likely outcomes. In judging the moral consequences of foreign policy decisions, it is tempting to focus on acts of commission. Causation seems more immediate, visible, and calculable. Yet omissions may have larger moral consequence for more people. Failure to develop or protect institutions in the 1930s affected millions of lives. The same may be true today.

Sometimes the distinction between acts of commission and omission has moral significance. Failure to save lives that could be easily saved is little different morally from causing deaths, but in other situations costly and heroic actions would be necessary and involve a high risk of failure. Walking by a shallow pond and refusing to rescue a drowning child because you do not want to get your shoes wet is very different from plunging into the surf during a riptide. In the latter cases, we might excuse a president's omission unless the United States had been a significant cause of the problem. General Colin Powell called this the "Pottery Barn principle"—if you broke it, you have an obligation to pay for it. Redressing an act of commission can add an additional moral dimension to consider.

Americans differ among themselves and over time about how prudent they want their presidents to be. Some want lions; others want foxes. Lions are big and have big ideas. Foxes are small, agile, and have many ideas. Machiavelli famously noted that leaders who are foxes cannot defend against wolves, but he also pointed out that those who act like lions are vulnerable to snares. Sometimes it is better that a leader be a lion, other times a fox, and that is the source of heated foreign policy debates. Moral behavior depends upon an accurate assessment of the circumstances— which is sometimes called "judgment" or "contextual intelligence." As Machiavelli warned, "those who rely simply on the lion do not know what they are about . . . He who has known best how to employ the fox has succeeded best."[38] FDR was a fox who eventually acted like a lion in response to Hitler; Lyndon Johnson was a lion who became ensnared in Vietnam.

MENTAL MAPS OF THE WORLD AND MORAL FOREIGN POLICY

How then should presidents avoid traps? What does the world look like? Is it so harsh that they must abandon their morals at the border? Do they have any duties to those who are not fellow citizens? Cynical political consultants might say "no problem because foreigners don't vote." Total skeptics would add that the notion of a "world community" is a myth, and where there is no community, there are no moral rights and duties. But three prevailing mental maps of world politics offer different answers to these questions.

Realism

Unlike skeptics, realists accept some moral obligations but see them as limited primarily to the virtue of prudence by the harsh nature of world politics. John Bolton, a lawyer who served at high levels in the George W. Bush and Trump administrations, has argued for "defending American interests as vigorously as possible and seeing yourself as an advocate for the US rather than a guardian of the world itself."[39] Hans Morgenthau wrote that "the state has no right to let its moral disapprobation . . . get in the way of successful political survival . . . Realism, then, considers prudence . . . to be the supreme virtue in politics."[40] In the words of John Mearsheimer, "States operate in a self-help world in which the best way to survive is to be as powerful as possible, even if that requires pursuing ruthless policies. That is not a pretty story, but there is no better alternative if survival is a country's paramount goal."[41] The realists draw a harsh mental map of the world.

In dire situations of survival, consequences may indeed justify what appear to be immoral acts. Robert D. Kaplan argues that "the rare individuals who have recognized the necessity of violating such morality, acted accordingly, and taken responsibility for their actions are among the most necessary leaders for their countries."[42] A frequently cited example is when Winston Churchill attacked the French fleet in 1940 and killed some 1,300 Frenchmen rather than let the fleet fall into Hitler's hands. Churchill referred to that crisis of British survival as a "supreme emergency," and Walzer argues that in such rare instances moral rules can be overriden even though "there are no moments in human history that are not governed by moral rules."[43]

For instance, some ethicists have justified Churchill's bombing of German civilian targets in the early days of World War II when Britain's survival was at stake, but condemned his later support for the fire-bombing of Dresden in February 1945 when victory in Europe was already assured.[44] In the early days of the war Churchill could claim the necessity of dirty hands as his justification for overriding the moral rules, but he was wrong to continue to do so in the later days of the war. In general, such dire straits of supreme emergency are rare, and most leaders are eclectic in selecting the mental maps with which they navigate the world. Often leaders have an incentive to exaggerate dangers and threats to justify their actions. For example, Donald Trump explained his mild reaction to the murder of Jamal Khasoggi with the comment "America First! The world is a dangerous place!"[45] As one defender put it, "Trump has sent the message that the United States will now look after its own interests, narrowly defined, not the interests of the so-called global community, even at the expense of long-standing allies. This world-view is fundamentally realist in nature."[46] But realists who describe the world in a way that pretends moral choices do not exist are merely disguising their choice. Survival comes first, but that is not the end of the list of values. Most of international politics is not about survival.

A smart realist also knows about different types of power. No president can lead without power, at home or abroad, but power is more than bombs, bullets, or resources. You can get others to do what you want by coercion (sticks), payment (carrots), and attraction (soft power), and a full understanding of power encompasses all three aspects. Because soft power is rarely sufficient by itself and takes longer to accomplish its effects, leaders find the hard power of coercion or payment more tempting. But when wielded alone, hard power can involve higher costs than when it is combined with the soft power of attraction. The Roman Empire rested not only on its legions, but also on the attraction of Roman culture. The Berlin Wall came down not under an artillery barrage, but from hammers and bulldozers wielded by people who had lost faith in Communism. A nation's soft power rests upon its culture, its values, and its policies when they are seen as legitimate in the eyes of others. It can be reinforced by the narratives that a president uses in explaining his foreign policy. Kennedy, Reagan, and Obama, for example, framed their policies in ways that attracted support both at home and abroad. Nixon and Trump were less successful in attracting those outside the United States. Trump declared himself a nationalist, but there is a moral difference between a national patriotism that includes others and a nativism that excludes others.

Cosmopolitanism

Common humanity is another important mental map of the world. While it is weak, nonetheless some degree of international human community exists. As we saw earlier, our intuitions about common humanity are hard-wired into us by evolution. Most Americans respond to pictures of starving children, even if not all would allow them to cross borders or take them into their homes (though some do). Cosmopolitans argue that basic human rights are universal: "They are not respecters of political boundaries and require a universalist politics to implement them; even if this means breaching the wall of state sovereignty."[47] Many Americans hold multiple loyalties to several communities at the same time in a series of widening concentric circles that extend beyond national boundaries. One can simultaneously feel part of a town, a state, a region, a profession, a transnational ethnic group, and humanity at large. However, the outer circles tend to be weaker and generate weaker moral duties than cosmopolitans often assume. One can be a strong inclusive nationalist and a moderate globalist at the same time. All large communities are imagined, but in today's world the imagined community of nationality is usually strongest. In the words of the philosopher Kwame Anthony Appiah, "cosmopolitanism is an expansive act of the moral imagination. It sees human beings as shaping their lives with nesting memberships: a family, a neighborhood, a plurality of overlapping identity groups, spiraling out to encompass all humanity. It asks us to be many things, because we are many things."[48]

I sometimes asked my students to test their moral intuitions about the existence and limits of cosmopolitanism with the following thought experiment. Suppose you are a good swimmer reading at the beach and notice a child drowning in the surf. Would you put down your book and rescue her? Most say yes. Would it matter whether she called "help!" or cried out in a foreign language? Most say the foreign language would make no difference. If she were somewhat farther out and you were not a strong swimmer, how much risk would you take? Answers range from the prudent to the heroic. If there were two children and you could rescue only one, would it matter whether it was yours? Most say yes.

In other words, your role as parent brings in additional moral rights and duties beyond the common humanitarian duty of rescue. Borders are arbitrary and sometimes unjust, but nations are communities that engender additional rights and responsibilities. As Stanley Hoffmann has written, "States may be no more than a collection of individuals and borders may be mere facts, but a moral significance is attached to them."[49] A cosmopolitan who ignores the moral, legal, and institutional significance of borders fails to do justice to the difficult job of balancing rights in the international realm as much as the blinkered realist who sees everything as national survival. Liberals (whom I discuss in greater detail next) see a moral meaning in national boundaries, though a humanitarian duty to rescue can co-exist with a preference for protection of fellow citizens.[50] The devil is in the details of how far and how much. Foreign policy is doubly difficult because it requires the reconciliation of domestic and foreign obligations. Leaders who promote a benign foreign policy but cannot develop support for it at home are failures. At the same time, presidents who focus only on domestic opinion are ducking the hard moral and political choices, including the moral discourse of their constituents.

Liberalism

As we have seen, international politics is often called anarchic, but anarchy simply means "without government" and does not necessarily mean the chaos of a frontier district in the Wild West before the creation of a sheriff or a mayor. Liberals argue that rudimentary practices and institutions such as balance of power, international law, norms, and international organizations can create enough order to establish a framework for meaningful moral choices in most cases.

Even in the extreme circumstances of war, law and morality can play a role. The just war doctrine originated in the early Christian church, as Saint Augustine and others wrestled with the paradox that if the good did not fight back, they would perish and the evil would inherit the earth. That doctrine of just self-defense became secularized after the seventeenth century, and today it provides a broad normative structure that considers all three moral dimensions: good intentions represented by a just cause; forceful means that are proportional to the situation and which discriminate between military and civilian targets; and good consequences that emerge from a prudent regard for the probability of success. Just war doctrine is more than theoretical. It is enshrined both in International Humanitarian Law (the Geneva Conventions) and the American Uniform Code of Military Justice. Soldiers who violated the moral principles that are enshrined in the law of armed conflict have been jailed in many countries, including the United States.

Different mental maps of the world portray anarchy differently, and that affects the way leaders frame their moral choices. Writing in 1651 after the bloody English civil war in which the king was decapitated, the realist Thomas Hobbes imagined a state of nature without government as a war of all against all where life was nasty, brutish, and short. In contrast, writing in a somewhat more peaceful period a few decades later, the liberal John Locke imagined a state of nature as involving social contracts that permitted the successful pursuit of life, liberty, and property.†† Today, liberals say that while there is no world government, there is a degree of world governance, and anarchy has limits. Liberals stress the role of institutions, both national and international, in advancing cooperation among sovereign states in today's world. They argue that "the variable that matters most for liberals is interdependence. For the first time in history, global institutions are now necessary to realize basic human interests."[51]

Cosmopolitans are more skeptical of national sovereignty than liberals and stress the common humanity of individuals. However, these simple mental maps are not exclusive and in practice, presidents have mixed all three mental maps of world politics in inconsistent ways in different contexts when they formulate foreign policies. As we shall see in the following cases, most presidents have been "liberal realists with a touch of cosmopolitanism."

The rise of human rights law after World War II, particularly in reaction to the horror of genocide, has complicated presidential choices. The American

---

†† Thomas Jefferson adapted this to "life, liberty, and the pursuit of happiness" in America's Declaration of Independence.

public wants some response, but is divided over how much. For example, in retrospect, Bill Clinton himself criticized his failure to respond to the genocide in Rwanda in 1994.[52] Yet had Clinton tried to send American troops he would have encountered stiff resistance in parts of his administration, the Congress, and public opinion. Particularly after the death of American soldiers in an earlier humanitarian intervention in Somalia in 1993, the public was not ready for another intervention. Clinton has acknowledged that he could have done more to help the UN and other nations to save some of the lives that were lost in Rwanda, but good leaders today are often caught between their cosmopolitan inclinations and their more traditional obligations to the followers who elected them.

Realism is the default position among the mental maps that most presidents use to chart their course in foreign policy, and given a world of sovereign states, realism is the best place to start. The problem is that many realists stop where they start rather than realizing that cosmopolitanism and liberalism often have something important to contribute to an accurate moral map. When survival is in jeopardy, realism is a necessary basis for a moral foreign policy, though not sufficient. The question again is one of degree. Since there is never perfect security, the moral issue is what degree of security must be assured before other values such as welfare, identity, or rights become part of a president's foreign policy. Most foreign policy choices involve questions like arms sales to authoritarian allies or criticizing the human rights behavior of another country. When some realists treat such trade-offs as similar to Churchill's decision to attack the French fleet, they are simply ducking hard moral issues. It is not enough to say that security comes first or that justice presupposes some degree of order. Presidents have to assess how closely a situation fits a Hobbesian or Lockean mental map, or more likely where an action lies on a continuum between security and other important values.

The Problem of Intervention

Take intervention, for example. What actions should the United States take that cross sovereign borders? Since 1945 the liberal Charter of the UN limits the use of force to self-defense or actions authorized by the Security Council (where the US and four other countries have a veto). Realists argue that intervention can be justified if it prevents disruption of the balance of power upon which order depends. Liberals argue that nations are groups of peoples with a sovereign right to determine their own fate that is enshrined in the UN Charter. Intervention can only be justified to counter a prior intervention or to prevent a massacre that would make a mockery of self-determination.[53] Cosmopolitans prioritize justice and individual human rights to justify humanitarian intervention.

In practice, these principles often get combined in odd ways. In Vietnam, Kennedy and Johnson argued that the United States was countering North Vietnamese intervention in the South, but the Vietnamese saw themselves as one nation that had been artificially divided for realist Cold War balance-of-power purposes. Ironically, today the United States enjoys good relations with the victors as the sovereign state of Vietnam. In the first Gulf War, George H. W. Bush used force to expel Iraq's forces from Kuwait in order to preserve the regional balance of power, but he did so using the liberal mechanism of a UN collective security resolution and a broad coalition to enhance American legitimacy and soft power. Bush 41 considered himself a realist and refused to intervene to stop the shelling of civilians in Sarajevo, but after devastating pictures of starving Somalis on American television in December 1992, he sent American troops on a cosmopolitan humanitarian intervention in Mogadishu, which subsequently became a problem for his successor.[‡‡] But humanitarian intervention is not a new or uniquely American foreign policy problem. Victorian Britain had debates about using force to end slavery, Belgian atrocities in the Congo, and Ottoman repression of Balkan minorities long before Woodrow Wilson became the American president.[54]

Public opinion also shows a similar pattern of mixed mental maps. Because foreign policy is usually a lower priority than domestic issues, the American public tends toward a basic realism. As we saw in the last

---

[‡‡] I use a shorthand to refer to George H. W. Bush, the 41st president, as Bush 41, and his son George W. Bush as Bush 43.

chapter, security from attack and economic security generally rank highest in opinion polls.[55] Elite opinion is often more interventionist than the mass public, leading some critics to argue that the elite is more liberal than the public,[56] but patterns of "strong, widespread public support for international organizations, multilateral agreements and actions, and collective international decision making suggest that most Americans are . . . 'neo liberals,'" and support for humanitarian assistance shows strands of cosmopolitanism.[57] As presidents look inward, no one mental map fits all circumstances. Since members of the public have mostly not reflected on these issues, there is little reason to expect the public to have a single consistent view. Moreover, as we shall see, some presidents have careers that were highly filtered through the political process and were thus familiar to the public, while others were outsiders whose character and actions involved more surprises.[58]

In the second Gulf War, American motives for intervention were mixed. Theorists have sparred over whether the 2003 invasion of Iraq was a realist or a liberal intervention.[59] Some key figures in the George W. Bush administration, such as Richard Cheney and Donald Rumsfeld, were realists concerned about Saddam Hussein's possession of weapons of mass destruction and the local balance of power, but "neoconservatives" in the administration (who were often ex-liberals) stressed the promotion of democracy as well as American hegemony. Outside the administration, some liberals supported the war because of Hussein's abominable human rights record, while others opposed Bush for failing to obtain the institutional support of the UN Security Council as his father had in the first Gulf War.

In its broadest definition, intervention refers to external actions that influence the domestic affairs of another sovereign state, and they can range from broadcasts, economic aid, and support for opposition parties at the low coercion end of the spectrum to blockades, cyberattacks, drone strikes, and military invasion at the high coercive end. From a moral point of view, the degree of coercion involved is very important in terms of restricting local choice and rights. Moreover, military intervention is a dangerous instrument to use. It looks deceptively simple, but rarely is. Prudence warns against unintended consequences.

Stephen Walt argues that "had realists been at the helm of US foreign policy over the past 20 years, it is likely that a number of costly debacles would have been avoided."[60] Perhaps he is right, but there are many variants of realism as well as of liberalism. Realism is a broad tendency, not a precise category with the clear implications for policy that he imagines. Certainly Cheney and Rumsfeld considered themselves realists. In the 2016 presidential debate, both Trump and Hillary Clinton said the United States had a responsibility to prevent mass casualties in Syria, but neither advocated military intervention. And while some commentators argue that the promotion of democracy has "grown into America's self designation as a special nation," there is an enormous difference between democracy promotion by coercive and noncoercive means.[61] Voice of America broadcasts and the National Endowment for Democracy cross international borders in a very different manner than does the 82nd Airborne Division. In terms of consequences, the means are as important as the ends. No single one of the mental maps of the world provides presidents with an easy answer or substitutes for their good judgment and contextual intelligence.

THE BEST MORAL CHOICE IN THE CONTEXT: SCORECARDS

How then should we judge presidential ethics in foreign policy? Presidents have their own values and convictions, but they are also leaders living in Max Weber's real world of nonperfectionist ethics. Arnold Wolfers, a Swiss American realist, argued after World War II that "the interpretation of what constitutes a vital national interest and how much value should be attached to it is a moral question. It cannot be answered by reference to alleged amoral necessities inherent in international politics." At the same time, leaders cannot always follow simple moral rules. The best one can hope for in judging the ethics of leaders in foreign policy, Wolfers concluded, is that they made "the best moral choices that circumstances permit."[62] This is true, but not completely helpful. It is a necessary but certainly not sufficient standard. Prudence is a virtue in an anarchic world, but such a broad rule of prudence can easily be abused.

How can we decide whether our presidents did indeed make the best moral choices under the circumstances? We can start by making sure we judge them in terms of our three-dimensional ethics, and we can draw from the wisdom of all three mental maps of realism, liberalism, and cosmopolitanism in that order. When we look at the goals the presidents sought, we do not expect them to pursue justice at the international level similar to what they aspired to in their domestic policies. In the August 1941 Atlantic Charter, which was one of founding documents of the liberal international order, Roosevelt and Churchill declared their devotion of freedom from want and from fear (though they disagreed about the British Empire). But Roosevelt did not try to transfer his domestic New Deal to the international level. After all, even a renowned liberal philosopher like John Rawls believed that the conditions for his theory of justice applied only to domestic society.[63]

At the same time, Rawls argued that there were duties beyond borders for a liberal society, and the list should include mutual aid and respect for rights and institutions that ensure basic human rights, while allowing people in a diverse world to determine their own affairs as much as possible.[64] Thus we should ask whether presidents' goals included a vision that expresses widely attractive values at home and abroad, but prudently balanced those values and assessed risks so that there was a reasonable prospect of their success. This means we judge the president not only on his character and intentions, but also on his contextual intelligence when it comes to promoting values.

Regarding ethical means, we can judge presidents by the well-established just war criteria of proportional and discriminate use of force that are the law of our land, as well as Rawls's liberal concern for minimal degrees of intervention in order to respect the rights and institutions of others. As for ethical consequences, we can ask whether a president succeeded in promoting the country's long-term national interests, whether he respected cosmopolitan values by avoiding extreme insularity and unnecessary damage to foreigners, and whether he educated his followers by promoting truth and trust that broadened moral discourse. These criteria are modest and derived from the insights of realism, liberalism, and cosmopolitanism. The resulting scorecard is by no means complete, but it provides us with some basic guidance that goes beyond a simple generality about prudence.

This 3D scorecard approach hardly solves all problems, but it encourages us to look at all dimensions of a president's actions as we make comparisons. Consider the example of Ronald Reagan and the two Bushes. When people sometimes call for a "Reaganite foreign policy," they tend to mean the moral clarity that went with Reagan's simplification of complex issues and his effective rhetoric in presentation of values. Not only is this inadequate one-dimensional moral reasoning for reasons explained earlier, but it also mistakes the success of Reagan's moral leadership, which included the ability to bargain and compromise as he pursued his policy. Nonetheless, clear and clearly stated objectives can educate and motivate the public. The key question is whether Reagan was prudent in balancing his aspirations and the risks of his goals and objectives. Some people have argued that his initial rhetoric in his first term created a dangerous degree of tension and distrust in US–Soviet relations that increased the prospect of a miscalculation or accident leading to war, but it also created incentives to bargain,

Table 2.1 What Is a Moral Foreign Policy Leader? A 3D Checklist.

Intentions: Goals and Motives
1. *Moral vision.* Did the leader express attractive values, and did those values determine his or her motives? Did he or she have the emotional IQ to avoid contradicting those values because of personal needs?
2. *Prudence.* Did the leader have the contextual intelligence to wisely balance the values pursued and the risks imposed on others?

Means
3. *Use of force.* Did the leader use it with attention to necessity, discrimination in treatment of civilians, and proportionality of benefits and damages?
4. *Liberal concerns.* Did the leader try to respect and use institutions at home and abroad? To what extent were the rights of others considered?

Consequences
5. *Fiduciary.* Was the leader a good trustee? Were the long-term interests of the country advanced?
6. *Cosmopolitan.* Did the leader also consider the interests of other peoples and minimize unnecessary damage to them?
7. *Educational.* Did the leader respect the truth and build credibility? Were facts respected? Did the leader try to create and broaden moral discourse at home and abroad?

which Reagan later put to good advantage when Gorbachev came to power in Reagan's second term. In terms of consequences, Reagan undoubtedly advanced the national interests of the United States, though most of the credit for ending the Cold War and the Soviet Union belongs to Gorbachev. In any event, Reagan took good advantage of the opportunity in a manner that was not limited simply to insular American interests.

By his own account, Bush 41 did not have a transformational vision, but was interested in avoiding disaster in a world that was changing dramatically at the end of the Cold War. While he referred to a "new world order," he never spelled one out. As he and his team responded to the forces that were largely outside of his control, he set goals and objectives that balanced opportunities and realism in a prudent manner. In each instance, Bush limited his short-run objectives in order to pursue long-term stability as a goal. Critics have complained that Bush did not set more transformational objectives.[65] In ethical terms, although Bush did not express a strong moral vision, it is difficult to make the case that he should have been less prudent and taken more risks. In terms of consequences, Bush was a worthy fiduciary in accomplishing national goals and managed to do so in a manner that was not unduly insular and with minimal damage to the interests of foreigners. He was careful not to humiliate Gorbachev and to manage the transition to Yeltsin in Russia. At the same time, not all foreigners were adequately protected, such as when Bush assigned a lower priority to Kurds in Northern Iraq, to dissidents in China, or to Bosnians embroiled in a civil war in the former Yugoslavia. In that sense, Bush's realism set limits to his cosmopolitanism. With a better set of communications skills, Bush might have been able to do more to educate the American public about the changing nature of world they faced after the Cold War. But given the uncertainties of history and the potential for disaster, Bush had one of the best foreign policies of the past century. He allowed the country to benefit from a rising tide and his skills avoided shipwreck during tempest.

In contrast, his son George W. Bush started as a limited realist with little interest in foreign policy, but his objectives became transformational after the terrorist attacks on September 11, 2001. Like Wilson, FDR, and Truman, Bush 43 was concerned about security but turned to the rhetoric of democracy to rally his followers in a time of crisis. Bush's 2002 National Security Strategy, which came to be called the Bush Doctrine, proclaimed that the United States would "identify and eliminate terrorists wherever they are, together with the regimes that sustain them." In this new game there were no rules. The solution to the roots of the terrorist problem was to spread democracy everywhere, and a freedom agenda became the basis of his 2006 National Security Strategy. But the removal of Saddam Hussein did not accomplish the mission, and inadequate understanding of the context plus poor planning and management undercut Bush's grand objectives.

Despite their shared genes, the policies of George W. Bush could not have been more different from those of his father. The greater similarities are between George W. Bush and Woodrow Wilson. Both were highly religious and moralistic men who initially focused on domestic issues without any vision of foreign policy. Both tended to portray the world in black and white rather than shades of gray when they responded to a crisis with a bold vision, and stuck to it. Both tried to educate the public, but good teachers need to be good learners, and Bush's impatience hindered his learning. Wilson succeeded initially in educating a majority of the American people about his League of Nations, but he failed because he refused to make compromises with the Senate. In the long term, Wilson's vision was partially vindicated by the creation of the United Nations, but he lacked the leadership skills needed for its execution and implementation in his own lifetime.

A big problem in foreign policy is the complexity of the context, and that is why contextual intelligence is such an important skill for presidents to have in framing an ethical foreign policy. Contextual intelligence is the ability to understand an evolving environment and capitalize on trends.[66] Sometimes prudence is dismissed as mere strategic self-interest and contrasted with moral conviction. But in 3D ethics, both are important. As Weber pointed out, conviction is important, but in a complex political environment like foreign policy, the president is a trustee who must follow an ethic of responsibility. In that context, weak contextual intelligence that produces negligent assessment and reckless risk-taking leads to immoral consequences. We live in a world of diverse cultures and still know very little about social engineering and how to build nations. When we cannot be sure how to improve the world, prudence becomes an important virtue in an ethic of responsibility, and hubristic visions can create grave damage. Prudence usually requires emotional intelligence, the ability to manage one's emotions and turn them to constructive purposes rather than to be dominated by them.[67] As we shall see, prudence often requires such self-mastery. Obama referred to this basic principle as "don't do stupid shit." He was criticized for not providing an adequate vision, but prudence is not a bad place to start. In foreign policy as in medicine, it is important to remember the Hippocratic oath: first, do no harm.

That raises again the role of institutions, public goods, and how broadly a president defines our national interest. The overall assessment depends not just on specific acts but also on how their pattern shapes the environment of world politics. A president may have a broad and long-term vision but be unable to convince the public, as with Woodrow Wilson in 1919. The disastrous decade of the 1930s was caused when the United States replaced Britain as the largest global power but failed to take on Britain's role in providing global public goods. The result was the collapse of the global system into depression, genocide, and world war. In domestic politics, governments produce public goods such as policing or a clean environment, from which all citizens can benefit and none are excluded. At the global level, where there is no government, public goods—such as coping with climate change, financial stability, or freedom of the seas—are provided by coalitions led by the largest power. Small countries have little incentive to pay for such global public goods. Because their small contributions make little difference to whether they benefit or not, it is rational for them to ride for free. But the largest powers can see the effect and feel the benefit of their contributions. Thus, it is rational and in the long-term national interest of the largest countries to lead. That is consistent with America First, but it rests on a broader historical understanding of the current context than President Trump has shown when he uses that term.

Humans are storytellers, and the narratives that presidents use to explain their foreign policies define national identity at home, and can expand the domestic political space for a more enlightened definition of the national interest. Such narratives can also generate the soft power of attraction abroad that creates an enabling environment for the United States. But presidential narratives that show lack of respect for other cultures and religions not only narrow moral discourse at home, they also weaken American soft power abroad and thus undercut our national interest. That is why the broadening of moral discourse is an important aspect in the assessment of presidents' foreign policies. Reagan had a natural talent for such stories.

Reagan's Secretary of State, George Shultz, once compared foreign policy to gardening—"the constant nurturing of a complex array of actors, interests, and goals." Derek Chollet, who later served in the Obama administration, pointed out that Shultz's later successor Condoleezza Rice wanted a more transformational diplomacy, "not accepting the world as it is, but trying to change it. Rice's ambition is not just to be a gardener—she wants to be a landscape architect."[68] There is a role for both images depending on the context, but we should avoid the common mistake of automatically thinking that the transformational landscape architect is a better foreign policy leader—in terms both of effectiveness and ethics—than the careful gardener. As Henry Kissinger put it, "To strike a balance between the two aspects of world order—power and legitimacy—is the essence of statesmanship. Calculations of power without a moral dimension will turn every disagreement into a test of strength . . . Moral prescriptions without concern for equilibrium, on the other hand, tend toward either crusades or an impotent policy tempting challenges; either extreme risks endangering the coherence of the international order itself."[69] Well-meaning interventions that lack realism can alter millions of lives for the worse. Shakespeare correctly warned about crying havoc and unleashing the dogs of war.

For presidents, prudence is a necessary virtue for a good foreign policy, but it is not sufficient. American presidents between the two world wars were prudent when they needed a broader institutional vision. Wilson had such a vision but without sufficient realism. Franklin Roosevelt started without a foreign policy vision but developed one on the job. In a world of rapid technological and social change, just tending the garden is not enough. A sense of vision and strategy that correctly understands and responds to these new changes is also crucial. In judging a president's record of pursuing a moral foreign policy that makes Americans safer but also makes the world a better place, it is important to look at the full range of their leadership skills, to look at both actions and institutions, commissions and omissions, and to make three-dimensional moral judgments. Even then, we will often wind up with mixed verdicts, but that is the nature of foreign policy as we shall see in the cases that follow.

3

The Founders

The presidents who created the American order after World War II did not enter office with a grand strategy for an American or a liberal international order. Foreign policy was the last thing on the mind of Franklin Roosevelt when he took office during the Great Depression. He paid little heed to a British invitation to an international conference to stabilize the monetary system in 1933, and although Secretary of State Cordell Hull favored more open trade, the American economy, like most of the world, was isolated behind high tariffs. After 1938 FDR began to focus on the security threat posed by Hitler, and in midst of the war, his administration began thinking about institutions for a postwar world. Their first concern was to avoid another Great Depression, and forty-four allied countries met in Bretton Woods, New Hampshire, in July 1944 to create an International Monetary Fund and International Bank for Reconstruction and Development. In the realm of security, FDR wanted a United Nations that strengthened Wilson's liberal League of Nations by adding a security council with "four policemen" (later increased to five) who would enforce collective security against aggressors. His grand design was premised on the assumption that wartime cooperation with the Soviet Union would continue, and there was little provision for the alternative when cooperation broke down and Soviet vetoes paralyzed the Security Council. FDR's grand design for the postwar order was missing many parts, particularly in a world where the balance of power had shifted from multipolar to bipolar. Most important, however, as FDR explained in his epitaph for isolationism near the end of his life, "we have learned to be citizens of the world, members of the human community."[1]

In 1945, Harry Truman inherited Roosevelt's partly formulated plans for economic institutions and a United Nations based on continued cooperation with the Soviet Union, but Truman had no plans for a Cold War world in which that cooperation broke down. While Truman had served in France in World War I, he had little foreign policy experience, and FDR rarely confided in him during Truman's few months as vice president. Moreover, "polls taken in the autumn of 1945 showed that the majority of Americans wanted their country to act to relieve the despair and poverty that had produced ideologies abhorrent to the American mind," but the vast majority also wanted troops brought home quickly and believed their government should concentrate on improving living conditions at home.[2] World War II weakened the economies of the other great powers while strengthening the United States, leaving it as nearly half the world economy. Nonetheless, there was no clear strategy or plan for American hegemony. The first years of Truman's presidency were marked by a good deal of uncertainty in foreign policy. Only after 1947 were most of the major institutions of the American order such as the Marshall Plan and NATO developed as responses to a series of crises, and even then the so-called American hegemony did not include half of the world's population.[3]

Dwight Eisenhower had served as supreme commander of allied forces in Europe during World War II, and Truman appointed him to be the first supreme commander in NATO in 1951, but in the 1952 election, Eisenhower was critical of Truman's policy of merely containing rather than defeating the Soviet Union. Some members of his Republican Party were still tempted by isolationism, while others campaigned on rolling back Communism. Nonetheless, Eisenhower's actions as president consolidated his predecessors' policy. In 1953, he convened a planning exercise in the solarium of the White House that compared a strategy of rolling back Communist gains in Europe with two variants of the existing strategy of containment of the Soviet Union. Given the risks and costs of nuclear war after the Soviets developed nuclear weapons in 1949, Eisenhower rejected the rollback option, and containment remained the American strategy. He argued in 1954 that a "modus vivendi—a means of living together—must be reached with the Russians if the world itself is to avert destruction . . . In response to his comments, Washington leaders debated 'coexistence.' What level would be desirable when it came to the Soviet Union, and indeed, what did the word really mean?"[4]

All three presidents were shaped by their experience of holding high-level positions in World War II and by their memories of the Great Depression of the 1930s. All three regarded isolationism as a serious mistake. FDR had worked for Woodrow Wilson as assistant secretary of the navy and tried to adapt Wilson's ideas about collective security in the design of the new United Nations. Truman also considered himself a Wilsonian and initially tried to continue Roosevelt's plans for a UN-centered world, but events confronted him with choices that led instead to a policy of containment of Soviet power and the permanent stationing of troops overseas. In the 1952 election campaign, Eisenhower joined with other Republicans in criticizing the strategy of containment as cowardly and initially saw troops overseas as a temporary measure, but he quickly came to adopt Truman's policies. In short, there was no grand design for the creation of the American era or the liberal international order, but the three founders shared a lesson learned from the failures of the 1930s.

FRANKLIN D. ROOSEVELT

When Mount Rushmore was carved in the 1920s, the reputations of Washington, Lincoln, Jefferson, and Theodore Roosevelt were set in stone.

If the mountain were recarved today, Franklin Roosevelt would almost certainly join them. In regular rankings of presidents by historians over the years, FDR usually comes in third (behind Washington and Lincoln) even among conservative historians.[5] At a time when democracies were collapsing in many European countries, he is often credited with helping to save liberal democracy in the United States. And, of course, he led the country into World War II, which profoundly transformed America's role in the world.

Roosevelt was initially very cautious in foreign policy. Given the strong isolationist sentiment among the American public, he "never lost sight of the proposition that foreign policy in a democracy, especially one necessitating painful sacrifices, could not survive without a national consensus."[6] In the beginning he continued the Western Hemisphere tradition, and his State Department focused on trade and his Good Neighbor policy toward Latin America. Only at the end of the decade did he see the need for a more global foreign policy.

Hitler and Roosevelt were both elected in 1932, but only gradually did FDR become aware of the threat that Hitler posed. In 1937, during the Spanish Civil War, Roosevelt carefully suggested a quarantine on both sides, but he quickly backed off when the domestic politics proved difficult. Roosevelt's policy was to slow the drift to war in Europe, and to avoid American involvement if war nonetheless occurred.[7] By the end of 1938, the Munich agreement and the Kristallnacht violence against Jews had changed FDR's personal views. While he publicly supported the Munich Agreement, which led to the partition of Czechoslovakia, he privately concluded that it was impossible to work with Hitler in any meaningful way.

FDR wanted Congress to repeal the Neutrality Acts and provide aid to Britain and France, but the American people were unwilling. Gallup polls conducted in 1936 and 1937 showed that 70 percent of Americans believed it had been a mistake to enter World War I. In 1940, no more than 10 percent of respondents said the United States should send its army abroad. In 1941, support for entering the war increased to 23 percent—but even then, the vast majority of the public opposed it.[8] Americans did not share FDR's perception of the Nazi threat. As Roosevelt told his speechwriter in

1938, "It's a terrible thing to look over your shoulder when you are trying to lead—and to find no one there."[9] Roosevelt's contextual intelligence was well ahead of the American public, but as a skilled politician in a democracy, he both followed and tried to lead public opinion.

While professing nonintervention in public, FDR was disingenuous in the measures he took to quietly support the allies and prepare the United States for a war when it came. To help Britain without violating the Neutrality Acts, he traded destroyers for British bases in the Caribbean, but he simply described it as a good deal for the United States. When he offered "lend-lease" aid to Britain in 1940, FDR compared it to a temporary loan of a garden hose to a neighbor even though he knew the analogy was misleading, because there was no prospect of its return. Despite Iceland's proximity to Europe, he sent troops there on the grounds that they were protecting the Western Hemisphere.

Roosevelt tried to educate the public and the Congress, but despite his impressive oratorical skills he was unable to persuade them to change the Neutrality Acts. When speeches and lobbying failed to change minds, he created crises to try to convince the public. FDR tried to engineer a number of incidents at sea, even outright lying about the alleged attack of a German submarine upon the USS destroyer *Greer*, but to little avail. He ran his 1940 election campaign with the deceptive slogan that "your sons will not go to war." In the end, despite his reputation as a great communicator, FDR's dilemma was only solved by Japan's attack on Pearl Harbor, and Hitler's mistake of declaring war on the United States in support of his Axis ally.

Conspiracy theorists suggest that Pearl Harbor was one of Roosevelt's engineered crises, but most historians discount that view.[10] FDR was actually focused on the threat to America from Europe, and his handling of relations with Japan showed considerable ineptitude both in strategic design and implementation. He described the US oil embargo on Japan as a noose to be jerked on from time to time, but failed to monitor the tighter bureaucratic implementation that made the embargo look like strangulation in the eyes of Tokyo.[11] At the same time, it is not likely that he deliberately tricked Japan into attack. As he told Interior Secretary Harold Ickes in July 1941, "It is terribly important for the control of the Atlantic for us to help to keep peace in the Pacific."[12] In contrast to his knowledge of Europe, FDR's contextual intelligence about Asia was not strong, but ironically it was Asia that solved his problem of how to enter Hitler's war. In this sense, despite the tragedy of lives lost, Pearl Harbor was a stroke of luck for Roosevelt. It allowed him to transform American foreign policy and ensured that the attitudes of the American public would support the dramatic change.

As the sheltered son of a wealthy and overbearing mother, Roosevelt learned early in life how to protect his independence through prevarication. Throughout his political career Roosevelt relied heavily on deception, which he practiced on his wife, his friends, and the public. He was a gifted actor, and became even more so after polio crippled him in 1921 at age thirty-nine. Garry Wills argues that "what polio did was make him preternaturally aware of others' perceptions of *him*. This increased his determination to control those perceptions. People were made uncomfortable by his discomfort. He needed to distract them, direct their attention to subjects he preferred; keep them amused, impressed, entertained. That meant he had to perfect a deceptive ease, a casual aplomb, in the midst of acute distress. He became a consummate actor." He used devices like the pince-nez, cigarette holder, and careful stage management to distract attention from his crippled lower body. "This regime of deception reached its climax in the 1944 campaign, when the terminally ill Roosevelt tried to show his strength in an open-car ride through New York City, where he was pelted by driving rain."[13] As another historian put it, "Roosevelt was a man to whom dissembling came easily, and who did not like to tell disagreeable truths boldly. He thus continued to lie about his broad foreign policy goals to enemies and allies alike well after Pearl Harbor."[14]

Franklin Roosevelt was also a man of compromise, often changing positions, and leaving followers and observers to wonder what he really believed. He was notorious for keeping subordinates in the dark, and referred to his leadership skills as that of a juggler trying to keep many balls in the air at once. In contrast to well-organized presidents like Eisenhower or George H. W. Bush, FDR wanted staff to compete with each other so that he had multiple lines of information, and yet remained in ultimate control.

One can see echoes of this style in Kennedy's or Trump's management of the White House.

FDR always remained close to public opinion and never let himself get too far ahead of it. Some see this timidity as a moral failing. For example, he could have saved many more Jews from Hitler's Europe if he had braved anti-Semitic reactions in the American public and loosened immigration restrictions before the war. At the beginning of the war, a similar attitude led to the violation of the human rights of Japanese American citizens, who were interned in camps. And even regarding his major objective of preparing the public to enter the war on the side of the allies, FDR quickly retreated when many of his trial balloons were punctured. Instead, he hoped that what seemed to be independent crises and incidents would educate public opinion in the direction he wished to move. But what is the line between trying to educate the public and immoral manipulation of the public? What degree of deception is morally permissible in a democracy?

As we saw in chapter 2, there is an important distinction between self-serving and group-serving deception. FDR was not above—and sometimes enjoyed—occasional self-serving lies. That was "in character." Most of his major deceptions, however, were for what he thought was the good of the public he was deceiving. A reasonable test is to ask how an impartial observer who shared his goals might judge the action, and how damaging the actions were to trust and institutions. FDR sometimes went too far. It was one thing to campaign in 1940 on a promise of no war or to use misleading labels like "destroyers for bases" or "lend-lease" as disguises for military aid programs. It was quite different to deliberately tell the American public in 1941 that the USS *Greer* had been attacked by a German submarine when it was the *Greer* itself that launched the attack.

In justifying the morality of FDR's foreign policy, one has to rely on the consequentialist argument that "in extremis it is sometimes necessary to violate the letter of the law in order to save the rule of law." Hitler posed such an existential threat that FDR had no alternative but to deceive the public. While forgiving FDR's lies at the beginning of the war, historian Cathal Nolan is critical of FDR's use of lies to support his wartime and postwar plans when the excuse of necessity was weaker. Later in the war, FDR deliberately deceived the American public about the internal character of the Soviet Union. The appropriate criticism is not that Roosevelt lied: "The real problem was that he may have lied *unnecessarily* before he tried an all-out campaign of using the presidential bully pulpit to convince anti-Soviet Americans that massive material aid to Russia was in the direct and vital interest of the United States."[15] Some historians argue that Roosevelt's public deception extended to self-deception in his appraisal of Stalin's motives.[16] One of the effects of the deception is that Americans were less well prepared for dealing with the Soviet Union at the end of the war.

In terms of the scorecard we developed in the last chapter, FDR does well on the first dimension of his intentions. Roosevelt articulated attractive values, and he had the emotional IQ necessary to keep his personal motives aligned with those values. In the famous words of Justice Oliver Wendell Holmes Jr., FDR had a "second-class intellect; first-class temperament."[17] FDR did not let grandiosity or insecurity or narcissism drive him off course. He also maintained a reasonable balance between risk and realism in his foreign policy, though his contextual intelligence was less clear in Asia than in Europe. But his ethical goals were limited by a degree of insularity, and a bolder position could have saved more Jews and done less damage to the rights of Japanese Americans.

On the second dimension of means, given the nature of World War II when he joined it, Roosevelt's use of force was necessary although not discriminate in the bombing of cities. His domestic means were constitutional, but the degree of deception he used may have been excessive and damaging for institutions in the long term. At the same time, his plans for a postwar United Nations and the Bretton Woods economic institutions, and his pressure on Britain for decolonization, showed a liberal concern for rights and institutions. As far back as 1941, when he and Churchill announced the Atlantic Charter, FDR espoused such goals.

It is in the third dimension of consequences that Roosevelt's foreign policy had the greatest ethical importance. His choice to see Hitler as a threat and to prepare America for entry into World War II rather than to accept the isolationist trend of public opinion was a major moral decision with enormous consequences for both the security of the country and the creation of the world order. The Japanese attack and Hitler's declaration of war were strokes of luck for FDR, but he had done the difficult political work of preparing to capitalize on that luck by peacetime measures such as aiding Britain, instituting a draft, and rebuilding the navy. FDR was also lucky that when he decided to run for an unprecedented third term in 1940, the Republican Party nominated a moderate internationalist, Wendell Willkie, rather than an America First isolationist like Charles Lindbergh.[18]

Equally important, after Pearl Harbor, FDR began a process of educating the American public for a sustainable role in the world. He understood the moral importance of institutions discussed in chapter 2. He saw the immoral consequences of the American free-riding in the 1930s (in which he participated), and realized that a better world would require institutions and the largest country would have to lead in the creation and sustaining of such institutions. In that regard FDR's moral vision was in Woodrow Wilson's liberal tradition, but he seasoned Wilson's institution with a dose of realism. Unlike Wilson's League of Nations, FDR's United Nations would have a Security Council where the veto powers—the four policemen later expanded to five—would punish aggressors.

For this grand design to work, the United States and the Soviet Union would have to maintain their wartime cooperation, and that vision was essential to Roosevelt's final efforts. In the effort to preserve that cooperation, Roosevelt did not always level with the American people about the Soviet Union. But in his final meeting with Stalin at Yalta in 1945, FDR was aware that the war-weary American public wanted the imminent return of troops and he "had to rely on charms more than arms to persuade Stalin to permit genuine political independence in the East," which Soviet forces controlled.[19] In helping to frame the postwar liberal international order, FDR broadened the American moral discourse about foreign affairs. As for truth, however, some of his lies could be justified by their long-term consequences, but not all. And he failed to educate public opinion or his poorly prepared understudy, Harry Truman, who would succeed him when the great actor died in April 1945. The following scorecard summarizes these judgments.

Roosevelt's Ethical Scorecard

Intentions and Motives

Moral vision: attractive values, good motives	good
Prudence: balance of values and risks	good

Means

Force: proportion, discrimination, necessity	mixed
Liberal: respect for rights and institutions	mixed

Consequences

Fiduciary: success for long-term US interests	good
Cosmopolitan: minimal damage to others	mixed
Educational: truthful; broad moral discourse	mixed

HARRY S. TRUMAN

Harry Truman was the "little man with glasses" from Missouri who never attended college and spent ten years working on his father's farm. At age thirty-three, he was a hands-on farmer. He was very different from his wealthy, Harvard-educated predecessor. Yet historians generally rank Truman among the top ten American presidents. His international experience was limited to brief service as an artillery officer in France during World War I and as a Senator from 1935 to 1945. During his two and a half months as Roosevelt's Vice President, FDR never consulted him about such important issues as the atomic bomb, the Yalta Conference—or much else. In biographer David McCullough's words, Truman was "a 19th century man,"[20] yet he made some of the most important foreign policy decisions of the twentieth century. If Wilson and FDR broke from America's Western Hemisphere tradition by sending large armies overseas, Truman proved pivotal to the postwar order by keeping them there. George Washington had warned about "no entangling alliances," but Truman's NATO alliance has lasted for seven decades.

In 1945, the dominant political concerns in the United States were not about international order but about domestic employment and whether the postwar economy would relapse into depression. Truman rapidly brought some three million US troops home from Europe. When a 1945 Gallup poll asked Americans what they thought the most important problem facing the country during the next year was, jobs and strikes topped the list.[21] Yet American public opinion was no longer isolationist in the way it had been in the 1930s. In October 1945, 71 percent of respondents believed it would be better for the future of the United States to take an active part in world affairs,[22] and surveys reveal that between 1945 and 1956 the share of respondents who believed the United States should take an active role in the world never dipped below 70 percent.[23]

Truman did not come into office with a clear foreign policy agenda. He admired Wilson and he wanted to implement Roosevelt's grand design for a postwar order based on the liberal idea of collective security bolstered by great powers ensconced as permanent veto-wielding members of a new UN Security Council. In June 1950, when the Soviets made the tactical mistake of boycotting the Security Council and thereby allowed collective security to work after North Korean armies crossed the 38th Parallel into South Korea, Truman responded in what historian Ernest May called "an axiomatic" reflection of his deepest beliefs.[24] As he told his advisors when he returned to Washington after learning of the invasion, he had been thinking about Mussolini and Hitler and now the Soviets: "By God, I'm not going to let them have it."[25] He had learned the lessons of the 1930s, and vowed not to allow aggression go unanswered again. Wilsonianism was his moral default option.

When Vyacheslav Molotov, the Soviet Foreign Minister, visited the White House in April 1945 shortly after Truman became president, Truman chewed him out for breaking promises, particularly about Eastern Europe. Some critics see that encounter as proof of Truman's Cold War orientation, but the incident can more accurately be seen as Truman's naïve American reaction to Soviet lies rather than a plan for a Cold War. If anything, like Roosevelt, Truman underestimated Stalin's malevolent intentions, and once mistakenly compared him to Kansas City political boss Tom Prendergast.[26] Early in 1946, the American diplomat George Kennan sent his famous Long Telegram from Moscow warning Washington about Soviet intentions, but Truman tried to preserve FDR's cooperation policy. In the summer of 1946, he asked his aide Clark Clifford to sample the views of people in the government. When Clifford reported that most experts agreed with Kennan, Truman ordered that the report be restricted to ten copies and locked up.[27] He did not want his hand forced, and had no alternative design.

The year and a half between the end of the war and what became known as the Truman Doctrine was "one of the most difficult and confusing periods in U.S. diplomatic history . . . [as] Americans gyrated between hopes of peaceful cooperation and fears of all-out strife."[28] As Russia specialist Chip Bohlen put it, "The United States is confronted with a condition in the world which is at direct variance with the assumptions upon which policies were predicated. Instead of unity among the great powers . . . there is complete disunity."[29] Finally, in February 1947, in the context of British withdrawal in the Eastern Mediterranean in the face of Soviet and Yugoslav pressure on Greece and Turkey, Truman agreed to the great transformational steps of the Truman Doctrine, followed months later by the Marshall Plan, and then NATO in 1949.

Truman was neither a charismatic leader nor a great communicator. Though he believed in heroic leaders from his reading of history, he feared that he did not measure up. Moreover, he was surrounded by strong advisors.[30] Under Secretary of State Dean Acheson and Michigan Republican Senator Arthur Vandenberg framed the issues at crucial White House meetings in 1947. George Marshall gave the famous Harvard commencement address that later led to his eponymous plan, and Truman revered Marshall. But the famous wise men of Dean Acheson, Averell Harriman, Robert Lovett, John McCloy, George Kennan, and Charles Bohlen each had blind spots and shortcomings; "No single one could have guided the country to its new role as world power." Yet collectively, they "brought to the immense task just the right mixture of vision and practicality, aggressiveness and patience."[31]

Some critics portray Truman as a mere conduit for the so-called wise men. Such a picture, however, misses his ability to select and command the respect of the impressive team, and underrates his on-the-job learning and his ability to develop his contextual intelligence while in office. It also misses Truman's willingness to make tough decisions. He stood up to the iconic Secretary of State George Marshall, who opposed the creation of the state of Israel; fired the imperious war hero Douglas MacArthur, who wanted to expand the Korean War; and resisted the use of nuclear weapons after the war bogged down.[32] While Truman did not lose sleep (in his words) over the use of atomic bombs to end World War II, his character made him very dubious about further use of nuclear weapons despite the political punishment he suffered at home after China entered the Korean War in November 1950. Truman can be seriously criticized for lack of prudence in not heeding China's warnings of war if the Americans entered North Korea and approached the Yalu River, but his optimistic assessment was shared by the intelligence community, many of his advisors, and above all by General MacArthur, who was in command in the field and difficult to control.[33]

Any description of Truman as a puppet misses the importance of his moral vision of America's role in the world. Truman had a Wilsonian view of American exceptionalism, and that made a difference to the way that the doctrine of containment was formulated.[34] It was Truman's decision to follow Acheson and Vandenberg's advice to frame containment as a defense of free people everywhere and "scare the hell out of the American people," rather than portray it as an issue of the balance of power in the Eastern Mediterranean. George Kennan was dismayed by this militarization and ideological expansion of his original concept. Some analysts complain that Truman's open-ended universal commitment led eventually to the disaster of the Vietnam War, but that is too simple. Truman provided aid to Tito's Communist Yugoslavia (even though it was a major supporter of Communists in Greece) after Tito broke with Stalin, and in Asia, Truman followed Marshall's advice and avoided becoming entangled in a losing effort to protect Chiang Kai-shek's nationalist regime in China despite domestic pressure from Republicans in Congress and the press.

Moreover, Truman's emphasis on the values embodied in his doctrine and in the Marshall Plan also contributed to the institutionalization of the Atlantic alliance. The democratization of Germany was crucial, and the liberal nature of American primacy in Europe made it more open and more stable than a traditional military alliance. In the words of a Norwegian scholar, America succeeded in maintaining the allegiance of postwar

Europe, because it was "an empire by invitation."[35] In addition to the Truman Doctrine, the Marshall Plan, and NATO, Truman added a fourth point of technical assistance for modernization in developing countries.

In any event, it was Truman's interpretation of the objectives of containment that guided foreign policy as the United States responded to the new geopolitical structure of bipolarity after World War II. Containment was a realist balance of power policy, but under Truman's tutelage, it also became part of a liberal international order. His moral outlook mattered. At the same time, he was pragmatic and willing to trade off liberal values for security interests. As Eleanor Roosevelt wrote to him, she did not believe in "taking over Mr. Churchill's policies in the Near East in the name of democracy." As one historian put it, "The Greek and Turkish regimes might well have firm anti-communist credentials, but that did not mean they were of themselves free or democratic."[36] The same could be said for President Syngman Rhee of South Korea.

Truman, the accidental president, had a very different character from Roosevelt. "He possessed little or no charisma, struggled with an ego more fragile than most observers have understood, and had extreme distaste for the need to manipulate others. He was, however, a good manager and, on the important things, a person of sound judgment, not least because he understood his weaknesses. Often dismissed by contemporaries as a 'little man' because his deficiencies were more apparent than his strengths, he actually was one of the more important and successful of twentieth-century presidents."[37]

In the words of another biographer, Truman "surrounded himself with people who were better educated, taller, handsomer, more cultivated, and accustomed to high-powered company, but that didn't bother him. He knew who he was."[38] This apparent contradiction suggests that there were different layers of Truman's self-confidence. Just below the surface were the sensitivity and insecurity that led him to write intemperate letters to critics, but below that was a sense of self that led him to stuff the letters into a desk drawer rather than send them, and eventually to have the character and courage to fire a disruptive military hero like Douglas MacArthur. Truman benefited from a good emotional IQ that gave him self-control over his personal needs and motives, and he understood that he had limited knowledge of international affairs. Unlike Roosevelt, he relied on delegation and institutionalizing foreign policy by creating the Central Intelligence Agency, the Department of Defense, and the National Security Council.

In terms of our three-dimensional ethics, Truman ranks high in the first category of intentions, goals, and motives. He came into office committed to implementing Roosevelt's grand design, but he also had a strong moral vision of his own. "He was a Wilsonian idealist who deeply believed in American international leadership; the duty of American foreign policy was to promote the betterment of mankind. He could speak with great eloquence of TVAs for remote parts of the world and of the progress yet to come in human affairs. He probably would have been at a loss in any attempt to discuss totalitarianism on a theoretical basis. But . . . he understood its challenge, whether Nazi or Soviet, better than did many of his contemporaries."[39] Truman was a man who expressed the proverbial basic values of the American Midwest, and his emotional intelligence enabled him to align his personal needs and motives with his publicly professed goals. He knew how to keep his ego in check, insisting that the Marshall Plan be named for the general rather than the president because it would sell "a whole hell of a lot better in Congress."[40]

Truman did a reasonable job of prudently balancing risk and realism in his goals. He was quite cautious in the early days after the war, and only developed his transformational objectives after learning from experience and in consultation with skilled advisors. Even then he was notable for his prudence. In his 1949 Inaugural Address, after listing military and economic measures to contain Soviet expansion, he included a note of humility: "We must deny ourselves the license to do always as we please."[41] While he expressed his doctrine in universalistic terms, he applied it with an awareness of the limits of American power, resisting pressures to try to reverse the outcome of the Chinese civil war. As Acheson said, the liberal rhetoric had to be "clearer than truth" to persuade the public and Congress, but the resources were budgeted just for Greece and Turkey. Until the Korean War, Truman was cautious in his expansion of the Pentagon budget.

Truman resisted suggestions that the United States use its nuclear monopoly to wage preventive war. In Truman's words, "Such a war is the weapon of dictators, not of free and democratic countries like the

United States."[42] Truman argued that nuclear weapons were not ordinary weapons, and refused to let the military have custody over them, putting them instead in a civilian Atomic Energy Commission. "Despite the US monopoly on the bomb, the man who had never expressed doubts about its use on Japan was now troubled by the possibility of having to use it again."[43] Truman's management of the Berlin Airlift in response to Soviet efforts to squeeze American troops out of the surrounded German capital was a model of balancing risk and realism among advisors that Jack Kennedy later emulated during the Cuban Missile Crisis in 1962.

Raymond Aron, a distinguished French intellectual, had characterized the twentieth century as "the century of total war."[44] Under the threat of nuclear weapons, it became instead the century of limited war. Nonetheless, history required critical human agents to make that moral transition, and Truman was a key to that process. The man who unleashed nuclear war at Hiroshima called for a study of nuclear options during the Berlin Airlift and rejected what he saw.[45] When he could have pressed harder against Soviet domination of Poland and Czechoslovakia at the time of the Marshall Plan in 1948, he opted for prudence rather than the risk of war.

In Korea, after Chinese troops crossed the Yalu River and pushed back the American Army in November 1950, Truman insisted on keeping the war limited and resisted MacArthur's requests to bomb Chinese targets and to use Chiang Kai-shek's troops that had just lost the Chinese civil war.[46] Truman acted incautiously in June 1950, given Acheson's earlier exclusion of the peninsula from America's defense perimeter and given the poor preparation of American troops. Truman wanted to implement Wilson's vision of collective security as embodied in the UN Charter, but a realist might have been more cautious about the risks involved and as Acheson later observed, it was Korea that ultimately "destroyed the Truman Administration."[47] For Truman, the moral lesson of the 1930s was to stand up to aggression and he did—and he paid the price. At the same time, he saw the moral disproportion of nuclear weapons and refused temptations to use them to rescue his position and reputation.

Unlike FDR, Truman was rarely deceptive. While his description of the intervention in Korea did not adequately prepare the public for the war, in general Truman respected the truth and built trust in institutions at home and abroad. He was also attentive to questions of autonomy and rights, and in 1948 the Universal Declaration on Human Rights was signed on his watch. Where Truman has been faulted in the category of means is the indiscriminate killing of civilians through the use of nuclear weapons to end the war in Japan. Given the momentum of the Manhattan Project, it would have taken a bold move by the new president to stop the program, and he saw no reason to do so, particularly given how little was known about nuclear weapons at that point. The principles of discrimination and proportionality had already been massively violated by the fire-bombings of cities, and the public was eager to end a war that Japan had started. The train had already left the station by the time Truman became president, and he went along with the consensus although he did decide against using a third bomb. When the question of nuclear use came up in Berlin and Korea, Truman knew more and refused to treat nuclear weapons as normal. In his farewell address of 1953, he warned that "starting an atomic war is totally unthinkable for rational men."[48] By sticking to his principles, he helped to begin a nuclear taboo.

As for moral consequences, Truman's decision to keep an American presence overseas and to build strong alliance institutions was crucial to the establishment of the American order. Some Republican isolationists complained about the risks related to engagement, but hawks railed at the immorality of his consignment of Chiang Kai-shek and Eastern Europeans to totalitarian Communist domination. Like MacArthur, they felt Truman should have pressed harder in challenging Stalin and faulted this sin of omission. Perhaps Truman left some money on the table by not exploiting America's nuclear monopoly, but the risks were high, and on balance he was a prudent fiduciary for American long-term interests. Moreover, he did so with attention to the needs of outsiders and programs to assist them, such as the Marshall Plan and technical assistance.

And while Truman was no great orator, he and his cabinet tried to educate the American people to the importance of maintaining American leadership in the reconstruction and stabilization of the postwar world. Some critics have faulted Truman for changing George Kennan's realist doctrine of containment to an overly universal liberal doctrine of defending free peoples everywhere that eventually set the scene for the Vietnam War. But it is difficult to blame Truman for Vietnam, and without his universalism the strategy would have been more difficult to sell to the American people, as Senator Vandenberg had warned. Truman indulged in American moralism, but it is also true that he conducted a largely ethical foreign policy that helped to create the post-1945 liberal international order. These judgments are summarized in the following scorecard.

Truman's Ethical Scorecard

Intentions and Motives

Moral vision: attractive values, good motives	good
Prudence: balance of values and risks	good

Means

Force: proportion, discrimination, necessity	mixed
Liberal: respect for rights and institutions	good

Consequences

Fiduciary: success for long-term US interests	good
Cosmopolitan: minimal damage to others	mixed
Educational: truthful; broad moral discourse	good

DWIGHT D. EISENHOWER

Though historians currently rank Truman among the top six presidents, he left office in 1953 with very low approval ratings, and his foreign policy was politically contested. The liberal Henry Wallace wing of the Democratic Party believed Truman was too uncompromising with the Soviet Union, and the Republican Party was divided between an aggressive group that attacked "the cowardly college of containment," and Robert Taft's isolationist wing that wanted to reduce American commitment abroad. Dwight Eisenhower had retired from the army as a five-star general and become president of Columbia University before returning to service as the first Supreme Commander of NATO. He did not originally intend to run for president, but decided to do so when he feared that Taft might get the Republican nomination in 1952.

Like Truman, Eisenhower came from a humble Midwestern background, but his opportunity to attend West Point (where he graduated in 1915) and his distinguished career in the army in World War II gave him a greater contextual intelligence about international affairs than any previous president. Unlike Truman, Eisenhower did not need on-the-job training. In 1953, at the beginning of his term, he held the famous White House Solarium exercise to examine basic options for foreign policy, but it was less to educate Eisenhower than for him to educate his cabinet and close staff. He fended off the two wings of his party that worried him (isolationists and advocates of rollback) and, not surprisingly, came down in favor of the middle option. The Republicans had removed George Kennan from the State Department, but Eisenhower used him to present the case for the containment option, though Kennan's policy had been called immoral and cowardly by some Republicans who wanted to roll back Communism.

Secretary of State John Foster Dulles had refused to give Kennan a new assignment, but Eisenhower was not limited by Dulles. As described by historian John Gaddis, Dulles's bluster made Eisenhower uneasy, but in a Republican Party still dominated by isolationists and McCarthyites, having Dulles at State was politically useful. Moreover, despite Eisenhower's military background, it was not his habit to discipline subordinates. He understood soft power. In his words, "You don't lead by hitting people over the head; that's assault, not leadership."[49] Instead he sought to educate Dulles and others within his administration about the probable risks, costs, and consequences of a more aggressive strategy. As Gaddis put it, Eisenhower used Kennan "to liberate Eisenhower from the 'liberation' strategy to which Dulles had tried to commit him during the 1952 campaign."[50]

Eisenhower came into office with modest objectives, and his style was transactional rather than charismatic. He consolidated the doctrine of containment and made it sustainable by a set of prudent judgments such as avoiding land wars in Korea and Vietnam that later trapped his successors. He cut overseas spending in order to support the domestic economy, and strengthened the new alliances with Europe and Japan. He was willing to negotiate with the Soviet Union, and exercised great prudence at the time of the Soviet intervention in Hungary in 1956 when he rejected a CIA proposal to air-drop arms to Hungarians.[51] While he relied on nuclear threats of massive retaliation to offset Soviet conventional superiority in Europe and to save spending on expensive land forces, he was simultaneously very careful in resisting the actual use of nuclear weapons against North Korea and China.

Eisenhower managed to maintain a broad public consensus on foreign policy. Public opinion expert Ole R. Holsti argues that "if the term 'internationalist foreign policy consensus' was ever a valid description of the domestic bases of American foreign policy it would appear to have been most applicable to the period between the traumas of the Korean and Vietnam wars." In 1956, 59 percent of Republicans, 58 percent of Democrats, and 58 percent of Independents approved of foreign aid to help stop Communism.[52] A 1954 Gallup poll showed that 62 percent of the public considered themselves internationalist, while 17 percent said they were isolationist. A large majority (76 percent) approved of the United Nations.[53]

Eisenhower often "led from behind" with gentle persuasion rather than command. Presidential expert Fred Greenstein called Eisenhower's a "hidden hand presidency" because he combined a visible monarchical style with a less visible prime ministerial role. While Dulles sounded rhetorical alarms, Eisenhower remained in control of foreign policy. Eisenhower had superb organizational skills, and was quite firmly in control of his government.[54] He improved Truman's institutional innovations such as the National Security Council and used it both to manage information and policy flows, but also to educate his top officials. But the cost of his low-key style was that he failed to educate the public on issues like civil rights and the spurious missile gap, which Democratic critics popularized.

Eisenhower understood the limits of American power, and managed crises well. Although he used the misleading metaphor of dominoes falling in Southeast Asia, he avoided letting the metaphor suck him into a major intervention in Vietnam because, in his words, it would "swallow up our troops by the divisions." However, having stated that Indochina must be held, Eisenhower risked a loss of credibility and the decision was not easy for him.[55] He considered intervening with air power, nuclear weapons, or ground troops, but finally ruled out acting unilaterally.[56] But he kept his emotional needs separate from his analysis and avoided the trap that later destroyed Lyndon Johnson, who lacked Eisenhower's emotional and contextual intelligence. One result of Eisenhower's prudence was eight years of peace and prosperity.

As biographer Stephen Ambrose noted, because Eisenhower's leadership was "firm, fair, objective, dignified, he was everything most Americans wanted in a president." If there was one word to describe reactions to him, it was "trustworthy."[57] Richard Nixon once said that when it came to decision-making, Eisenhower was "the most unemotional and analytical man in the world," and Greenstein argued that what was striking about his leadership was "not his lack of passion, but the freedom of his public actions from extraneous emotion."[58] He had the emotional intelligence to manage his motives. While he could be skillful in the Machiavellian politics of indirect action against opponents like Joseph McCarthy (or even allies like his vice president, Richard Nixon), Eisenhower was generally respectful of the truth. At the same time, he had strong moral convictions. He was a free-market Republican, a staunch anti-Communist, and committed to America's role in the world.

Though he titled his war memoirs *Crusade in Europe*, Eisenhower was no moral crusader. In 1952, when he accepted the Republican nomination, he called for the party to join him in a crusade to clean up Washington, but this was run-of-the-mill political rhetoric. Critics later "found it difficult to discover what his crusade was aiming at. There was no stirring call to arms, no great moral crusade, no idealistic pursuit of some overriding national goal." In 1953, Eisenhower had wanted "to provide moral leadership that would both draw on and illuminate America's spiritual superiority to the Soviet Union, indeed to all the world."[59] But he did not take a strong public lead on the great domestic moral issues of the day that affected American soft power—civil rights and McCarthyism.

With regard to the Third World, Eisenhower showed little respect for democracy or the human rights of others in his approach to containing Soviet influence. There were no liberal restraints when it came to overthrowing elected regimes.[60] He did reject advice to send troops to Vietnam, because "in the eyes of Asiatic peoples [we would] merely replace French colonialism with American colonialism."[61] At the time of the British, French, and Israeli invasion of Egypt in the Suez Crisis of 1956, he used economic pressure to force British withdrawal because he said he would not condone armed aggression—no matter who is the attacker and no matter who is the victim. Although Eisenhower used liberal rhetoric about the free world, which he hoped would line up countries with the Western democracies, his overthrow of popularly elected governments in Iran and Guatemala, and his hostility toward Nasser, Castro, and Patrice Lumumba in the Congo, contributed to mistrust of the United States in the Third World. Even in the context of Cold War bipolarity, it is difficult to see many of Eisenhower's covert interventions as proportionate or necessary, and even a sympathetic biographer concluded that "unfortunately, Eisenhower's CIA did far more harm than good to American interests."[62] Moreover, he was faulty in his expectation that covert actions would remain covert.[63]

Managing crises was what Eisenhower did best, whether it be Korea in 1953, Dien Bien Phu in 1954, Quemoy and Matsu in 1955, Hungary and Suez in 1956, Sputnik in 1957, Berlin in 1959, or the Soviet shootdown of a U-2 spy plane in 1960. "Eisenhower managed each one without overreacting, without going to war, without increasing defense spending, without frightening people half out of their wits. He downplayed each one, insisted that a solution could be found, and then found one. It was a magnificent performance."[64] His wartime experience and emotional self-control provided the necessary contextual and emotional intelligence to avoid disaster.

In ethical terms, Eisenhower's vision and goals were modest and balanced, and his emotional IQ kept his motives and public values aligned. He was prudent in balancing values and risk, but his record on means was mixed. The covert actions that overthrew the elected regimes of Arbenz in Guatemala and Mossadegh in Iran violated local autonomy, and Eisenhower by his own admission "realized full well that United States intervention in Central America and Caribbean affairs had greatly injured our standing in all of Latin America."[65] He allowed CIA Director Allan Dulles to engage in covert actions that included attempted assassinations in a number of countries because in a bipolar Cold War, he felt it essential to forestall any possible Communist advances.[66] But one can question whether these leftist nationalist regimes would have led to Communist states, and the long-term memories and repercussions were not good for the United States or the local peoples. Moreover, he left his successor with bad advice about involvement in Laos and Vietnam, as well as plans for a covert invasion of Cuba that became the 1961 debacle known as the Bay of Pigs. Biographer William Hitchcock asks, "Why did Eisenhower order such brutal and ultimately damaging secret operations?" and attributes it "to a failure of moral imagination."[67]

Despite his dubious means with covert intervention, Eisenhower deserves a great deal of moral praise for resisting numerous recommendations for the use of nuclear weapons in the Korean War, to prevent the Vietnamese defeat of French forces at Dien Bien Phu, or to defend the Nationalist forces on the islands of Quemoy-Matsu off the coast of China. He rejected a plan by the Joint Chiefs of Staff to use atomic weapons in Vietnam with the comment: "You boys must be crazy. We can't use those awful things against Asians for the second time in less than ten years. My God." At another point in 1954, Eisenhower turned to Admiral Radford, Chairman of the Joint Chiefs of Staff, and said: "Suppose it would be possible to destroy Russia. I want you to carry this question home with you: gain such a victory, and what do you do with it? Here would be a great area from the Elbe to Vladivostok . . . torn up and destroyed, without government, without its communications, just an area of starvation and disaster. I ask you what would the civilized world do about it? I repeat that there is no victory except through our imaginations."[68] Eisenhower went beyond mere prudence about insular American interests and included a cosmopolitan element in his moral reasoning about not using nuclear weapons.

Ironically, these private moral decisions were strongly at odds with his public statements on nuclear weapons. Nuclear deterrence requires an opponent's belief in the possibility of use. Eisenhower was a fiscal conservative who warned against the "military-industrial complex" in his farewell address, and by 1958 had brought Pentagon spending down to 10 percent of GDP from the 14 percent it had been when he took office. Nuclear deterrence offered a defense policy with "more bang for the buck."[69] Unlike Truman, he wanted nuclear weapons to be perceived as a normal part of the arsenal—"like bullets"—and feared the development of a taboo that would delegitimize them and remove them from the arsenal. His defense posture was designed to save money on conventional forces by having tactical nuclear weapons backed by the threat of massive retaliation. At the same time, he wanted to retain presidential control.

Eisenhower's refusal to use nuclear weapons did not prevent him from threatening to use them for the sake of deterrence and coercion. He hinted at nuclear use to help achieve an armistice in the stalemated Korean War, and was ambiguous about nuclear use in the Taiwan offshore islands crises of 1954 and 1958. Would Eisenhower have used nuclear weapons? His close advisor General Andrew Goodpaster thought not, but others disagreed, and Eisenhower never answered the hypothetical question. His objective was deterrence, and in the words of biographer Evan Thomas, he accomplished it "by cleverness, indirection, subtlety, and downright deviousness—and by embracing the very weapon he could never use—to safeguard his country and possibly the rest of mankind from annihilation."[70]

While no one knows for sure whether Eisenhower would ever have used nuclear weapons, his private decisions were "no" at crucial points, while his public posture built a massive apparatus of nuclear risk.[71] Those private choices reinforced the taboo that he feared would undercut his public options, and his successors worried that the elaborate machinery of massive retaliation left presidents with very few real options. At the same time, he tried to advance arms control agreements with the Soviets. By the very nature of his deterrent bluff, however, Eisenhower could never level with the American people about his real view on nuclear weapons. As he once told his press secretary, "Don't worry, Jim. If that question comes up, I'll just confuse them."[72]

Eisenhower's nuclear policy was consistent with his general style of posing publicly as a benign monarch above the fray, while carefully controlling like a prime minister behind the scenes. As Fred Greenstein points out, "He was no Machiavellian; he recognized the importance of honesty and intellectual clarity in private deliberations but took it as an unspoken axiom that public language was to be adapted to the circumstances at hand and toward the best possible consequences."[73] Such an approach to deception is far down the scale from the deception practiced upon the public by Franklin Roosevelt's lies or Donald Trump's tweets, but such questionable means limited Eisenhower's ability to educate the public. In general, however, Eisenhower's foreign policy leadership produced eight years of peace and prosperity for Americans and many others by prudent avoidance and management of crises. Those are pretty impressive moral consequences, and his record is summarized in the following scorecard.

Eisenhower's Ethical Scorecard

Intentions and Motives

Moral vision: attractive values, good motives	good
Prudence: balance of values and risks	good

Means

Force: proportion, discrimination, necessity	good on nuclear
Liberal: respect for rights and institutions	poor

Consequences

Fiduciary: success for long-term US interests	good
Cosmopolitan: minimal damage to others	mixed
Educational: truthful; broad moral discourse	mixed

******

In surveying the role of ethics in the decisions by the three presidents who founded the American liberal international order, several things stand out. All three were liberal realists who drew upon both traditions in constructing their mental maps of the world. While they were Wilsonian in their views of institutions and collective security, and believers in American exceptionalism, they were not ideologues or crusaders. None used the populist nationalist tradition represented in their time by Governor Huey Long of Louisiana or Senator Joseph McCarthy of Wisconsin. All three were quite prudent in their balancing of risks and values. All three exhibited good emotional intelligence in their motives and good contextual intelligence in their mental maps of the world. While Truman's doctrine spoke of "free people everywhere," he did not apply it in hard cases like China, and while Eisenhower's Republican Party criticized the immorality of containment and spoke of rolling back Communism in Europe, he was quite prepared to abandon the Hungarians in their 1956 uprising.

At the same time, the language of American exceptionalism and values was important in shaping policy. As Chip Bohlen observed about his friend George Kennan's proposals to simply divide Europe into spheres of influence, "they may well be optimum from an abstract point of view. But as practical suggestions they are utterly impossible. Foreign policies of that kind cannot be made in a democracy."[74] And de facto, Europe did become divided. Both Truman and Acheson quickly saw that Michigan Senator Arthur Vandenberg, a former isolationist who became a key Republican internationalist, was correct that to get Congress to fund the Truman Doctrine they would need to stress values and "make things clearer than truth." The appeal to morality was critical to recruiting support for policy.

Another point to note is the enormous moral importance of omissions as well as acts of commission. At the end of World War II, the United States had nearly half the world's product and a monopoly on atomic weapons. Some policymakers were tempted by the idea of preventive war and aggression for peace. Truman rejected such ideas as immoral. Moreover, during the decade of crises from Berlin in 1948 to the offshore islands in 1958, Truman and Eisenhower rejected military advice to use nuclear weapons. At the time, nuclear weapons were new and poorly understood, and had Truman or Eisenhower decided to use them, the ensuing world would look very different today. There would likely be many more nuclear weapons states and more prospect of use. Nobel Laureate Thomas Schelling argued that development of a nuclear taboo was one of the most important normative developments of the past seventy years. It was the dog that did not bark—or bite. While Eisenhower resisted a formal taboo that would weaken his strategy of deterrence through massive retaliation, at crucial moments he resisted recommendations of tactical use. In part, like Truman, his reasoning was based on strategic prudence, but both men also expressed views in private that were also based on intuitive moral concerns. The continuing strength of the nuclear taboo is debated today, and there are different moral views at the public, elite, and presidential levels, but the existence of both the taboo and a debate can be traced back to these presidential decisions in the 1950s.[75]

Finally, in terms of institutions, all three presidents valued the United Nations but quickly saw its limitations when faced with Soviet vetoes. They were institutionalists without being prisoners of institutions. They understood soft power and the role of institutions in shaping expectations. The Marshall Plan placed a strong emphasis on European economic integration, and the presidents faced numerous frustrations in dealing with bickering European allies. They also recognized that an American security framework would be necessary in which European economic integration could develop, and that led to the creation of NATO. The founders understood that hard and soft power can reinforce each other. Imperfect as their grand strategy was and often uncertain in its implementation, the founders nonetheless created a framework that led to a better world for many, both in and outside the United States.

4

The Vietnam Era

The 1960s began with Cold War anxieties at a peak. A summit meeting between Eisenhower and Khrushchev had been cancelled after the Soviets shot down a U2 spy plane; Americans worried about the developing Soviet nuclear arsenal as well as about expanding Soviet influence in Africa and Latin America, particularly after Fidel Castro came to power in Cuba. In Europe, the Soviets pressed for change in the status of Berlin, the isolated Western enclave within East Germany. In Asia, a Communist insurgency threatened the American-backed government of South Vietnam, and the issue of Vietnam came to dominate the decade.

There is a difference, however, between foreign policy moods and realities. The Soviet launch of *Sputnik* in October 1957 shocked both the elite and broad public's sense of American technological superiority. Intelligence reports overestimated Soviet capabilities, and Democrats including Kennedy criticized Eisenhower for allowing a missile gap to develop. Eisenhower knew the United States was well ahead, but he said little for fear of jeopardizing the U2 flights that provided critical intelligence. The missile gap was real, but contrary to the partisan rhetoric, it was in America's favor by a ratio of nearly six to one. Some of the national mood at the beginning of the decade was related to generational change. Kennedy charged that global trends were leaving the United States behind and Eisenhower had allowed "the Communists to evict us from our rightful estate at the head of this world-wide revolution," offering a future for developing countries (such as Vietnam) that was "far more peaceful, far more democratic, and far more locally controlled."[1]

To the contrary, however, the 1960s turned out to be traumatic in American foreign policy. The Vietnam War led to more than 58,000 American deaths, millions of Vietnamese killed, riots in American cities and campuses, the early retirement of one president, and the near-impeachment of another. The war ended in defeat, and the mental and political scars lasted decades. The origins of American involvement in Vietnam went back to the Truman and Eisenhower era, but the presidents most centrally involved were John F. Kennedy, Lyndon B. Johnson, and Richard Nixon. All three had lived through the paranoid period of McCarthyism in the early 1950s, and the bitter domestic political debates over who "lost China to Communism." Each feared the political onus of being the president who "lost" Vietnam, yet none really had any in-depth understanding of the country.

The dominant metaphor about Vietnam—the domino theory that Eisenhower ironically created but avoided—became a trap for his successors. The prevailing image in Washington was that if the North Vietnamese Communists took over South Vietnam, it would precipitate knock-on effects that would topple other Asian countries into the Sino-Soviet bloc in a bipolar world. Even when some leaders privately realized the limits of the metaphor, their public use of the imagery became a trap that constrained their options. And linked to the metaphor was a broader concern about the credibility of global commitments in the Cold War. As Assistant Secretary of Defense John McNaughton famously estimated in March 1965, 70 percent of our reason to stay in Vietnam was "to avoid a humiliating US defeat to our reputation as a guarantor. 20 percent—to keep

SVN and adjacent territory from Chinese hands. 10 percent—to permit the people of SVN to enjoy a better, freer way of life."[2]

With 20/20 hindsight, if American presidents had paid more heed to nationalism instead of Communism in their rhetoric, they might have used a better metaphor—the game of checkers in which red and black squares alternate. Dominoes is an ideological metaphor in which everything turns red. Checkers is a realist metaphor in which "the enemy of my enemy is my friend." China had already begun to chafe against Russian tutelage, and the fighting in Vietnam had started as a nationalist struggle against French colonialism. After the French defeat, the dividing line between North and South Vietnam that was established by the Geneva armistice of 1954 was supposed to be temporary, but neither side properly observed its plan for elections in 1956 and two decades of war ensued. Many Vietnamese continued to think in terms of one nation rather than the two states that the United States portrayed. In the years that followed the final withdrawal of American troops and the unification of Vietnam under Communist control in 1975, fighting erupted between Russia and China, China and Vietnam, and Vietnam and Cambodia. The realist checkerboard metaphor based on nationalism proved to be a better predictor of political alignment and conflict than the domino theory, and today Communist Vietnam welcomes port calls by the US Navy to balance pressure from Communist China.

JOHN F. KENNEDY

Jack Kennedy was forty-three when he was inaugurated in 1961. Not only was he the first Catholic president to be elected, but also the youngest, and his rhetoric rang with images of youth and renewal. He was not only twenty-seven years younger but radically different in style from Eisenhower. He had run against Eisenhower's "eight years of drugged and fitful sleep," and promised a "new frontier" that would "get the country moving again." His charismatic call to "ask what you can do for your country" inspired many in the younger generation, as did such initiatives as the Peace Corps and the mission to send a man to the moon. In November 1963, the world was shocked when his thousand days in office were suddenly cut short by assassination.

That tragic ending and the brevity of his presidency gave rise to myths and countermyths about what might have happened if Kennedy had lived. By the fiftieth anniversary of his death, an estimated 40,000 books had been written about him and he had become a popular celebrity myth more than a clearly defined historical figure.[3] His foreign policy was dominated by Cold War crises over Laos, Berlin, Cuba, and Vietnam. Some he handled well; others poorly. He will always be remembered, however, for his skill in handling the 1962 Cuban Missile Crisis when the world came closest to the prospect of nuclear war. As former British Prime Minister Harold Macmillan said, "He earned his place in history by this one act alone."[4]

After that scare, JFK went on in 1963 to change the tone of the Cold War competition with a conciliatory speech at American University and began a process of nuclear arms control with the Limited Test Ban Treaty. At the same time, it must be remembered that his dealings with Khrushchev over Berlin and his failed covert actions in Cuba (both the Bay of Pigs, which he inherited from Eisenhower, and Operation Mongoose, a covert action program that his administration initiated) helped to set the scene for the Cuban Missile Crisis. And in Vietnam, he increased the number of American military advisors from 685 to over 16,000 while also abetting a clumsy coup against the Diem government. As historian Alan Brinkley summarized, "It would be hard to call him a great president, but neither was he a failure."[5]

Jack Kennedy was born to a wealthy Irish Catholic family in Boston in 1917, and attended private schools before graduating from Harvard. His early political career was helped by his father's money and connections, but JFK also showed great courage as a war hero in the Pacific and in his lifelong battle with illness, which he carefully disguised and hid from the public. He was staunchly anti-Communist but not rigidly ideological. When Eisenhower told Kennedy that the new president might have to intervene to prevent a Communist takeover in Laos, JFK neatly sidestepped the crisis and agreed to its neutralization. At the peak of the Cold War in his American University speech of June 10, 1963, Kennedy declared that while Americans found Communism "profoundly repugnant as a negation of personal freedom and dignity," he also believed that "no government or social system is so evil that its people must be considered as lacking in virtue."[6] Echoing an earlier speech he had given in Seattle in 1961, Kennedy appealed to a larger cosmopolitan vision. "If we cannot end now our differences, at least we can make the world safe for diversity. For in the final analysis, our most basic common link is that we all inhabit this small planet."

JFK was aware of the growing strength of nationalism and anti-colonialism. With programs like the Alliance for Progress in Latin America and support for the government of South Vietnam, Kennedy hoped to channel Third World nationalism away from Communism and toward democracy. He was attracted by the ideas of modernization theorists such as MIT economist Walt Rostow (whom he brought into his government), who argued that democracy could be encouraged through nation-building plus counterinsurgency to combat indigenous guerilla movements. However, in the words of a British assessment of American democracy promotion, "The fallacy that lay at the heart of the Kennedy administration's embrace of counterinsurgency . . . was similar to that which was undermining the efforts of nation-builders to promote democracy through strategic economic aid and investment. Developing nations often lacked the political culture in which democratic institutions could be established."[7] America lacked the power to change that in Vietnam. Regime change through support for coups such as the overthrow of President Ngo Dinh Diem proved counterproductive. While the postwar democratization of Germany and Japan had been of profound importance to the creation of the liberal international order, both cases occurred under years of occupation after their governments were totally defeated in World War II. Kennedy's nation-building and counterinsurgency were efforts at democratization on the cheap.

Kennedy's style was charismatic and his rhetoric was inspirational. He was also innovative as a communicator. Just as Theodore Roosevelt had used public speeches as a bully pulpit and Franklin Roosevelt used radio for his fireside chats (and Donald Trump later used tweets), Kennedy pioneered in the use of live television. Not only did he use it successfully in his 1960 presidential debates with Richard Nixon, but his televised press conferences from the White House were widely watched and admired.

While Kennedy's rhetoric was transformational, his policies were mostly incremental. Although he took some risks in his public behavior, he was generally rather prudent. He is said to have estimated the risk of nuclear war during the missile crisis as one in three, and one can question whether he should have imposed such a risk on the American people, but he reasoned that to acquiesce in Khrushchev's adventure in Cuba would mean a higher risk of war over Berlin later. And he was prudent in his compromise settlement of the crisis.

His private behavior, however, was quite the opposite, including relations with the mistress of a mob boss and a woman thought to be an East German spy. All this was well known to his close aides as well as to J. Edgar Hoover, the director of the FBI (which intervened in the second case). Whatever one's moral judgment of his marital duplicity, the political risks that Kennedy took in bringing such women into the White House blurred the line between what could be considered private and public behavior by a president.

Kennedy's management style was more similar to FDR than to Eisenhower. He dismantled Eisenhower's elaborate advisory staff and foreign policy process and returned the National Security Council to a small informal group. After Eisenhower visited the White House early in the Kennedy years, he complained to a friend about "the damnedest bunch of boy commandos running around."[8] The result was that some important balls were dropped. JFK, by his own admission, failed to adequately scrub the plans for the covert invasion of Cuba that he inherited from Eisenhower, and he initially gave casual approval rather than careful attention to the coup that removed the Diem government in 1963. In Kennedy's words, "I feel that we must bear a good deal of responsibility for it."[9] It is unclear whether JFK approved the details of the CIA's Operation Mongoose and plans to assassinate Fidel Castro, but CIA Director Richard Helms later testified that he was under pressure to do something about Castro, and the circumstantial evidence is strong.[10]

After the Bay of Pigs failure, JFK was a quick learner and showed impressive organizational skills as well as emotional control in the management of the Cuban Missile Crisis when he resisted military advice for a pre-emptive strike that might have escalated to nuclear war.[11] Instead, he bought time and instituted a naval blockade of the island, which placed the burden of initiating conflict on the Soviets. It is interesting to listen to tapes that were made at the time and compare JFK's restraint with the remarks by Vice President Lyndon Johnson, who wavered "back and forth between seeking a negotiated compromise and using military force."[12] This was a clear case where the moral character of the president made a huge difference in the outcome of American foreign policy.*

The Cuban Missile Crisis was as much about Berlin as about the island ninety miles off the coast of Florida. Ever since the Berlin blockade and airlift during the Truman administration, the Soviet Union had been trying to consolidate its position in Eastern Europe by squeezing the Western powers out of their sectors in the former German capital. Kennedy and his advisors were more cautious than Eisenhower about relying on threats of nuclear deterrence. They tried to increase the president's options in Europe by increasing conventional forces and developing a doctrine of "flexible response." At the same time, between 1960 and 1963 the United States increased its nuclear warheads from 20,000 to 29,000 (while the Soviet arsenal went from 1,600 to 4,200).[13] Kennedy also tried to encourage West European defense cooperation, and in contrast to Eisenhower's cuts, Kennedy increased the defense budget by 17 percent in his three years in office.

The situation in Europe was exacerbated by the flow of political refugees from East Germany escaping through West Berlin. When Kennedy met with Khrushchev in Vienna in June 1961, Berlin was a central issue. Despite JFK's warnings, Khrushchev bullied Kennedy and came away from the meeting with the impression that "this man is very inexperienced, even immature."[14] Kennedy was realistic about the summit, telling a journalist that Khrushchev had "savaged" him. When the Soviets erected the Berlin Wall a few months later to stem the flow of refugees, Kennedy quietly accepted it.

---

* Some question whether this was a moral or prudential question, but as argued in chapter 2, in complex foreign policy issues with unpredictable consequences, prudence becomes a reasoned virtue in a three-dimensional ethics.

Fearing Khrushchev was underestimating American nuclear strength, Kennedy had the Pentagon make a public statement about the vast strategic advantage held by the United States. Khrushchev's placement of missiles in Cuba may have been partly to defend the Castro regime, but also to redress the strategic balance and add to the pressure regarding Berlin. In the final settlement of the missile crisis, JFK had his brother Robert secretly agree that after the Soviet missiles were removed from Cuba, the United States would quietly remove the intermediate-range nuclear missiles that Eisenhower had placed in Turkey. Rather than "shoot 'em out," he quietly "bought 'em out." Kennedy was a prudent leader who understood the virtue of compromise in an ethic of consequences.

The major unknown about Kennedy's foreign policy is what he would have done about Vietnam had he lived. In October 1963, he issued National Security Action Memorandum 263 aiming at the withdrawal of the bulk of US military personnel by the end of 1965. Some supporters swear he intended to get out after re-election in 1964 and point to remarks to that effect made to Senator William Fulbright. In the 1990s, former advisors like Secretary of Defense Robert McNamara and National Security Advisor McGeorge Bundy said they believed JFK would have gotten out, but like other alumni, their judgment may have been affected by concern about their roles in history.[15] Memoirs are not history; they are efforts to shape history. Critics note that Kennedy never discussed such a plan with Robert Kennedy, his brother and closest advisor, who continued to support the war in the early years of the Johnson administration. The debate continues among historians to this day, and the answer remains indeterminate.[16]

Kennedy was always ambivalent about Vietnam. The historian Fredrik Logevall believes that "Kennedy, more than most national political figures of the time, might have gone against the grain and ordered a full-scale review of Vietnam policy."[17] After a visit in 1951, and again at the time of the French defeat at Dienbienphu, he spoke out against US intervention, but in 1956 he gave a speech declaring Vietnam to be "the cornerstone of the Free World in Southeast Asia, the keystone to the arch, the finger in the dike." As president, he wisely rejected Eisenhower's advice to become involved in Laos, and he consistently resisted his advisors who urged him to send combat troops, though he greatly increased the number of military advisors to 16,000.

In the view of biographer Robert Dallek, JFK's refusal to send anything more than military advisors "was a stance that was a likely prelude to complete withdrawal." Dallek believes the coup against Diem in November 1963 pressed Kennedy further in that direction, and "it was hardly conceivable that Kennedy would have sent thousands more Americans to fight in so inhospitable a place as Vietnam."[18] On the other hand, by using the rhetoric of the domino theory he was caught in a dilemma, and how he would have resolved that dilemma is unknown. Logevall's assessment is "that Kennedy at the time of his death was leaving his Vietnam options open, playing a waiting game." Nonetheless, "the better argument is that JFK most likely would *not* have Americanized the war but instead would have opted for some form of disengagement."[19]

How should we judge the morality of Kennedy's brief but event-filled foreign policy? In terms of his goals and motives on my scorecard, he ranks well. His moral vision expressed broadly attractive values of promoting democracy and liberty, nuclear arms control, and economic development (enshrined in his "Alliance for Progress" in Latin America). His emotional intelligence was sufficient to ensure that his motives were generally aligned with his expressed values, though the motive of escaping domestic political punishment was at odds with his proclaimed goal of preserving freedom in Vietnam. If, as he told Senator Mike Mansfield in May 1963, he could not withdraw until after the 1964 election, "it is hard to credit his willingness to let boys die in Vietnam for the sake of his reelection. What seems more plausible is that Kennedy never forgot that politics and policy-making were the art of the possible."[20] American military advisors killed and were killed, but by refusing to send combat troops he drew a line that had kept casualties low. At the time of Kennedy's death, 108 American military personnel had died.[21] In terms of broader goals, Kennedy was also able to inspire others with his call to service, appealing in his inaugural address not just to fellow Americans but to "fellow citizens of the world" to work together for "the freedom of man."

Equally important, Kennedy generally understood the limits of American power in practice if not always in his rhetoric. He was prudent in balancing risks and values. After his early mistakes on Cuba, he showed a willingness to compromise that was crucial to avoiding war in the Missile Crisis. And his ensuing American University speech in 1963 set a different tone in the Cold War competition. He spoke of peace "as the necessary rational end of rational men." While he remained anti-Communist, he accepted a cosmopolitan view of humanity and launched a process of nuclear arms control. He appealed not for Wilson's "world made safe for democracy," but for a world "made safe for diversity" (though this seemed inconsistent with his actions in Vietnam).

Kennedy's record on the second ethical dimension of means is more mixed. He was willing to threaten to use force in the naval blockade, but careful and proportionate in its actual use, as shown both by his cautious approach to nuclear issues as well as his resistance to the large-scale introduction of ground forces both in Cuba and Vietnam. Where he can be faulted was in his failure to respect the rights and institutions of others. His plea to make the world safe for diversity was hardly consistent with the covert actions (including assassination) in Cuba and the coup against the Diem government in Vietnam. According to aide Michael Forrestal, the unexpected killing of Diem in the coup "bothered him as a moral and religious matter."[22] In the words of Chester Bowles, the liberal Under Secretary of State whom Kennedy removed in 1961, "the question that concerns me most about this new administration is whether it lacks a genuine conviction about what is right and what is wrong."[23] Kennedy authorized the spraying of the herbicide Agent Orange, which created massive ecological and health damage in Vietnam. Historian Niall Ferguson accuses Kennedy of callous and reckless interventions with his abortive invasion of Cuba, attempted assassination of Castro, and bloody coup in Vietnam.[24]

Assessing the dimension of ethical consequences, Kennedy's actions also merit a mixed review. Was he a good fiduciary for America's interests? Harold Macmillan's judgment is surely correct that JFK forever earned his place in history through his adept handling of the Cuban Missile Crisis. From his taped remarks, we can suspect that Johnson would have done worse. But against this praise, skeptics point out that some of Kennedy's earlier actions from the Bay of Pigs to the Vienna Summit to Operation

Mongoose helped to bring him to that moment of peril in October 1962.[†] On the side of exoneration is his subsequent change of the tone of the Cold War and reaching the first nuclear arms control agreement in 1963. On Vietnam, Kennedy allowed himself to get sucked into the domino theory rhetoric and greatly increased American involvement, but we do not know if he would have redeemed himself after the 1964 election. We do know that Lyndon Johnson plunged further into the abyss.

On other aspects of ethical consequences, JFK does well. His prudence was far from perfect and his covert actions were damaging, but he sometimes minimized the unnecessary dangers to others. Perhaps his strongest suit was in the educational consequences of his legacy. While he sometimes lied, his inspirational rhetoric broadened moral discourse at home and abroad, as did programs like the Peace Corps and the program to send a man to the moon. Many young people were recruited to public service by Kennedy's vision. He was good for American soft power. Cities around the world have streets named after him, and his ideals still inspire many of those he called "fellow citizens of the world." His mixed scorecard follows.

Kennedy's Ethical Scorecard

Intentions and Motives

Moral vision: attractive values, good motives	good
Prudence: balance of values and risks	mixed

Means

Force: proportion, discrimination, necessity	good/mixed
Liberal: respect for rights and institutions	mixed/poor

Consequences

Fiduciary: success for long-term US interests	mixed
Cosmopolitan: minimal damage to others	mixed
Educational: truthful; broad moral discourse	good/mixed

---

† In October 1987, I moderated a discussion at Harvard between Soviet policy makers and Kennedy officials on the twenty-fifth anniversary of the Crisis. McGeorge Bundy and Robert McNamara swore Kennedy had no intent of again invading Cuba, but McNamara admitted "if I were on your side, I'd have thought otherwise. I can very easily imagine estimating that an invasion was imminent." James G. Blight and Janet M. Lang, The Fog of War. (Lanham, Rowman and Littlefield, 2005), 40-41.

LYNDON BAINES JOHNSON

Lyndon Johnson became president in November 1963 after Kennedy's assassination. The two men were not close, and JFK had chosen him for vice president (against the advice of brother Robert) for purely tactical reasons. The two men had very different backgrounds. While JFK had been born in Boston with a silver spoon in his mouth, Johnson's family had struggled with poverty in Southwest Texas. Kennedy graduated from Harvard; Johnson from Southwest Texas State Teachers College in San Marcos. Johnson once complained to a journalist, "I don't believe I'll ever get credit for anything in foreign affairs, no matter how successful it is, because I didn't go to Harvard."[25] Johnson's experience teaching poor Mexican American children in the segregated town of Cotulla left a strong impression on him that later affected his presidential policies on voting rights and the anti-poverty program he called "the Great Society."

Johnson was a decade older than Kennedy and first went to Washington as a Congressional aide in 1931, spending most of his life in the capital as an aide, a Congressman, and a Senator, working effectively with FDR, Truman, and Eisenhower. After a controversial Senate election in 1948, Johnson rose to become the minority leader and then majority leader. While Kennedy had an indifferent record as a Congressman and Senator, Johnson's political skills transformed the institution, and he became what his biographer Robert Caro termed "the master of the Senate."[26]

While JFK was a great communicator and master of television, LBJ did poorly on TV. In smaller political settings, however, he had extraordinary transactional political skills ranging from bullying to personal charm. Johnson was a large man at six feet three and a half inches who used his size to dominate others, looming over them with what became known as "the Johnson treatment." He often enjoyed using his power to deceive and humiliate others, including his wife and his staff. People who worked for him described him with adjectives such as "brave and brutal; compassionate and cruel; driven, tyrannical, crude, insensitive, petty, empathic, shy, sophisticated, witty and magnanimous." Presidential historian Fred Greenstein summarizes LBJ as "a brilliant behind-the-scenes politician and a complex and flawed human being."[27] His close aide Bill Moyers reported that "I both loved and loathed him at the same time."[28] Caro refers to LBJ's "terrifying pragmatism" and his "seemingly bottomless capacity for deceit, deception and betrayal."[29] According to Johnson's former press secretary George Reedy, "As a human being, he was a miserable person—a bully, sadist, lout and egotist." LBJ mistrusted the press, accused them of lying, and blamed them for his unpopularity. He would watch several television stations at the same time, but he never received from the media the confirmation of his self-image that he craved. Yet this same egotist would also appear in the White House operations center at 5 a.m. to "check on the casualties from Vietnam, each one of which took a little piece out of him."[30]

Johnson was a typical anti-Communist of the time, but not an ideologue, and he had the courage to stand up to Senator Joseph McCarthy in 1954. Over the decades, Johnson adjusted his views from New Deal supporter to member of the conservative Southern bloc in the Senate, but he was prepared to desert his Southern colleagues in helping the Eisenhower administration pass the Civil Rights Act of 1957. Caro describes LBJ as "unencumbered by philosophy or ideology."[31] His subsequent championing of civil rights had much to do with his presidential ambitions, but underneath the ambition and pragmatism was his youthful experience with the injustice of discrimination and poverty in South Texas. As he said when he promoted the landmark Voting Rights Act of 1965, "You never forget what poverty and hatred could do when you see the scars on the hopeful face of a young child."[32]

While he was helped in part by the outpouring of public sympathy for JFK after the assassination, Johnson was able and willing to pass and surpass Kennedy's civil rights proposals, even though he fully recognized the risk of delivering "the South to the Republican Party for a long time to come."[33] Many historians believe that Johnson did more for civil rights than any president since Lincoln, and this alone would assure his place in the top ten American presidents.

But Johnson's place in the presidential pantheon was spoiled by his Vietnam policy, which became so unpopular that he withdrew from the race for re-election in 1968. As Doris Kearns Goodwin writes: "'If it hadn't been for Vietnam'—how many times this phrase has been spoken in conversations assessing Johnson's place in history." She goes on to recount that Johnson told her in 1970, describing the early weeks of 1965, "I knew from the start that I was bound to be crucified either way I moved. If I left the woman I really loved—the Great Society—in order to get involved with that bitch of a war on the other side of the world, then I would lose everything at home. . . . But if I left that war and let the Communists take over South Vietnam, then I would be seen as a coward and my nation would be seen as an appeaser and we would find it impossible to accomplish anything for anybody anywhere on the entire globe."[34]

LBJ's political skills were better suited to the small chamber of the Senate than for the national stage of the White House, and his contextual intelligence was well honed for domestic politics but not for foreign policy. Some aspects of his foreign policy were successful, such as his careful handling of French President Charles de Gaulle's withdrawal of French troops from under NATO command in 1966, and his prudent handling of the North Korean capture of the USS *Pueblo* in 1968. Somewhat more controversial was his sending of 22,000 troops to the Dominican Republic in 1965 after a coup raised fears that a left-wing government there might align with Cuba. On the other hand, he continued JFK's arms control initiatives with the Soviets and persuaded the Senate to ratify an Outer Space Treaty in 1967, and negotiated the Nuclear Non-Proliferation Treaty of 1968. But everything else came to be overshadowed by the war in Vietnam. Johnson agreed with Kennedy on modernization theory. His "support for the administration's ambitious attempts at democracy promotion abroad was genuine and visceral, sincere and personal."[35]

Initially, Johnson was reluctant to escalate the Vietnam War. He did not want to do anything to jeopardize his election campaign in November. In May 1964, Johnson told McGeorge Bundy, "I don't think it's worth fighting for and I don't think we can get out. It's just the biggest damned mess."[36] In August, however, when it appeared that two American destroyers had come under attack from North Vietnamese coastal patrol boats under ambiguous circumstances, Johnson ordered a retaliatory attack and persuaded Congress to pass the Tonkin Gulf Resolution that authorized "all necessary measures." Later he confessed to one aide that "those dumb, stupid sailors were just shooting at flying fish," but in his August 4 speech to the nation "he decided to lie" and said the attacks were unprovoked.[37] He used the incident to increase his options by getting a blank check from Congress.

In January 1965, two Kennedy holdover officials, McGeorge Bundy and Robert McNamara, sent Johnson a memo recommending step-by-step military escalation. When Vietcong guerillas killed nine US advisors at Pleiku on February 6, Johnson began a process of escalation that he increased dramatically in July and eventually culminated in 536,000 US combat troops in Vietnam by the end of his presidency. With the failure of each increment of escalation to solve the problem, Johnson's dilemma deepened. "Apparently hoping his words would conceal or even change established facts, and in an effort to halt the erosion of his support, Johnson indulged more and more freely in distortion and patent falsehoods: constant reference to the progress made in Vietnam, describing things as he wanted them to be."[38] At the same time, he narrowed his circle of advisors, while allowing some token dissent, intimidated others, and became "a prisoner of his own propaganda. Screening out options, facts, and ideas, Lyndon Johnson's personality operated to distort truth much the same way as ideology works in a totalitarian society."[39] A careful comparison of Eisenhower's and Johnson's advisory systems describes the absence of give-and-take in Johnson's informal and personalized processes.[40] Johnson dug himself deeper and deeper into the hole of the domino metaphor. "Oh sure, I recognize your argument about the diversity of Communism and your claim that nationalism is strong as well as Communism," he said, "but the question is which is stronger? . . . I knew that if the aggression succeeded in South Vietnam, then the aggressors would keep on going until all of Southeast Asia fell into their hands."[41]

The situation was made doubly complex by Johnson's personalizing the issue. He was deficient in emotional intelligence, and his personal needs became disastrously intertwined with his public goals. Despite his bullying demeanor, he was an insecure man, and he desperately feared being seen as a coward. "Nothing was more important to Johnson than being seen as courageous."[42] He became obsessed with proving that Kennedy never planned to abandon Vietnam, and in 1967 he instructed Walt Rostow to compile JFK's statements to show that he would have seen things through whatever the costs.[43] After careful study in 1997, H. R. McMaster, who later became National Security Advisor under President Trump, concluded that "the president's fixation on short-term political goals, combined with his character and the personalities of his principal civilian and military advisors, rendered the administration incapable of dealing adequately with the complexities of the situation in Vietnam."[44]

Johnson believed that his Great Society legislation was key to his legacy. But this contributed to LBJ's deliberate deception and failure to educate the public about the war. According to Francis Bator, his former deputy national security advisor, the reason Johnson agreed to a major increase in troops in July 1965—but announced it as "no change in policy" and refused to call for a tax increase to support it—was that he feared that raising the issue of "guns vs. butter" would lead to the Congressional defeat of his Great Society legislation. "Johnson thought that hawkish Dixiecrats and small-government Republicans were more likely to defy him . . . if he could be made to appear an appeaser of communists."[45]

But Fredrik Logevall argues that Johnson had more options. Vietnam did not engage the public that much in early 1965; senior senators were skeptical about escalation, and Johnson had just decisively prevailed over the hawkish Barry Goldwater in the 1964 election. When Johnson consulted his closest friend in Congress in May of that year, Senator Richard Russell of Georgia recommended a coup to "get some fellow in there that said he wished to hell we *would* get out. That would give us a good excuse for getting out. . . . Vietnam isn't important to us a damn bit except from a psychological standpoint."[46]

In the retrospective view of McGeorge Bundy, if Johnson had decided to cut our losses, "he was sufficiently inventive to do that in a way that would not have destroyed the Great Society."[47] Why then did LBJ choose to escalate and Americanize the war even though other savvy politicians like Vice President Hubert Humphrey warned him about the possible domestic political implosion that eventually occurred in 1968? According to Logevall, "The issue was credibility, not merely in national terms but also domestic partisan terms and personal terms. Credibility cubed." LBJ's personal motives complicated the equation. "He feared the personal humiliation he imagined would inevitably accompany a defeat."[48] In Bundy's view, the dramatic difference between Kennedy and Johnson on the question of Vietnam was that "Kennedy didn't want to be dumb; Johnson didn't want to be a coward."[49]

How should we summarize the ethics of Johnson's foreign policy? In terms of publicly stated goals, at an abstract level LBJ's moral vision of preserving South Vietnamese from Communist tyranny was similar to Kennedy's, but it becomes more complex because of Johnson's personality and character. To the extent that his motives were to preserve his own self-image as courageous, his moral intentions were flawed. As for prudence, Johnson vacillated between realism and optimism in Vietnam. His decision to enter negotiations in 1968 was a prudent step, but before that his faulty estimates of progress led to many deaths. At the same time, in the other aspects of his foreign policy involving the USSR and Europe, Johnson deserves good marks for prudence.

In terms of means, it is hard to argue that he used force discriminately, or even proportionately. The strategy of attrition was a brutal meat-grinder, and spraying defoliants on the Ho Chi Minh Trail had unintended but foreseeable consequences. Too many civilians were killed, and as Goodwin argues, "his means were subordinated to his ends."[50] At the same time, Johnson made major efforts to keep the war limited and prevent it from spreading to China or the USSR, despite pressure from the military and hawks in Congress to expand bombing targets. He rejected Eisenhower's gratuitous advice that he consider tactical nuclear use, and when he was alerted that the military was developing a contingency plan for the use of nuclear weapons in Vietnam, he ordered an immediate stop to the planning.[51] As for a liberal respect for the rights and institutions of others, Johnson's practice was mixed or poor, both in Vietnam and in the sending of 22,000 troops to the Dominican Republic in 1965.

Regarding consequences, Johnson was a good trustee of American interests in many aspects of foreign policy, but it is impossible to make that case with regard to Vietnam. He did not get us into Vietnam, but his massive escalation of the war in 1965 imposed large and long-term costs on the United States. As for minimizing the damage to others, even though the burden for the millions of Vietnamese deaths must be shared by Vietnamese leaders like Ho Chi Min and Le Duan, Johnson scores poorly on this dimension. Nor is he reprieved by any beneficial educational effect of his foreign policy discourse at home or abroad. Johnson repeatedly lied to the American public (of which a majority supported the war until 1968), and delayed a broader appreciation of the conflict.

McGeorge Bundy once noted that incidents justifying military retaliation "are like streetcars." If you miss one, you can always climb aboard another. Ironically, there were several attacks on US forces in 1964, but LBJ chose to dramatize the convenient August 4 Tonkin Gulf incident, which was not real. When that was later exposed to be a "phantom streetcar," Johnson lost the faith of "people whose trust the president needed very badly."[52] As Robert Caro summarizes, the weakening of constitutional restraints on the presidency and the public credibility gap "which were to affect the nation's history profoundly, were to a considerable extent a function of this one man's personality."[53]

Truman's refusal to escalate in Korea marked the end of the century of total war. One of the moral benefits of a limited war is the reduction of damage through escalation, but such wars involve an element of bluffing. To maintain credibility for bargaining, a president has to maintain a relentless optimism that serves to mis-educate the public. But in Johnson's case this tactic was reinforced by his personal needs. Logevall argues that in Shakespeare, "tragedy lies in the very choices the protagonist makes. His Macbeth is no mere victim: he contributes to his own demise. The same must be said of Lyndon Johnson."[54]

His poor foreign policy scorecard shows the results.

Johnson's Ethical Scorecard

Intentions and Motives

Moral vision: attractive values, good motives	mixed/poor
Prudence: balance of values and risks	mixed/poor

Means

Force: proportion, discrimination, necessity	poor
Liberal: respect for rights and institutions	poor

Consequences

Fiduciary: success for long-term US interests	poor
Cosmopolitan: minimal damage to others	poor
Educational: truthful; broad moral discourse	poor

RICHARD M. NIXON

All three presidents of the Vietnam era were highly complex characters with mixed records, but Richard Nixon is the most puzzling. His ethical lapses led him to resign in 1974 to avoid impeachment, but he was also the most innovative and strategic foreign policy thinker of the three. A shy man, he sometimes described himself as an introvert in an extrovert's profession. Despite these limitations, he was a very successful politician who won two presidential elections, narrowly lost the 1960 election to Kennedy, and was featured on the cover of *TIME* magazine fifty-six times. Nixon had great abilities, but "he was not a natural; it was all hard, lonely work."[‡] He saw himself as an idealist, but "trusted almost no one. He assumed the worst in them. . . . He clung to the word and idea of being 'tough.' He thought that was what had brought him to the edge of greatness."[55]

As one presidential historian put it, "Nixon was a source of mystification even to his close associates. The puzzle resulted from his highly private nature, the coexistence in his political personality of a corrosive cynicism and a desire to bring about constructive achievements, and the paradox that a political figure with so many strengths could take actions that were so self-destructive."[56] Some observers have tried to solve the puzzle by speaking of "two Nixons," but biographer Evan Thomas argues that "there was only one Nixon. In Nixon the light and dark strains are inextricably intertwined, impossible to disentangle. They fed each other. Nixon's strengths were his weaknesses, and vice versa. The drive that propelled him also crippled him. The underdog's sensitivity that made him farsighted also blinded him. He wanted to show he was hard because he felt soft. He learned to be popular because he felt rejected."[57]

David Gergen, a former aide, describes Nixon as hardworking, patriotic, and raised in a Quaker tradition. "Nixon sincerely wanted to be a model president. In private notes for himself that he kept at the White House, he once wrote, 'I have decided my major role is moral leadership.'" But Gergen

---

[‡] I had occasion in the early 1980s to ask former president Nixon how he managed to deliver hour-long speeches analyzing Soviet behavior to large audiences without using any notes. His reply: "I type it all out, memorize it, and rehearse it." That's work.

goes on to say that although "Nixon could speak in moral terms. . . . He did not bring a moral framework to politics. He did not see his role as one of teaching people the 'spirit of their constitution,' nor did he see that he should encourage 'a disposition to virtue and his performance of virtuous actions.' He was much too fascinated by the exercise of raw power and left the preservation of democratic institutions to others."[58]

Born in the small town of Yorba Linda, California, in 1913, Nixon was six years younger than Johnson and four years older than Kennedy. Like Johnson, but unlike Kennedy, his family's financial circumstances were modest. He graduated from nearby Whittier College. All three men grew up in homes where there was tension between the moral aspirations of a religious mother and a less moral father. All three served in the navy during World War II and in Congress after the war. All entered politics at an early age, with Nixon becoming Eisenhower's vice president at the age of forty. All three were typically anti-Communist, but basically pragmatists rather than strict ideologues. In his early campaigns Nixon developed the reputation as a red-baiting anti-Communist, but he later helped Eisenhower in the taming of Joseph McCarthy. Unlike Johnson, Kennedy and Nixon preferred foreign policy to domestic policy, though Nixon also had a number of significant domestic policy accomplishments such as the earned income tax credit and creation of the Environmental Protection Agency.

Nixon liked to read history. His role models were the pragmatic conservative British Prime Minister Benjamin Disraeli on the domestic side, and French President Charles de Gaulle in foreign policy. Nixon also admired Charles de Gaulle's aloof status and treatment of foreign policy as an executive prerogative. Nixon's management style was to isolate himself behind a small staff in the White House. On foreign policy he turned to Harvard professor Henry Kissinger, a former advisor to Nelson Rockefeller, and encouraged Kissinger to centralize foreign policy in the White House while isolating the State Department under William Rogers. He encouraged Kissinger to have back-channel conversations with Soviet Ambassador Anatoly Dobrynin without informing the State Department, and similarly encouraged Kissinger's secret trip to China. But people who think that Kissinger controlled Nixon are mistaken. On China, for example, Nixon was well ahead of Kissinger, publishing an article in 1967 that looked ahead to the end of China's isolation.[59]

Nixon can be credited with three major successes in foreign policy: the famous opening to China, the management of the Cold War through détente and arms control with the Soviet Union, and the ending (albeit too slowly) of the Vietnam War. The opening to China was a well-executed reversal of alignments that took advantage of the growing Sino–Soviet friction, and refocused attention away from American defeat in Vietnam and the expansion of Soviet and Cuban influence in Africa. Nixon deserves the credit, foreseeing the possibility in 1967 and deftly managing the politics at home and abroad. It is not surprising that this legacy gave rise to the diplomatic term "a Nixon to China maneuver."[60]

Although all three accomplishments were important, there was also a frequently forgotten debit side of the ledger in Nixon's foreign policy. For a man who prided himself on his long-term vision, Nixon was astonishingly uninterested and myopic in his foreign economic policy (as was Kissinger). When alerted to currency instability in Italy, Nixon famously responded, "I don't give a shit about the lira!"[61] By 1971 the abnormal US share of the world economy had returned to its prewar 25 percent, and an adjustment of the dollar's dominance was necessary. Nixon could have curbed pressures on the dollar by raising taxes and curtailing demand at home, but he did not want to pay a political price in the 1972 election. Instead, he allowed Treasury Secretary John Connally to export the American domestic economic problem by unilaterally breaking the framework of the Bretton Woods institutions and imposing tariffs on allies without consultation. Connally famously told the allies that the dollar is our currency, but your problem.[62] While this obviously had major foreign policy implications, neither Kissinger nor Secretary of State Rogers were even invited to the Camp David meeting where the decision was made.[63] The results were not trivial and Nixon's decision bequeathed a major problem of inflation that weakened the United States and bedeviled the presidencies of both his successors, Gerald Ford and Jimmy Carter.

Critics also fault Nixon for not paying sufficient attention to the conditions for human rights abroad. His tacit support for the coup in

Chile that replaced the democratically elected president Salvador Allende with the repressive military regime of Augusto Pinochet in 1973 is a frequently cited example. Another was his support for the heavy-handed military government of Pakistan in trying to put down the secession of what is now Bangladesh in 1971. Nixon and Kissinger were relying on the Yahya Khan government for help with their China initiative, but they were "not just motivated by dispassionate realpolitik," but also disdain for the leftist regime in India; "the White House tapes capture their emotional rage."[64] And their prioritization of détente over pressure to rescue Soviet Jews led to criticism by senators like Henry Jackson, which helped to stimulate the neoconservative movement. The neoconservative criticism also included charges that Nixon was not tough enough in the bargaining with the Soviet Union, including the Strategic Arms Limitation Treaty of 1972, the first bilateral arms control treaty between the superpowers.

On Vietnam, Nixon inherited a difficult situation from Johnson, albeit he has been charged with encouraging the South Vietnamese to delay the Paris peace negotiations that Johnson had begun.[§] Although Nixon denied such sabotage, historian Henry Farrell concludes that Nixon lied, and in October 1968 ordered his aide H. R. Haldeman to "monkey wrench" Johnson's initiative.[65] When Nixon came into office in 1969 he believed that a precipitous withdrawal would topple the dominoes in Southeast Asia, and also undercut American credibility in the rest of the world. He also knew he had to wind down the war, and by abolishing the draft he removed some domestic pressure on the timetable. And internationally he prepared the way for Vietnamization by declaring the "Nixon Doctrine" that urged regional powers to become more responsible for their own security.

In 1968, 61 percent of Americans believed that the United States was either losing ground or at a standstill in Vietnam.[66] Nixon interpreted public opinion as wanting an American victory but not at the cost of a long land war, and he reduced the rate of American casualties over time. At first, he

---

§ Since the South Vietnamese had other sources of information, the incident is more likely indicative of Nixon's unethical choices about means rather than proving major long-term causal significance.

toyed unsuccessfully with what he called a "madman theory," hoping for a quick victory by convincing the North Vietnamese that he might do anything, including the use of nuclear weapons.[67] Nor were his hopes of linking arms control issues to Vietnam able to produce sufficient Soviet pressure on Hanoi. When these hopes proved illusory, he and Kissinger settled for gradual "Vietnamization" and a negotiated solution that would produce a "decent interval" between American withdrawal and the collapse of the Thieu government in Saigon.

In searching for that solution Nixon expanded the war to Cambodia in April 1970, producing chaos in that country and riots (including the Kent State University shootings) on American campuses. At the end of the year, his "Christmas bombing" campaign finally produced a peace deal at Paris in late December 1972, but it was not very different from what the North Vietnamese had agreed to in October—a cease fire allowing them to leave their armies inside South Vietnam. When Kissinger was asked privately how long he thought the South Vietnamese government could survive, he responded, "If they're lucky, they can hold out for a year and a half."[68] In August 1972, Kissinger told Nixon: "We've got to find some formula that holds the thing together for a year or two."[69] In the event, it was twenty-eight months.

Nixon ended the Vietnam War, but at a high moral cost. Although he reduced the number of American troops and casualties over time, 21,194 Americans died during his three years of stewardship compared to 36,756 under Johnson, and 108 under Kennedy. Sixty percent of American casualties during Nixon's presidency occurred in 1969, and thus some of those deaths must be charged to Johnson's account.[70] Credibility is an important asset in international affairs, but how many lives is a "decent interval" worth? (And how does one count the millions of Vietnamese and Cambodian lives?)

Nixon was not alone in wrestling with this dilemma. As mentioned earlier, during the Johnson administration John McNaughton, a Harvard law professor serving as the assistant secretary of defense for international security affairs, estimated that 70 percent of the reason for fighting was to avoid a humiliating defeat to our reputation as a guarantor. As we saw in chapter 2, dirty hands problems are not choices between right and wrong. The moral choice is the lesser of evils. Credibility was related not just to Vietnam but to Southeast Asia, and even Berlin. If Nixon (or Johnson before him) had followed the advice of senators like Fulbright or Aiken and accepted the reality of defeat earlier, how serious would the damage to American global power have been, given its ultimate recovery after the United States was defeated in 1975? Were there not other ways to establish credibility besides spending more lives in Vietnam? To some extent, Nixon began to provide an answer to this question with his opening to China in 1971. Ending wars is always difficult, and Nixon's policy of Vietnamization did reduce the rate of American casualties. Accepting defeat and declaring withdrawal over the course of 1969 would have been a bold and politically costly move. Nixon showed himself capable of such moves when it came to China, though not Vietnam. Instead, his policy of gradualism and deception did not alter the ultimate outcome but proved costly in lives and credibility.

The costs of a decent interval that merely delayed defeat cannot be measured solely in casualties. As Gergen concludes, "The Johnson administration had already told the country a pack of lies about Vietnam, but that did not justify the continued deceptions of the Nixon years. . . . One can also draw a direct line from Vietnam to Watergate. The obsession with secrecy and stopping the flow of leaks led first to the wiretapping of journalists and administration officials and then to the formation of 'the Plumbers.' "[71] The means that Nixon used to create his decent interval had high costs for trust in the United States, both at home and abroad.

What is the net assessment of the morality of Richard Nixon's foreign policy? Nixon's publicly expressed goals were good. According to Kissinger, underlying Nixon's realism was a Wilsonian view of the United States as a moral leader in the world.[72] Unfortunately, while Nixon had a very high level of contextual intelligence about international affairs, he lacked the emotional intelligence to keep his personal vindictiveness and insecurity from corrupting his public goals, as could be seen in not just in his construction of an enemies list that included journalists and staff, but also in his negative reaction to democratically elected leftist leaders like Allende or

Indira Gandhi. In general, he was prudent in balancing values and risks, but not in cases like Bangladesh or the bombing of Cambodia.

With regard to moral means, Nixon's use of force observed some limits of proportion and discrimination. He restricted the army's production of biological weapons and signed the biological warfare convention. Despite his madman theory of intimidation, he avoided nuclear use in Vietnam, and the possible escalation of the violence of Vietnam to China, though not to Cambodia. But his use of force in Vietnam cannot be called proportionate and discriminating. And his actions in Chile and Bengal failed the test of liberal respect for rights and institutions of others.

In terms of moral consequences, Nixon was a good fiduciary for the interests of the American people in his opening to China and his management of the Cold War competition with the Soviet Union, including the Middle East, but in foreign economic policy he was negligent, and in ending the Vietnam War one can quarrel with the time he took and the costs he incurred. His cosmopolitan efforts to minimize damage to others were poor both in Vietnam and in cases like Bangladesh and Chile. Some realists rate Nixon highly because they focus only on his opening to China and forgive him everything else. They are uninterested in his poor legacy on inflation, or on human rights. Others weigh those factors more heavily, and also find it difficult to forgive his spending 21,000 US lives (and countless others) to create a reputational decent interval that in any event turned out to be brief.

Nixon's educational consequences for truth, trust, and broadening moral discourse were poor. While Nixon was not alone responsible for the decline in trust in government, in Gergen's view, "the lying and deceptions in Vietnam by two administrations, along with Watergate, seriously undermined public confidence in government and have handicapped presidents ever since."[73] At the beginning of the 1960s, three-quarters of respondents to polls in the United States replied that they had a great deal of confidence in our institutions; a decade later that had declined to just one-quarter. The causes of such a change were complex, and not attributable just to the leaders of the 1960s or to the Vietnam War, but some significant part of the costs must be charged to Richard Nixon.[74]

Nixon's Ethical Scorecard

Intentions and Motives

Moral vision: attractive values, good motives	mixed
Prudence: balance of values and risks	mixed

Means

Force: proportion, discrimination, necessity	poor
Liberal: respect for rights and institutions	poor

Consequences

Fiduciary: success for long-term US interests	mixed
Cosmopolitan: minimal damage to others	poor
Educational: truthful; broad moral discourse	poor

*****

None of the three Vietnam-era presidents get as good grades as the founders. Some might say the exam was tougher because conditions in the world were rougher, but this is not convincing. The Vietnam-era presidents shared a misleading mental map of the world that overestimated American power and underestimated the power of nationalism and local culture. Even when they expressed private reservations about the domino metaphor, they dug themselves in deeper by using it in their public rhetoric. To continue the exam metaphor, they misread the key question and then cheated on their answers.

The presidents saw their goal of combatting Communism globally and in Vietnam in moral terms, but their personal motives complicated the moral status of their intentions. All feared domestic political punishment for being the president who "lost Vietnam" and were willing to sacrifice the lives of many others to avoid that personal cost. It is one thing to spend lives and treasure on a misguided but well-intended metaphor about preserving American credibility in a bipolar world. It is another thing to sacrifice so many lives for domestic political advantage, or as in the cases of Johnson and Nixon, for a personal image of toughness. As senators like William Fulbright of Arkansas or George Aiken of Vermont argued at the time, there were political alternatives, albeit unpleasant ones, that were lesser evils. Neither the bipolar Cold War nor domestic politics made the Vietnam imbroglio inevitable. The tragedy also required bad moral choices.

Perhaps Kennedy would have avoided Americanizing the war, but we can never be certain. By restricting troops to advisory rather than combat roles he had avoided the huge casualties incurred by his successors, but he helped to prepare the way despite the fact that by November 1963 he thought the odds of winning were only one in a hundred. According to McGeorge Bundy, as a political issue in his second term Kennedy intended to "flush it," and when asked how he would engineer a withdrawal, he told his advisors, "Easy. Put a government in there that will ask us to leave." He did not think it a big test of the balance of power, but of American political opinion.[75]

Some observers credit Johnson's and Nixon's massive use of force—including bombing, chemical defoliation, attrition, strategic hamlets, and other instruments—as having saved Southeast Asia from Communism, but this was not true. The biggest domino, Indonesia, had already fallen in the opposite anti-Communist direction after a military coup toppled President Sukarno, well before Johnson's 1965 escalation of the Vietnam War. On the other hand, what can be said in their favor is that none of the three presidents seriously considered the use of nuclear weapons, and all three sought to keep the war from escalating to a larger conflict with China or the Soviet Union. For that one can be grateful, but in terms of lives lost and costs to the nation one must judge the Vietnam presidents as ethical failures.

5

Post-Vietnam Retrenchment

After Richard Nixon resigned in disgrace in August 1974, his successor Gerald Ford told the nation that "our long national nightmare is over." But overcoming the effects of Vietnam and Watergate was not so easy. Trust in institutions had declined, and American foreign policy attitudes were entering a phase of recovery and retrenchment.[1]

Although Nixon had won the 1972 election by a landslide, the 1974 midterm Congressional elections were swept by the opposition, and a new group of Democratic politicians known as "the Watergate babies" entered office. A combination of press leaks, official commissions, and a Senate committee chaired by Frank Church of Idaho exposed many of the covert tactics used by the CIA during the Cold War, including attempted assassinations. The economy was slowed by a combination of inflation and slow growth that was dubbed "stagflation." That problem that plagued both Ford and Carter stemmed from Johnson's "guns *and* butter" policy in which he refused to choose between his Great Society program and the Vietnam War. Nixon exacerbated the problem by imposing wage and price controls in 1971, and their subsequent removal resulted in an explosion of inflation.

Social and cultural norms regarding race, gender, gay rights, abortion, and environmental issues began to change dramatically at the end of the 1960s and throughout the 1970s. As Lyndon Johnson had predicted when he signed the Civil Rights and Voting Rights Acts, the problems of race began the long process of turning the "solid South" from solidly Democratic to solidly Republican. The cultural changes produced a conservative counterreaction that Nixon called "the silent majority" and that Ronald Reagan championed unsuccessfully in his challenge to President Ford in 1976 for the Republican Party nomination, but successfully in defeating Carter for the presidency four years later. As one observer put it, the 1970s was "an epic period of change in the American political landscape. The centrist political consensus of the postwar era was unraveling under the combined pressures of a ruinous decade of the Great Stagflation and military defeat in Vietnam."[2]

The structure of the international system remained bipolar. The American share of the world economy had declined from its abnormal high of 1945 to about a quarter of world product in 1970, which had been the prewar share. The United States was still far larger than any other economy, but despite its smaller economy, Soviet military investments had given them a lead in the number of nuclear warheads. In the aftermath of the Cuba Missile Crisis the United States had slowed its nuclear buildup, but the Soviet Union accelerated theirs. Many analysts argued that "nuclear overkill" was not a good measure of relative power, but new groups like the Committee on the Present Danger argued that the Soviet Union now had nuclear superiority, and there was considerable anxiety about the issue. The Soviets also became more supportive of revolutionary regimes in Africa. Along with the loss in Vietnam, critics cited these events as evidence of American decline and criticized efforts at arms control and détente with the Soviet Union. Gerald Ford and Jimmy Carter confronted rough seas in their efforts to restore trust and guide foreign policy.

GERALD R. FORD

Gerald Ford was a unique president. He had the shortest presidency (895 days) of modern times, and he was the only president who was never elected as either president or vice president. A moderate Republican congressman from Michigan, Nixon had chosen Ford to replace Vice President Spiro Agnew, who resigned after a corruption scandal related to his prior service as governor of Maryland. Ford was confirmed by the Senate in 1973 under the procedures of the new 25th Amendment to the Constitution.

Ford was the same age as Nixon, and had also served in the navy in World War II and entered Congress after the war. He graduated from the University of Michigan, where he was a football star, and then from Yale Law School. He was re-elected to Congress twelve times and rose to become the House Minority Leader. Popular with his colleagues, "he was seen as an uncomplicated personification of such virtues as integrity, decency and steadiness—an invigorating contrast to the emotionally convoluted Johnson and Nixon."[3]

Ford was initially accepted with relief by the public with approval rates of 71 percent, but those ratings plummeted to 49 percent when without warning or political preparation he announced a full pardon for Nixon a month after taking office. While many critics suspected a corrupt deal, former aide David Gergen argues that Ford was trying to clear the decks and move ahead, but failed to do the necessary preparatory work for the announcement. In his words, "More than one of our modern presidents has been a congenital liar; Jerry Ford was a congenital truth-teller."[4] His aspirations were to be a good president rather than a great one. In choosing portraits to hang in the cabinet room, Nixon had selected Eisenhower, Theodore Roosevelt, and Woodrow Wilson. Ford replaced Roosevelt with Lincoln and Wilson with Truman.[5]

Like Truman, Ford was a pragmatic legislator rather than a great communicator, and his rhetoric did not promote a broad public vision. On the other hand, he had good emotional intelligence, picked a first-rate cabinet, and developed a well-organized White House process that encouraged the free flow of ideas.[6] Ford was concerned about the need for stability in foreign policy. He kept Henry Kissinger in his dominant role as Secretary of State, but in 1975 required him to give up his simultaneous occupancy of the role of National Security Advisor to his able deputy Brent Scowcroft. The major foreign policy issues during Ford's short tenure were the collapse of South Vietnam, the management of relations with the Soviet Union, the use of force after the Mayaguez and Panmunjom incidents, and the growing importance of economic interdependence that followed the Organization of the Petroleum Exporting Countries (better known as OPEC) quadrupling of oil prices near the end of 1973.

Early in 1975, the United States still had six thousand troops in and near Saigon, but the South Vietnamese government was losing ground to the Communist offensive. Ford asked Congress to provide a $722 million military aid package to strengthen the Thieu government along the lines that Nixon had promised at the time of the Paris negotiations of 1973. By a large margin, Congress refused to provide the funding. On April 21, Thieu resigned and by April 30, Saigon had fallen. The US role was limited to evacuation of American and some Vietnamese personnel, with humiliating photos of helicopters taking off from the rooftops to ferry people to naval ships offshore. Whether Ford could have done anything differently or whether the promised American assistance could have saved the South Vietnamese regime was doubtful, but the outcome and images were of American promises broken. At the same time, the Ford administration oversaw a significant humanitarian response. The 1975 Refugee Assistance Act appropriated $455 million for Indochinese refugees, and 130,000 Vietnamese came to the United States in 1975 alone. Thousands more arrived in subsequent years.

Ford was more successful in managing the relationship with the Soviet Union. He continued Nixon's policy of détente with both the USSR and with China, paying visits to both countries. However, his efforts to negotiate a trade agreement with the Soviet Union were blocked by Congress, and the results of his 1974 SALT II negotiations were delayed in Congress by Senator Henry Jackson and other critics of Kissinger's détente policy. In July 1975, Ford met again with Soviet leader Leonid Brezhnev in Helsinki at the Conference for Security and Cooperation in Europe, where almost every European country agreed to uphold human rights and sovereign boundaries in Europe. Ford was criticized for accepting Soviet domination of Eastern Europe, but in the long term the Helsinki language on human rights contributed to the weakening of Soviet control. Ironically in light of subsequent events, many years later an aide disclosed that at their meeting, Brezhnev had offered to help Ford with his 1976 re-election campaign. Ford declined the offer.[7] Accepting Brezhnev's offer of foreign help would have been "out of character" for Ford's sense of morality.

In 1975 and 1976, Ford used military force in two incidents in Asia to demonstrate American credibility. In the first instance, in May 1975 shortly after the fall of Saigon, the Khmer Rouge in Cambodia seized the American merchant ship *Mayaguez* in international waters and Ford sent Marines to rescue the crew. The total of forty-one American servicemen who died in the operation was greater than the number of crew members who were rescued, but the action also had symbolic value. Although Ford was warned that the capture of the ship was the act of an immature Khmer government and patience might make sense, he acted to assert American credibility in the wake of the humiliating evacuation of Saigon. In his words, though he said he felt terrible about the loss of lives, he felt that "decisive action would reassure our allies and bluntly warn our adversaries that the US was not a helpless giant."[8] That was the moral price of credibility.

In August 1976, after North Korean troops killed two US soldiers who were clearing trees in the border village of Panmunjom, Ford responded with a major show of force and sent a large number of ground forces to clear the trees. North Korea did not react. A third issue related to military force was Ford's continuation of military aid to Indonesia after President Suharto, an ally in Vietnam, invaded the newly independent territory of East Timor, which had gained independence from Portugal in 1975. The Indonesian military was criticized for human rights violations, but human rights were not a high priority in the Ford administration, and in his memoirs he criticized the "amateurism" of Carter's human rights campaign, and its efforts to "normalize" relations with Cuba and Vietnam."[9] At the same time, the Helsinki Final Act, which he signed at a thirty-five-nation summit in 1975, had enshrined human rights for the first time as a core issue in East-West relations in Europe.

Ford was also attentive to the importance of international institutions. Economic interdependence had been increasing with rapid growth in Japan and Europe, and in 1973 OPEC had shocked the world by quadrupling the price of oil and setting off a recession. Ford conciliated Iran and Saudi Arabia, which had led the disruption, but proposed an organization of oil-consuming nations that became the International Energy Agency in Paris. In 1975, he proposed that the French economic summit at Rambouillet be made an annual meeting of the seven leading economies (G-7). In heading off Marxist demands at the UN for a "New International Economic Order," he supported a UN World Food Program, strengthening the IMF, and increased development assistance in Africa.[10]

Ford's overall ethical scorecard is good, but the results of his foreign policy were modest because his tenure was brief. He scores well given the difficult circumstances he inherited. His goals and moral vision were good and typical of the time. Unlike his predecessor, his emotional intelligence and good character enabled him to keep his motives aligned with his publicly stated goals and values. He tried to maintain negotiations and arms control with the Soviet Union to moderate the Cold War competition, though critics complained he was not tough enough with the Soviets. He was prudent in balancing values and risks, accepting the harsh reality of defeat in Vietnam.

With regard to means, Ford's use of force in the Mayaguez and Panmunjom incidents was proportional and discriminating. One could debate his use of force and the lives lost to restore credibility, but it was far more proportionate than the lives Nixon spent to create credibility with his ephemeral "decent interval" in Vietnam. Ford's liberal respect for rights and institutions was well illustrated by his participation in the Helsinki process, despite opposition from conservatives in his party. Ford's willingness to push for and sign the Helsinki Accords, even though he had political advisors concerned about its electoral impact, showed his courage in doing what he considered the morally right course.

In terms of consequences, Ford was a good trustee of American interests and showed a cosmopolitan concern for minimizing damage to others, as manifested in his treatment of Vietnamese refugees. On foreign economic policy issues, Ford was remarkably consistent in preserving and enhancing the global trading system, even in the face of considerable protectionist pressure in dealing with the recession he inherited. According to a key economic advisor, this was partially because he considered this wise economic policy in addressing inflation, but also because he viewed an open trading system as a powerful tool benefitting developing countries in expanding their economies.[11] He saw the importance of institutional responses to growing economic interdependence. Perhaps his most important consequences, however, were in his educational impact on restoring a respect for truth and a broad moral discourse at home and abroad.

Ford's Ethical Scorecard

Intentions and Motives

Moral vision: attractive values, good motives	good
Prudence: balance of values and risks	good

Means

Force: proportion, discrimination, necessity	good/mixed
Liberal: respect for rights and institutions	mixed

Consequences

Fiduciary: success for long-term US interests	good
Cosmopolitan: minimal damage to others	good/mixed
Educational: truthful; broad moral discourse	good

JAMES EARL CARTER

Born in 1924 in the tiny hamlet of Plains, Georgia, Jimmy Carter was a decade younger than the prior postwar presidents. He graduated 60th in his class of 820 midshipmen at the Naval Academy at Annapolis in 1946, and subsequently served in Admiral Hyman Rickover's nuclear navy, renowned for its strict standards. Unlike his predecessors, Carter never served in Congress and was an outsider to Washington. He was a successful one-term governor of Georgia, but when he declared his presidential candidacy in 1974, he was virtually unknown and unfiltered by the national political process. People asked, "Jimmy Who?" His success as a relentless campaigner in the Democratic Party primaries and in the 1976 general election owed a great deal to his promise of reform. His campaign slogan was "I will never lie to you." Years later, researchers discovered that Carter lived up to his slogan, and his public utterances were consistent with the written record. As the historian Douglas Brinkley concluded, Carter was able to return from Washington to Plains with his moral decency and integrity intact.[12]

Carter was socially liberal but fiscally conservative, and he had a hard time uniting the fractious groups in his party and in the Congress. Although he was gifted campaigner, he was not a natural politician in terms of compromise and coalition-building. His manner was more that of a moralist and an engineer who focused on the trees rather than the forest. Rather than treating compromise as essential to politics, Carter tended to regard it as doing what one knows is wrong.[13] In the words of a top aide, Carter never nurtured an effective national coalition. "Time and again, he would say, 'leave the politics to me,' while in fact he disdained politics. He believed that if he only did 'the right thing' in his eyes, it would be self-evident to the public, which would reward him with reelection. However, politics cannot be parked at the Oval Office door only to be brought up at election time."[14] As a political leader, Carter was more like an honest version of Richard Nixon than a natural politician like Bill Clinton, the gregarious younger Southerner who would later succeed him.

One biographer describes Carter as "consistently remembered as a president who failed to articulate a compelling political vision and who was unable to hold his party together . . . This memory of his presidency is not inaccurate. If FDR and Reagan demonstrated how to hold a fractious coalition together, Carter's legacy was just the opposite."[15] Another biographer concludes that Carter is underestimated, and while not a great president, was a good and productive one who took on intractable problems with comprehensive solutions while disregarding the political consequences and refusing to change his principles or abandon his personal loyalties He is ranked by historians in the middle of the pack.[16]

These characteristics make Carter a particularly interesting case for this book on ethics and foreign policy. Carter was a Wilsonian who saw the United States as a witness to morality in the relations among nations. He felt particularly strongly about human rights.[17] Carter himself says that of the presidents who served during his lifetime, he admired Harry Truman most, and studied his career more than any other because Truman was direct, honest, and somewhat old-fashioned.[18]

Carter was a born-again Southern Baptist, but he despised shows of religiosity such as those Johnson and Nixon put on with the Reverend Billy Graham. Carter considered such showmanship to be pseudo-religion. Instead, he followed his religious principles to guide his life—witness his quietly teaching Bible classes even when president. But can a man be too good to be a good president? As former speechwriter Hendrik Hertzberg put it, "Reagan had a fixed political ideology, and Carter did not—at least he had much less of one. A political ideology is a very handy thing to have. It's a real time-saver, because it tells you what you think about things you know nothing about." Carter was the moral engineer who wanted to figure out the right answers to policy problems rather than the political salesman who would implement them. Historian Betty Glad described him as pursuing "the old 'city on the hill' tradition, sharing some of its virtues as well as its flaws." However, his Wilsonian moralism never led him into blind triumphalism.[19]

Carter had a moral ideology that led to a strong sense of right and wrong. In Hertzberg's words, "It is wrong to kill people for no reason other than political gain or political fear. Lyndon Johnson and Richard Nixon did that. They escalated and continued the Vietnam War . . . long after it became clear that the war could not be won—and they did this not because they seriously believed that their actions would help America to be secure or Vietnam to be free, but because they were afraid of looking weak. . . . In the Mayaguez incident, even the gentle Ford sent a number of men to their deaths needlessly. Jimmy Carter never did that."[20] Carter was proud that no Americans died in combat during his presidency, though some were lost in the accident that aborted Carter's effort to rescue American diplomats held hostage in Iran in 1979.

Other critics are more harsh about Carter's morality. The foreign policy writer Robert Kaplan, for example, argues that "had it not been for the tough decisions that Nixon, Ford and Kissinger made, the United States might not have withstood the damage caused by Carter's bouts of moralistic ineptitude."[21] Kaplan cites Carter's 1977 curtailment of arms deliveries to Ethiopia because of human rights violations. He argues that the link between Carter's decision not to play power politics in the Horn of Africa and the mass deaths that followed in Ethiopia is more direct than the link between Nixon's incursion into a rural area of Cambodia and the Khmer Rouge atrocities six years later. However, counterfactuals about American actions in Africa are difficult to prove. The Soviet Union and its Cuban proxy intervened in a number of revolutions on the continent, but it remains unclear how much the United States would have been able to control events in Ethiopia, or for that matter how much Nixon or Ford had prevented or abetted deaths in Angola or Mozambique.

In general, the 1970s is seen as a period of retrenchment in American foreign policy. Military defeat had hurt the country's credibility as well as its self-image; the Soviet Union was building its nuclear forces and supporting leftist revolutions in the Third World; the 1973 Arab oil embargo had created energy crises and rising gasoline prices; the high rates of post-1945 economic growth of the world economy had begun to slow; and terrorist attacks in Europe and Japan were raising concerns about the stability of democracies. At the end of the decade an Islamic revolution overthrew the Shah of Iran, and the Soviet Union invaded Afghanistan.

Despite these problems, Carter had a number of foreign policy successes, including a peaceful return of the Panama Canal that improved relations in Latin America; negotiation of the Camp David Accord between Egypt and Israel; the slowing of nuclear proliferation that Kennedy had expected to accelerate rapidly; raising the profile of human rights issues in American diplomacy; full diplomatic recognition of China; and arms control negotiations with the Soviet Union. After the Soviet invasion of Afghanistan at the end of 1979 Carter reversed the post-Vietnam decline in military spending, developed new weapons systems, and promulgated the Carter Doctrine, which declared that an assault on the Persian Gulf region would be repelled by any means necessary including military force.

The return of the Panama Canal to Panama is a good illustration of Carter's approach. It had been a symbol of American power since the days of Theodore Roosevelt and a sensitive issue in conservative politics.

California Republican Senator S. I. Hayakawa famously quipped that "we stole it fair and square." But independent commissions and American intelligence warned that rising nationalist resentment in Panama could lead to terrorism and guerilla warfare, and Ford had tried but failed to resolve the issue. Carter's political advisors told him to defer the Panama issue to his second term, but Carter decided it was the right thing to do, and he made it the subject of his first Presidential Review Memorandum. Carter spent considerable political capital to get a narrow Senate vote of ratification in April 1978, but his actions ushered in improved relations with most of Latin America as well as Panama.[22] Without the Panama Canal Agreement, anti-American terrorists might have found much more fertile ground in Latin America.

When the Middle East peace process bogged down and negotiations between Egypt and Israel reached a stalemate in 1978, Carter invited Anwar Sadat and Menachem Begin to Camp David and worked intensively with them to mediate their differences. Many observers believe that agreement could not have been reached without Carter's persistence and attention to detail. He was deeply involved for thirteen days and twenty drafts before his negotiations were successful. Once again, political advisors had warned Carter against the risks he was taking, and he overruled them. Similarly, Carter pushed ahead with the full diplomatic recognition of China despite the political costs imposed by the Taiwan lobby that had prevented such action in the previous administration.

Carter also felt strongly about slowing the proliferation of nuclear weapons. At the time of the Test Ban Treaty in 1963, Jack Kennedy had expressed fear that there might be twenty-five states with nuclear weapons a decade later. After the OPEC oil embargo and the quadrupling of oil prices in 1974, the conventional wisdom was that plutonium and breeder reactors were the key to energy security, even though separated plutonium would introduce a weapons-usable material into international commerce. In May 1974, India became the seventh nuclear country when it exploded what it called a "peaceful nuclear device." At the same time, France and Germany were exporting reprocessing and enrichment plants that could produce weapons-grade material to Pakistan and Brazil, and it looked like

Kennedy's prediction was coming true. Carter, with his background in nuclear engineering, understood the danger of the situation. In his words,
"Despite the opposition from some of the other suppliers of advanced technology, I wanted to do everything possible to prevent this capability from
spreading to any additional nations."[23] He defied the consensus of the energy industry by cancelling reprocessing and breeder reactor plants in the
United States, and at considerable diplomatic cost, successfully pressed for
termination of the French and German sales. He also successfully achieved
a Nuclear Suppliers' Agreement where supplier countries agreed that they
would exercise restraint in the export of sensitive nuclear facilities.[24,*]

Another of Carter's innovations was to raise the priority of human rights
in American foreign policy, and it marked a change from the "Nixon-Ford-
Kissinger concept of balance of power as the organizing principle of world order."
Although the Ford administration had agreed to the 1975 Helsinki principles
that included human rights, Kissinger's priority was détente with the Soviets. In
1973, he commented to Nixon that the treatment of Jews in the Soviet Union
and their emigration is "none of our business," to which Nixon responded "we
can't blow up the world because of it."[25] But despite an inherent tension, Carter
decided to pursue both détente and human rights at the same time.

Carter's human rights policy was not an easy policy to implement consistently. Carter made exceptions for some Cold War authoritarian allies,
but he took steps against the apartheid regime in South Africa and military
juntas in Argentina, Chile, and elsewhere, and openly criticized the human
rights practices of the Soviet Union. Critics accused him of undercutting
Cold War allies such as the Shah of Iran and Anastasio Somoza in Nicaragua,
but over the long term, Carter's emphasis on the soft power of human rights
produced substantial returns for the United States.

The human rights policy illustrated one of the central problems for
Carter's foreign policy: how to manage the Soviet Union. Despite a serious
underlying economic erosion that was poorly estimated by the intelligence
community, the Soviet Union gave the spurious impression of being a rising

---

* I was responsible for this policy and that may bias my view, but the export of sensitive
nuclear facilities definitely declined under Carter.

power because of its military investments, particularly in nuclear weaponry, and its support for left-wing revolutions in Africa, often implemented through Cuban proxies. Carter often seemed to vacillate between the more détente-oriented policies of Secretary of State Cyrus Vance, and the hardline policies of his National Security Advisor Zbigniew Brzezinski. Carter claimed to benefit from hearing opposing viewpoints from the two advisors, but their positions were imperfectly integrated. "He tried to decide too many things himself. . . . Disagreement between Vance and Brzezinski therefore did not bother Carter because, he, Carter would make the decisions. Foreign policy decision making on the central issue of US-Soviet relations had an ad hoc, serial quality."[26] But the differences between the two major advisors sometimes gave a public impression—as well as a reality—of disarray.

Carter's insistence in 1977 on going for deeper cuts in nuclear weapons rather than merely accepting Ford's almost complete Vladivostok treaty, and his criticisms of human rights in the Soviet Union, delayed agreement on a SALT II agreement. Critics argued that his pursuit of the best prevented the achievement of the merely good. Eventually Carter signed a SALT II agreement in June 1979, but that turned out to be too late when the Soviet invasion of Afghanistan in December destroyed the political climate for détente. Some critics believe that Carter's human rights policy interfered with his arms control efforts, but others argue that "Carter's human rights policy gave the United States moral credibility around the world—no small feat after Vietnam—while putting Moscow on the domestic defensive."[27]

After the invasion of Afghanistan, Carter imposed an embargo on the Soviet Union, boycotted the Moscow Olympics, and issued the Carter Doctrine warning the Soviets against moving toward the oil-rich Persian Gulf. Again, critics complained the invasion proved he had been naïve, but few noticed that Carter had been increasing the defense budget by three percent a year even before Afghanistan, and that his able Defense Secretary Harold Brown had been investing in a new generation of technologies such as stealth and precision-guided weapons that later gave the United States a decisive conventional advantage that it displayed at the time of the Gulf War. Some attribute Carter's growing hard line to the influence of his Polish-born national security advisor, but as aide Robert Pastor noted, "the return of the Cold War was due to Soviet assertiveness, not to Brzezinski's tactics."[28]

Despite such successes, Carter's foreign policy is often described as weak. In his memoirs, Brzezinski described Carter as "tough, cool and determined . . . but reliance on force was not instinctive with him. And that showed. This sense of reluctance which Carter conveyed was translated in the public mind into a perception of weakness."[29] In 2010, Walter Meade referred to a "Carter Syndrome" as being too much in the tradition of Thomas Jefferson, minimizing overseas commitments and supporting peace simply by becoming an example of democracy at home and moderation abroad.[30] But that assessment was later challenged by French diplomat Justin Vaisse, who argued that Carter had very real successes but that they were obscured by his leadership style, and his "persistent inability to explain and promote his administration's decisions and achievements."[31]

Despite his four major foreign policy accomplishments, and his mixed performance with regard to managing the Soviet problem, Carter's presidency was finally undone by Ayatollah Khomeini's Islamic revolution in Iran. In Brzezinski's view, Carter's "only fatal error was in regard to Iran." Not only was the fall of the Shah a political calamity for Carter, but Iran's Islamic Revolution has affected American policy in the Middle East to this day. Brzezinski urged Carter to support a military coup in Iran but Carter (and Secretary of State Cyrus Vance) thought it "historically and morally wrong" to do so. In Brzezinski's view, "Their most persuasive argument, I think, was the moral one. They felt the United States—and notably the President himself—should not assume the responsibility for plunging another country into a bloody and cruel confrontation."[32]

Critics blamed Carter's human rights policies for weakening the Shah, but it is doubtful that Carter was the main cause of the Iranian revolution. In Vance's words, "A difficult question is whether there was anything the United States could have done to influence the direction of the Iranian Revolution during November and December of 1978 and early January of 1979. My answer is perhaps . . . but even then it may have already been too late for the forces that unleashed the revolution were deep seated and long in the making."[33] It is not clear that the half-conscript army could have held together in staving off the revolution, and the Shah was already physically and psychologically weakened by a fatal cancer.

Ironically, once the Shah had fallen and was in exile, Carter made another moral decision that worsened the situation. Brzezinski told him that "we simply had to stand by those who had been our friends," and Carter felt "morally ill at ease with the exclusion of the Shah" from the United States. Despite Vance's opposition and intelligence warnings of probable demonstrations in Teheran, Carter agreed with Brzezinski (backed by calls from Henry Kissinger and other Republicans) and admitted the Shah to the United States for medical treatment.[34] Subsequently, radical students in Teheran took American embassy personnel hostage, and the bad luck of an accidental collision in the desert destroyed Carter's efforts to rescue the hostages.

Carter became fixated on the hostages: "It is impossible for me to put into words how much the hostages have come to mean to me." Like an engineer, Carter focused on various plans designed to solve the problem rather than attending to the political task of managing the images and domestic politics of the hostage crisis.[35] Those events, combined with Carter's brave move to appoint Paul Volcker as Chairman of the Federal Reserve Board with instructions to tame the double-digit inflation even at the cost of recession, meant that Carter was challenged both from Senator Edward Kennedy on the left and Ronald Reagan on the right and decisively lost the 1980 election.

Summarizing the ethics of Carter's foreign policy is more complex than for Ford. In terms of intentions and a moral vision, Carter's emphasis on human rights had wide appeal and it increased American soft power that had been damaged by the Vietnam War. "Carter brought to the presidency a world view that might be called Wilsonian in the high value it placed on co-operation among nations to secure human rights, and to achieve peace. . . . He also brought a determination personally to address long-standing unresolved problems such as the Panama Canal and the Middle East conflict."[36] Had he used more political ideology and Machiavellian skills in addition to moral ideology, he might have knit his vision together more effectively. Carter's publicly expressed values were attractive, as were his private motives overall, but he may have been too concerned about avoiding dirty hands. Greater attention to Weber's advice about politics would have increased his achievement of his goals. Nonetheless Carter understood prudence, and he did not let his Wilsonianism become a crusade. He balanced values and risks, as can be seen in his tempering of his human rights policy in the Middle East and Southeast Asia, and he did not indulge in large-scale risks in managing Soviet behavior. At the same time, his willingness to take high personal political risks in the cases of Panama and Camp David produced significant successes that had evaded others.

In his choice of means, Carter clearly preferred diplomacy to force. He prided himself on avoiding the use of American troops in combat. At the same time, the view of Carter as a pacifist is exaggerated if one considers his increases in the defense budget and development of new weapons systems. While he had campaigned on removing troops from South Korea, he changed that position in office after aides remonstrated and explained the complexity of the situation on the Korean peninsula. Critics cite Carter's reluctance to use force as a serious moral omission, but whether more military assistance to authoritarian regimes in Ethiopia, Angola, Iran, or Nicaragua would have led to better outcomes is debatable. In terms of a liberal respect for the rights and institutions of others, Carter scores very well.

In terms of consequences, there is more debate about whether Carter was good for American interests. His successes were real, and it is debatable whether a pure Brzezinski or a pure Vance approach to Brezhnev's Soviet Union would have made much difference. The coming collapse of the Soviet Union was already ripening in the Soviet economy, and the soft power of Carter's human rights policy contributed to the change that eventually culminated with the fall of the Berlin Wall in 1989. As for a cosmopolitan concern to avoid unnecessary damage to the interests of others, Carter also scores well. But perhaps most impressive was his educational effect in showing respect for truth and his broadening of moral discourse with his concern for human rights. In the battles of partisan politics it became fashionable to belittle Carter's foreign policy, but time has shown there was more substance than was often realized.

Carter's Ethical Scorecard

Intentions and Motives

Moral vision: attractive values, good motives	good
Prudence: balance of values and risks	good/mixed

Means

Force: proportion, discrimination, necessity	good/mixed
Liberal: respect for rights and institutions	good

Consequences

Fiduciary: success for long-term US interests	mixed
Cosmopolitan: minimal damage to others	good
Educational: truthful; broad moral discourse	good

*****

Ironically, both Ford and Carter were men of good character who receive quite good grades on the ethics of their foreign policies, yet many people judge the 1970s as a weak period in foreign policy. But judgments have to be made in context and rendered "as compared to what." Given the aftermath of Vietnam and Watergate, the economic stagflation, and the cultural revolutions of the decade, it may be that the problems lay in the context rather than the leaders. And after the decade of the 1960s where presidential deceit damaged public confidence, it is interesting that both Ford and Carter built their reputations on telling the truth. The consequences for confidence at home and soft power abroad should not be underestimated.

One can argue that Reagan did better in the next decade, as we shall see, but only after a rocky start and the fortuitous arrival of Gorbachev as the new Soviet leader in 1985. As the British philosopher Bernard Williams once observed, there is such a thing as "moral luck."[37] If the geriatric Brezhnev generation had cleared out a decade earlier and the weakness of the Soviet economy been revealed sooner, the 1970s might be remembered for the ending of the Cold War rather than merely the recovery from Vietnam. As historian Robert Strong speculates, "How much more would a Carter-Gorbachev matchup have accomplished? What would two 'outsiders' have done if given the opportunity to reshape Soviet–American relations and the world?"[38]

6

The End of the Cold War

The American mood at the beginning of the 1980s was depressed. In 1979, Jimmy Carter had spoken to the nation about a "crisis of confidence" that was threatening our "social and political fabric." Analysts wrote of American decline, and a major magazine cover featured the Statue of Liberty with a tear running down her cheek. In addition to the hostage crisis, the Iranian revolution produced a further spike in energy prices. Economic stagflation persisted. Respected Washington lawyer Lloyd Cutler suggested that the United States might have to consider changing to a parliamentary rather than a presidential system. The Soviet Union appeared to be growing in power, both in nuclear weaponry and in left-wing revolutions in Africa and Central America.

By the end of the decade, none of this was true and America was about to end the Cold War and enter its unipolar moment. Part of the credit goes to the 1980s presidents Ronald Reagan and George H. W. Bush. But it can also partly be explained by the misperceptions of Soviet power that marked the beginning of the decade. In reality, the Soviet Union was the country suffering serious economic decline.

In the 1950s, Stalin's centrally planned economic system focused on rebuilding heavy industry, and Soviet growth rates were higher than those in America. In his visit to the United States in 1959, Khrushchev famously used such buoyant numbers to boast that the Soviets would prevail. But the Soviet central planning system failed to respond to change in the global information economy. It was slow and inflexible—all thumbs and no fingers. As the economist Joseph Schumpeter argued, capitalism embraces creative destruction, a way of responding flexibly to major waves of technological change. At the end of the twentieth century, the major technological change of the "third industrial revolution" was the growing role of information as the engine fueling economic growth.

The Soviet central planning system was designed for the slow pace of heavy industry of the second industrial revolution. Now with Moore's Law doubling the capacity of computer chips every two years, new centrally planned plants were obsolete before they could be completed. The Soviets were inept at handling information. The deep secrecy of its political system meant that the flow of information was slow and cumbersome. As Foreign Minister Eduard Shevardnadze told his officials, "You and I represent a great country that in the last 15 years has been more and more losing its position as one of the leading industrially developed nations."[1] Moreover, the Soviet economy could no longer sustain its military power, and the defense budget accounted for 24 percent of GDP (compared to 5.9 percent for the US during the decade). The distinguished British historian Paul Kennedy wrote that the United States was suffering from "imperial overstretch," but it turned out to be the Soviet Union, not the United States, that was experiencing imperial overstretch.[2] Reagan and Bush were good captains, but they also had the benefit of favorable winds.

RONALD REAGAN

Reagan was born in the small town of Tampico, Illinois, in 1911, making him older than all the 1960s presidents except Johnson. His family's means were modest. His father had a drinking problem, while his mother was strictly religious. He attended Eureka College, a small Protestant liberal arts school where he was an indifferent student. Like Carter, he came to the presidency through a governorship (California) and never served in Congress. His service in World War II was not overseas but involved motion pictures for the military. Prior to politics his career was in Hollywood, and between 1937 and 1964, he appeared in fifty-three films. In his early days he was an active Democratic admirer of FDR, and carried out effective leadership and collective bargaining as president of the Screen Actors Guild. He switched to the Republican Party in 1962 and honed his conservative ideology while speaking before various industry groups.

Reagan's ideology allowed him to simplify matters, but he never allowed it to prevent him from working across the aisle, or making pragmatic compromises when bargaining. Reagan believed "there are simple answers to many of our problems—simple but hard. It's the complicated answer that's easy because it avoids facing the hard moral issues."[3] While he called the Soviet Union an "evil empire" in 1983, he was pragmatic and prepared to negotiate with Gorbachev when they met in Geneva in 1985. At their final summit in Moscow in 1988, he said in reference to those earlier years that "I was talking about another time, another era."

Reagan was not as simple as he made himself out to be. He was a popular man but preferred his own company; a champion of small towns who lived in big cities; an exponent of family values who divorced his first wife and had distant relations with his children. He was "a true believer who lacked the usual personality defects of the type: a sectarian with an ecumenical style."[4] Like FDR, Reagan lacked a first-class intellect, but made up for it with great emotional intelligence. He radiated optimism, was adept at using humor, and a master of telling parable-like stories, some true and some illusory.

Reagan changed how Americans thought about themselves, but as one aide wrote, he could be so dreamy and inattentive to detail that he allowed dramatic mistakes to occur. Nonetheless, David Gergen considered him the best leader since FDR.[5] While some critics dismissed Reagan as a "mere actor," he once shrewdly observed that he did not see how anyone could do the job well who was *not* an actor. FDR would certainly have agreed with this sentiment, although Carter might not.

Reagan's style restored American self-confidence when some establishment figures were questioning whether the country was governable. One of his greatest leadership skills was his ability to present a vision that was attractive to American followers by stressing the "moral clarity" of good versus evil. As Reagan told his speechwriter Peggy Noonan, "There is no question that I am an idealist, which is another way of saying I am an American."[6] He used the "city-on-the-hill metaphor" and saw Americans as a chosen people, but as Gergen put it, Reagan did not feel a messianic urge to spread American ideas and culture to other countries, as did some of his predecessors. But he did think the country had to set an example and that it should nurture democracy and freedom in other lands.[7] He had the best ability to communicate with the public of any president since Franklin Roosevelt. While acknowledging his cognitive weaknesses, in a retrospective summary, *The Economist* called him one of the most consequential presidents of the twentieth century even though "this champion of simplicity was himself surprisingly hard to make sense of."[8]

In addition to his cognitive knowledge base, Reagan's weakness was in his organizational capacity. While he was not a prisoner of his staff, he depended heavily on those he appointed, and after delegation was almost irresponsibly inattentive. Like Eisenhower, Reagan reigned, but he lacked Eisenhower's hidden-hand prime ministerial skills. He was no dullard, and people who worked for him reported he could be attentive to good arguments but "if a subject didn't interest him—many did not—he breezed by it. . . . His inattention to details and hands-off stance could be dangerous for his leadership."[9] When his able and pragmatic Chief of Staff James Baker traded positions with Secretary of the Treasury Donald Regan in 1985, Reagan failed to understand fully the implications for management of the White House, and that set the scene for a scandal that nearly destroyed his presidency. Despite six NSC advisors over eight years, Reagan was never able to manage inter-agency battles between Secretary of State George Shultz and Secretary of Defense Caspar Weinberger.

Failure to monitor highly risky appointees like CIA Director William Casey, National Security Advisor John Poindexter, and staffer Oliver North nearly led to the destruction of his presidency in the Iran–Contra scandal, which involved trading arms for hostages with Iran and then illegally using the proceeds to fund covert action by the Contra rebels against the Marxist regime in Nicaragua. Reagan saw the big picture in simplified terms of his values, but he was unable to understand the details.[10] According to Ambassador David Abshire, who helped to clean up the Iran–Contra mess in 1987, Reagan's first inclination was to deny the scandal and sweep it under the rug, but he eventually agreed to full disclosure. As Abshire concluded, "In Ronald Reagan, perhaps, the United States has never had a president with such great talent for transformational and so little interest in transactional leadership."[11]

Reagan is often credited with ending the Cold War, but the story is more complex. His initial objectives were to reverse the détente that had characterized containment since Nixon and get tougher with the Soviet Union, though his initial objectives did not include rollback or regime change.[12] Reagan did not like the Cold War status quo, and his combination of a rhetorical offensive plus a military build-up was designed to put pressure on the Soviet Union. But the gap between intuition and knowledge was well illustrated by the case of his anti-missile shield or strategic defense initiative (SDI). He allowed the NSC staff to put it in a 1983 speech, even though his Secretary of State warned that "we don't have the technology to say this," and the Chair of the Joint Chiefs said, "the necessary policy groundwork had not been laid." But despite the disarray among American policymakers at home, the Soviets worried about joining an arms race they could not win while financially strapped.[13] SDI turned out to be more successful as a diplomatic than as a military weapon.

One of Reagan's stated objectives was to rid the world of nuclear weapons, which he saw as a moral imperative. When advisors urged caution in negotiation, he replied in moral terms: "I've been reading my Bible and the description of Armageddon talks about destruction, I believe, of many cities and we need absolutely to avoid that. We have to do something new."[14] He made progress on the nuclear issue at the 1986 Reykjavik

Summit, but failed when he refused Gorbachev's request to constrain SDI testing to the laboratory. Ironically, Reagan failed in part because of his cognitive misunderstanding. While many members of his administration saw SDI as a bargaining chip, Reagan really believed it would work as a shield as promised and thus refused limits that would not have mattered seriously to its development. And when it came to slowing the proliferation of nuclear weapons, the Reagan administration eased the pressure that Carter had put on Pakistan because he prioritized Pakistani assistance in countering the Soviet presence in Afghanistan.

Did Reagan really end the Cold War? His actions contributed to the outcome, in part through his rhetoric and military build-up that put stress on the Soviet system, but Reagan's real skill was in shifting from harsh rhetoric to practical negotiations. He intuited the willingness of Gorbachev to bargain well before other members of his administration did, and then was able to establish a good working relationship.

In causing the end of the Cold War, however, Reagan's actions were not nearly as crucial as those of Gorbachev. Gorbachev was truly transformational in his effects, though not in achieving his objectives. Gorbachev's goal was to reform rather than destroy the Soviet Union. Without him, the Soviet Union might have limped along for another decade or more. Ultimately, however, the deepest causes of Soviet collapse were structural: the decline of Communist ideology and the failure of the Soviet economy. This would have happened eventually even without Gorbachev or Reagan. Reagan had the intuition and political skills to see Gorbachev as a bargaining partner, and that helped to account for part of the timing if not a major part of the causation of the end of the Cold War. If Yuri Andropov, a noted Soviet hard-liner, had not died of kidney disease, or if Gorbachev had come to power five years earlier when Jimmy Carter was president, Reagan's strategy and causal role would not have mattered. Reagan enjoyed the moral luck that Gorbachev was the king in the deck of cards that was dealt to him, and Reagan played those cards well. But the root causes of Soviet collapse were structural and the proximate causes were Gorbachev's policies of perestroika, glasnost, and new thinking in foreign policy. He was like a man standing on the stage of history who noticed a loose thread in his sweater and kept pulling on it until he had no sweater left. Gorbachev did not intend to undo the Soviet Union, but he did.

Ronald Reagan is often cited as an example of a moral foreign policy leader par excellence. A movement conservative, he is remembered for speeches that issued a strong call for moral clarity—at Westminster in 1982, where he predicted that the spread of freedom would "leave Marxism-Leninism on the ash heap of history"; or in Berlin in 1987, where he demanded, "Mr. Gorbachev, tear down this wall." His appeal rested on "knowing that mere reason, essential though it is, is only half of the business of reaching momentous decisions. You also need solid-based instincts, feelings, whatever the word is for the other part of the mind. 'I have a gut feeling,' Reagan said over and over again, when he was working out what to do and say." When people refer to a "Reaganite foreign policy" they usually mean the moral clarity that went with Reagan's simplification of complex issues and his effective rhetoric in the presentation of values. But this one-dimensional assessment overlooks the importance of Reagan's means—an ability to bargain and compromise as he pursued his policy. In the judgment of historian Melvyn Leffler, "Reagan's emotional intelligence was more important than his military buildup; his political credibility at home more important than his ideological offensive abroad; his empathy, affability and learning more important than his suspicions. . . . He was Gorbachev's minor, yet indispensable partner, setting the framework for dramatic changes that neither man anticipated happening anytime soon."[15]

Nonetheless, in terms of expressing values and vision, Reagan's clear and clearly stated objectives educated and inspired. The key question is whether Reagan was prudent enough in balancing aspirations and risks in his goals and objectives. Some people have argued that his initial rhetoric in his first term created a dangerous degree of tension and distrust in US–Soviet relations that increased the danger of a miscalculation or accident leading to war. Some analysts believe that several nuclear crises in the early 1980s were much closer calls than realized at the time, but it is not clear that Reagan was fully aware of the risks he was creating.[16] In the sense of imposing unexamined risks, he may have been morally deficient, but Reagan's hard-line policies created incentives to bargain, which he put to good advantage when Gorbachev came to power in Reagan's second term. But suppose there had been no second term?

As for cosmopolitan vision versus insularity, Reagan expressed his values in universal terms, though he was sometimes accused of hypocrisy for focusing on Soviet violations of human rights while ignoring the violations perpetrated by a number of American client regimes. He intervened in the Caribbean island of Grenada, and was quite prepared to live with apartheid in South Africa; he supported regimes that used death squads in Central America; and he took two years after the first protests before he reduced his support for the Marcos regime in the Philippines. He believed in human rights, but wielded them mostly as a Cold War weapon.

With regard to means, Reagan had a mixed record. The circumvention of legal means during the Iran–Contra issue set a bad precedent in terms of domestic as well as international norms and institutions. And the Reagan Doctrine of using covert action to fight wars against leftist regimes in Central America not only raised legal issues with Congress, but also included the mining of harbors in Nicaragua, a country with which the United States was officially at peace. When the International Court of Justice ruled the American actions contrary to international law, Reagan ignored the verdict. Whether these transgressions of autonomy and institutional restraints were justified by realist necessity is disputable, but the damage was real.

In terms of consequences, Reagan undoubtedly advanced the national interests of the United States, though as we saw earlier, most of the credit for ending the Cold War and the Soviet Union belongs to Gorbachev. In any event, Reagan took good advantage of the opportunity in a manner that was not limited just to insular American interests. On other issues, such as placing Marines in Lebanon and then withdrawing them when they were attacked, or bargaining for the return of hostages, some analysts argue that he set bad precedents for dealing with terrorism that had unfortunate long-term consequences.

Reagan's parables and fables often stretched the truth, and critics debated whether he deliberately distorted the truth or just subverted it to the values in which he wanted to believe. In general, his rhetoric broadened moral discourse at home, but his educational effect was sometimes subverted by actions that were at odds with his words such as support for apartheid in South Africa. He spoke of freedom and human rights but supported brutal authoritarian governments in Central America and Africa. While Carter sometimes had to compromise his human rights policies in cases like Iran, Reagan's use of human rights as a weapon against leftists while excusing non-Communist authoritarians often appeared hypocritical to foreigners in terms of the values that Reagan proclaimed for himself and for his country. By and large, however, Reagan had an ethical foreign policy in terms of intentions such as the goals he set and his motives, as well as in many of the larger consequences to which he contributed. Where he sometimes fell short was in terms of the means he used. These judgments are summarized in the following scorecard.

Reagan's Ethical Scorecard

Intentions and Motives

Moral vision: attractive values, good motives	good
Prudence: balance of values and risks	mixed

Means

Force: proportion, discrimination, necessity	mixed
Liberal: respect for rights and institutions	mixed

Consequences

Fiduciary: success for long-term US interests	good
Cosmopolitan: minimal damage to others	mixed
Educational: truthful; broad moral discourse	good

GEORGE H. W. BUSH

The dissolution of the Soviet Union occurred in December 1991 under the presidency of George H. W. Bush, and at that point the United States became the world's sole superpower. Bush managed to negotiate the end of the Cold War with Germany united inside NATO and not a shot fired between East and West. This alone would solidify Bush's legacy in the way that JFK's avoidance of disaster in the Cuban Missile Crisis did for his place in history.

Son of a Republican senator from Connecticut, Bush had a patrician background, a happy family, and an Ivy League education at Andover and Yale, where he was a star athlete. He may have been born with the proverbial silver spoon in his mouth, but he used it well. He fought with distinction in World War II in the Pacific and survived having his plane shot down. His mother brought him up on Yankee modesty and WASP values of noblesse oblige. After the war, he left the East Coast and entered the oil business in Texas. Bush later served in Congress for two terms, as ambassador to the UN, envoy to China, and director of the CIA. He ran against Reagan for president in 1980, but after he lost the primary contests, Reagan selected him as vice president to appeal to moderate voters. Bush later summed up his attitude toward the presidency as "I want to do the most good I can and the least harm."[17]

Reagan and Bush were contrasting personalities. Where Reagan was long on vision but short on detail, Bush was excellent on execution but short on vision. He famously mocked what he called "the vision thing." Bush was neither a great communicator nor an accomplished actor, and that gave him a very transactional style on most issues. Bush was a distinguished combat veteran, while Reagan's military life was imagined in films. Although Bush was elected to Congress from Texas, he was no stranger to Washington, and his family was part of the moderate Eastern Republican establishment while Reagan built his career in California and pioneered the new conservative challenge within the party. Nonetheless, Bush was loyal to Reagan.

Like Eisenhower, Bush was among the most experienced men in international affairs to occupy the presidency, and that helped him to develop quite extraordinary contextual intelligence. He also shared with Eisenhower an important ability to pick able subordinates, and to organize an effective national security process. These skills plus emotional intelligence served Bush well in his adept management of the dismantling of the Cold War, as well as the creation of a coalition that revived UN collective security (for the first time since 1950) in the 1991 Gulf War. His emotional intelligence allowed him to resist braggadocio and the temptation to gloat that would have been popular at home, but counterproductive to working with Gorbachev. On the other hand, these same character traits limited Bush's ability to use his office to educate the public. Unlike JFK or Reagan, he did not have an inspirational style. While he spoke about a "new world order" and a democratic peace, he never articulated or communicated these concepts as a vision that could capture public opinion.

When the Bush administration came into office, it was skeptical of Reagan's infatuation with Gorbachev, and Bush was initially cautious in picking up where Reagan left off. In particular, Bush did not share Reagan's nuclear abolitionism. After the Malta summit in 1989, however, Bush found he could work with Gorbachev. Aided by an able team of Secretary of State James Baker and National Security Advisor Brent Scowcroft, Bush demonstrated extraordinary skill in managing the unification of Germany within NATO (against the advice of many advisors and allies) and the eventual peaceful dismantlement of the Soviet Union in 1991. As for later Russian complaints that Bush misled them with assurances that NATO would not expand, there were some misunderstandings and some ambiguity in the early verbal stages of negotiations in 1990, but no written agreements or broken formal promises.[18]

Few people predicted in 1989 that within a year the two German states would be reunited, much less within NATO. But 1989–1990 was one of those moments of rare fluidity in international politics that bubble up out of domestic changes. Two transformational leaders with different objectives, Gorbachev and German Chancellor Helmut Kohl, took advantage of that fluidity to change the world. Bush made an important bet in backing his friend Kohl while skillfully handling the relationship with Gorbachev. In that sense he contributed greatly to the transformation.

Some historians fault Bush for not having made a bigger bet that might have avoided the later alienation of Russia. In the words of one, "Bush had told the American electorate that he was not enamored of grand visions and he remained true to his word. What resulted from his foreign policy leadership as a result was by no means unfortunate, but it was not ideal. He defended the interests of the United States but . . . the decision to extend prefabricated settlement architecture only to Eastern Europe, not Russia, seemed a throwback to an earlier era."[19]

Zbigniew Brzezinski, who had served under Jimmy Carter, later praised Bush for his skillful management but faulted him for failing to set more transformational objectives in his foreign policy. Bush was reluctant to follow Reagan's ambitious objectives or rhetorical style. Bush's vision of a new world order was that of a modest realist. He borrowed the liberal Wilsonian language of UN collective security when he organized a coalition to reverse Iraq's invasion of Kuwait in 1990–1991, but he did not develop a new or broader vision that set new objectives. Brzezinski faults Bush for not seeing the potential for a vision that promoted democracy in Russia, not pushing harder for a solution to the Israel/Palestine dispute that roiled the Middle East and Muslim world, and taking a stronger position on North Korean and South Asian nuclear proliferation.[20]

Bush's defenders question whether anyone could have solved these problems. They note that Bush took the initiative on Israel and Palestine at the 1992 Madrid Conference, and say that he might have done more had he been able to win a second term. Critics complained that too much caution was a moral omission at such a time of rare fluidity. Things were now possible that had been frozen in place by the Cold War. But juggling so many balls in the air, Bush had to worry about dropping any of them: the fall of the Berlin Wall, nuclear issues, Iraq's invasion of Kuwait, the Tiananmen Square repression in China, civil war in Yugoslavia, and others.

Bush's objectives were based on prudence. The decline of the Soviet Union and the rise of Europe created a situation where the administration could look at the collapse of Yugoslavia and conclude that the United States "had no dog in that fight." This position was not based on lack of contextual intelligence since many top administration officials were very knowledgeable about Yugoslavia. Both Brent Scowcroft and Deputy Secretary of State Lawrence Eagleburger had served there. National intelligence estimates correctly forecast the coming civil war, but Bush's priority was to preside over extraordinary and favorable external change without dropping any of the balls. He decided to let the Europeans take the lead in the former Yugoslavia, and they were not up to the task. On the other hand, it is uncertain if a more active American role could have prevented the subsequent humanitarian crisis and genocide in Bosnia, though the Clinton administration eventually was able to limit the carnage.

According to his staff, Bush's leadership style was "restless but unassuming, at once both relaxed and reserved ... His style with foreign leaders bordered on the indirect, but sooner or later he would make his point. His managerial style was equally disciplined. He would discuss issues individually with top subordinates, clearly conveying the principles he cared about. But he would almost never visibly intervene in subcabinet or even some cabinet-level policy discussions." Bush surrounded himself with "people who shared his penchant for low-key rhetoric and careful attention to details ... who could get along and keep their egos in check," and keep him constantly informed.[21] His political organizational skills were impressive, and his National Security Advisor Brent Scowcroft, a veteran of the Ford administration, and deputy Robert Gates were renowned for running a fair and prudent process.

Bush was not transformational in his objectives but he presided successfully over a major structural transformation from a bipolar to a unipolar world. If any of the issues had been botched, the consequences could have been disastrous for the world. Bush's defenders ask the critics who complain that he presided over a transformation but did not sufficiently build upon it whether it is better to have a prudent leader who is guilty of possible moral omissions or a transformational leader with an unusual vision and willingness to take greater risks. Would Reagan have done better with his lofty vision, inattention to detail, and disorganized foreign policy process?

Although Bush is ranked as a middling president by historians, he excelled in foreign policy. As the veteran foreign service officer Nicholas Burns argued, "Bush's accomplishments in ending the Cold War, unifying Germany, amassing the Gulf War coalition that defeated Saddam Hussein in that same year, and in then pivoting to start Israeli-Palestinian negotiations at Madrid make him arguably the most successful foreign policy president of the last 50 years."[22] As Bush and Scowcroft argued in their co-authored memoir in 1998, "What Harry Truman's containment policy and succeeding administrations had cultivated, we were able to bring to final fruition. Did we see what was coming when we entered office? No, we did not, nor could we have planned it. . . . The long-run framework of Bush foreign policy was very deliberate: encouraging, guiding, and managing change without provoking backlash and crackdown. In the short run, the practical effort included as well a certain amount of seat-of-the-pants planning and diplomacy. . . . We eluded the shadow of another Versailles."[23]

Bush did take a big risk on the unification of Germany. At the time, many experts and foreign leaders thought it a reach too far, because the division of Germany had been a stabilizing factor in postwar Europe. For over a century after Bismarck unified the multiple German states, the great European question was how many German states in the center of Europe was consistent with a stable balance of power. Bismarck's answer was two (he left Austria independent); Hitler's answer was one, and that proved disastrous. The post-1945 answer was three, and this had been locked in place by the Cold War.

However, Bush supported the reunification of East and West Germany, resisting the advice of Margaret Thatcher, Francois Mitterand, Scowcroft, and others, apparently out of a sense of fairness and responsiveness to his friend Helmut Kohl. After a visit with Kohl in 1983, Vice President Bush concluded that "Germany was a solid democracy that had done penance for its sins and that 'at some point you should let a guy up.' "[24] In October 1989, even before the opening of the Berlin Wall, Bush responded to a call from Kohl by publicly stating that "I don't share the concern that some European countries have about a reunified Germany." At the same time, he was careful to let Kohl and others take the lead. In November 1989 when the Berlin Wall was opened (partly by an East German mistake) Bush was criticized for his low-key response, but he had made a deliberate choice not to humiliate the Soviets. "I won't beat on my chest and dance on the wall" was his response—a model of emotional intelligence and self-restraint. It helped to set the stage for the successful Malta Summit with Gorbachev a month later.[25]

Bush was concerned about avoiding disaster in a world that was changing dramatically. As he and his team responded to the forces that were largely outside of his control, he set goals and objectives that balanced opportunities and realism in a prudent manner. For example, some critics have faulted him for not being more forthcoming in proclaiming moral support for the national aspiration of Soviet republics like Ukraine in 1990, or for failing to go all the way to Baghdad to unseat Saddam Hussein in the Gulf War, or for sending Scowcroft to Beijing to maintain relations with China after the Tiananmen Square massacre of students in 1989, but in each instance, Bush was limiting his short-run objectives in order to pursue long-term stability as a goal.

In his final year, Cheney's Pentagon produced a long-term Defense Planning Guidance outlining a goal of maintaining American primacy in a time of change.[26] In response to public criticism of its arrogance, the White House toned down its presentation, but the goal remained while Bush's rhetoric about a new world order was otherwise never fleshed out. Bush remained focused on questions of stability more than new visions. In ethical terms, although Bush did not articulate a strong moral vision, it is difficult for a liberal realist to make the case that he should have been less prudent and taken more risks. One exception to his prudent realism came at the very end of his term, when he sent American troops to ensure delivery of food aid to starving people in war-torn Somalia. He saw it as "an opportunity to put American power to work to save, in his words, 'thousands of innocents.' "[27] Ironically, this uncharacteristic cosmopolitan intervention set the scene for the first major crisis for Bill Clinton.

As for means, Bush was respectful of institutions and norms at home and abroad, going to Congress for authorization of the Gulf War, and to the United Nations for a resolution under Chapter 7 of the Charter, something his son later failed to accomplish in 2003. Although a realist in his thinking, Bush could be Wilsonian in his tactics. In terms of proportionate and discriminate use of force, Bush's termination of the ground war in Iraq after only four days was motivated in part by humanitarian reactions to the slaughter of Iraqi troops as well as the concern that Iraq not be so weakened that it could not balance the threatening power of its neighbor Iran. He also worried that advancing on Baghdad might produce a quagmire as well as dissolve the coalition he had created. Neoconservative critics thought he should have taken the risk and removed Hussein.

Bush did intervene in Panama to capture (and later put on trial) Manuel Noriega. This use of force violated Panamanian sovereignty, but it had a de facto legitimacy given Noriega's notorious behavior related to drug trafficking and human rights violations. And when Bush organized his coalition to prosecute the Gulf War, he not only worked with the United Nations, but included a number of Arab countries that were not needed for military purposes but for the soft power legitimacy that they added to the coalition. He was attentive to institutions. With his careful combination of hard and soft power, Bush established a policy that raised moral standards at home and abroad and was capable of being sustainable in the future.

In terms of consequences, Bush was a good trustee in advancing American interests, and he did so with minimal damage to the interests of foreigners. He was careful not to humiliate Gorbachev, and to manage the transition to Yeltsin in Russia. At the same time, not all foreigners were adequately protected, such as when Bush assigned a lower priority to Kurds and Shia in Iraq, to dissidents in China, or to Bosnians who were embroiled in a civil war in the former Yugoslavia. But these moral omissions did not outweigh his moral commissions. On issues of global public goods, he reversed Reagan administration policies on the environment and signed the UN Framework Convention on Climate Change that eventually led to the 2015 Paris Climate Agreement.

Could Bush have done more? Was he guilty of important sins of omission in his intentions and vision? Possibly, or perhaps he might have done more in a second term, and losing that opportunity was just bad moral luck. And with a better set of communications skills, Bush might have been able to do more to educate the American public about the changing nature of world they faced after the Cold War. But given the uncertainties of history, prudence may be the most important foreign policy virtue in turbulent times, and greater ambition might have courted disaster. Overall, Bush's foreign policy record ranks near the top.

Bush 41's Ethical Scorecard

Intentions and Motives

Moral vision: attractive values, good motives	good/mixed
Prudence: balance of values and risks	good

Means

Force: proportion, discrimination, necessity	good
Liberal: respect for rights and institutions	good

Consequences

Fiduciary: success for long-term US interests	good
Cosmopolitan: minimal damage to others	good
Education: truthful; broad moral discourse	mixed

*****

Ending the Cold War without significant bloodshed was a major accomplishment in American foreign policy. Since 1945, the United States had lived with a bipolar balance of power, and for four decades the ideological and nuclear threat from the Soviet Union had been the central issue in US foreign policy. At the beginning of the 1980s, the Committee on the Present Danger and other groups of foreign policy notables were warning about the growing threat from the Soviet Union. By the end of 1991, both the Soviet Union and the Cold War were over. As it turned out, the perceptions of Soviet strength were misleading.

How did an empire end without war? By a combination of luck and skill. If the tough KGB chief Yuri Andropov had not died of kidney failure and Gorbachev not come to power in 1985, the Soviet threat might have continued for another decade or so. Though it was not what he intended, Gorbachev's efforts at perestroika (restructuring) and glasnost (opening) accelerated the Soviet decline.

Some people attribute the successful outcome to the combination of Reagan's harsh rhetoric and Bush's prudent negotiations, but that summary is too simple. Reagan's early rhetoric may have frightened Soviet leaders, but it increased nuclear risk and in retrospect we learned we were lucky in avoiding a crisis. Once Gorbachev came to power it was Reagan's personal and negotiating skills, not his rhetoric, that was crucial. And Reagan was guided by his moral vision of ending the Cold War and removing the threat of nuclear weapons. Similarly, though the Bush administration came into office concerned about Reagan's overtures, Bush's contextual intelligence, prudence, and understanding of the importance of not humiliating Gorbachev were crucial. Some people say that in life, it is more important to be lucky than to be skillful. Fortunately, Reagan and Bush were both.

The Unipolar Moment

When the Soviet Union dissolved in December 1991, the United States became the world's only superpower. For forty-six years, the structure of world politics had been bipolar, and Soviet military power balanced and limited what the United States could do. Although the 1952 Republican platform spoke of rolling back Communism, Eisenhower stood by when Soviet troops crushed an anti-Communist rebellion in Hungary in 1956; Kennedy traded away NATO missiles in Turkey rather than risk nuclear war in 1962; Johnson watched Soviet troops crush reform in Prague in 1968; and Nixon reversed American policy toward China in order to balance what was seen as growing Soviet power.

In the 1990s, these restraints began to relax. When George Bush sought a UN Security Council resolution to repel Iraq's invasion of Kuwait, Gorbachev's willingness to forgo a Soviet veto allowed UN collective security to function for the first time since the Korean War in 1950. Instead of a tense military stand-off in Berlin, the wall came down in 1989 and Germany was united within NATO. While Russia retained a formidable nuclear arsenal, its economy and conventional military capabilities atrophied, the Warsaw Pact dissolved, and the old Soviet state lost half of its population and economy. Bill Clinton and George W. Bush had far more leeway for choice in foreign policy, including the option of military intervention. For four decades, containment of the Soviet Union had been the North Star by which American leaders could navigate foreign policy. With the end of the Cold War, Georgi Arbatov, director of the Institute of US and Canadian Studies, quipped that the United States would also suffer through the loss of the enemy that helped concentrate its efforts. The conservative columnist Charles Krauthammer celebrated this era of American foreign policy as "the unipolar moment."[1]

Realist critics argue that Arbatov got it right. Without a balance of power, there were few restraints on American hubris. The mood was captured by the popularity of Francis Fukuyama's famous 1989 article "The End of History?," which argued that liberalism had defeated fascism in the first half of the century and Communism in the second half, and there was no major ideological alternative left to liberal democracy. Some critics believe that "the Clinton, Bush and Obama administrations, each in control of American foreign policy for eight years, were fully committed to pursuing 'liberal hegemony.'"[2]

But the hegemonic temptation was initially more tentative than this picture implies. Opinion polls did not show a significant change in the proportion of the public wanting a more active involvement in foreign policy until after the dramatic shock of the terrorist attacks on September 11, 2001. Clinton hesitated for two years before dealing with the humanitarian crisis in Bosnia, and George W. Bush campaigned in 2000 on the importance of a humble foreign policy. Among the foreign policy elites who paid close attention to foreign policy, some realists wanted retrenchment and a peace dividend; some liberals wanted more multilateralism, while neoconservatives wanted fewer restraints on intervention to promote democratic values. This was the context in which Bill Clinton had to find his way.

WILLIAM JEFFERSON CLINTON

Bill Clinton represented a major generational change. The man he defeated in 1992, George H. W. Bush, had fought in World War II before Clinton was even born. Later, Clinton avoided service in Vietnam. He was also the first president whose term was entirely after the Cold War.

Clinton was born in 1946 in the small town of Hope, Arkansas. His mother was a nurse and his stepfather a car salesman. Like Ronald Reagan, he had a number of traits common to the children of alcoholics. In his words, "I grew up with much greater empathy for other people's problems than the average person. . . . If you grow up in an environment that causes you to want to avoid trouble, you try to keep the peace at all costs."[3] A compulsive need to have people like him contributed to impressive political skills and a capacity to charm others. As summarized by presidential expert Fred Greenstein, "Besides being political to the core, Clinton was notable for his intelligence, energy, and exceptional articulateness. He also was marked by a severe lack of self-discipline that led him into difficulties, and a resilience and coolness under pressure that enabled him to extricate himself from many of his predicaments."[4]

In the words of a former advisor, David Gergen, "To friend and foe, Bill Clinton is a mass of contradictions. He is one of the smartest men ever elected president and has done some of the dumbest things. . . . He genuinely wanted, as he pledged, the most ethical administration in history, and enters history as the first elected president ever impeached."[5] Though Clinton was subsequently acquitted by the Senate, his lies about his affair with White House intern Monica Lewinsky absorbed a year of his presidency and contributed to a climate of mistrust. While his sexual behavior was reminiscent of John F. Kennedy, his failure to adjust to the changed climate of press reporting was a serious lapse in his political judgment. As he later explained to his confidant, Taylor Branch: "I cracked; I just cracked."[6] Though he lied to his cabinet and staff about the Lewinsky affair and others, there is no evidence that the incidents had a direct effect on his foreign policy.* However, they certainly competed for his time, and lowered trust in his presidency.

---

* Clinton was adept at public compartmentalization. I once attended a White House meeting between Clinton and British Prime Minister Tony Blair soon after the Lewinsky scandal hit the press. During coffee breaks, Clinton would huddle with his political advisors in the corner of the room. He could then return to the table and resume a cogent conversation as if nothing had happened. It was an impressive performance.

Like Carter, Clinton came to the office from a Southern governorship. He styled himself a "new Democrat," but he was never as much an outsider to Washington as Jimmy Carter. Clinton attended Georgetown University; he was a Rhodes Scholar at Oxford and a graduate of Yale Law School. He served on the staff of Arkansas Senator William Fulbright before returning to Arkansas where he was first elected governor at the age of thirty-two. Despite superficial similarities, Clinton and Carter were a study in contrasts. Both men had very high traditional IQs, but differed greatly in temperament and emotional IQ. Carter was the stern moralist; Clinton the pragmatist. Clinton had excellent political skills and an inspirational style that allowed him to become the first Democrat to be elected to a second term since Truman. Carter lacked these skills. Some go further and say Carter defied public opinion while Clinton merely followed it, but that underrates Clinton, who supported NAFTA and eventually intervened in Bosnia despite negative public opinion on both issues.

Clinton came into office intending to be an "assertive multilateralist" who would strengthen UN peacekeeping. His first National Security Advisor, Anthony Lake, declared himself a "pragmatic neo-Wilsonian." But this vision quickly succumbed to the harsh reality of Somalia, where mission creep had allowed Bush's humanitarian intervention to morph from providing food for starving refugees into stopping battles among the competing warlords who were trying to exploit the food distribution. When eighteen Americans were killed and one dragged through the streets after a failed mission in Mogadishu in October 1993, public opinion in the United States was strongly for withdrawal, which Clinton acceded to, albeit with a six-month timetable. He also commissioned an internal study that scaled back support for UN peacekeeping and imposed several tests for future peacekeeping operations, including clear objectives, a definite exit date, and consent of the warring parties to a ceasefire. Within the first year, Clinton's multilateralism became less assertive.

But the new guidelines for participating in UN peacekeeping did not solve the dilemma of liberal interventionism. A few months later, in April 1994, another African crisis arose. Fighting broke out in Rwanda that eventually led to some 800,000 deaths, primarily of the Tutsi minority. The UN

Security Council, including the United States, voted to remove most of its small 2,500-person peacekeeping force in Kigali, and the State Department was careful to avoid calling the killings a "genocide," which might have led to cosmopolitan calls for intervention. Congress would not have supported sending American troops, and while prompt action in support of the UN peacekeepers would not have saved all the victims, it might have saved some. But such modest options were not tried. Nonintervention in Rwanda was the product of the failed humanitarian intervention in Somalia. Later, Clinton would say his inaction in the face of genocide was one of his worst mistakes.[7]Contrary to conventional wisdom, his moral mistake was a sin of omission rather than hubris bred by the unipolar moment.

To make matters more difficult, Clinton was wrestling with two other cases of intervention during the same time. In October 1993, a military coup and the overthrow of President Jean-Bertrand Aristide was creating flows of Haitian refugees to the United States, and activist groups demanded that the United States intervene in Haiti to remove the military junta and restore the elected president. Clinton sent a ship with engineers and civil affairs experts but was humiliated when the ship was turned away by an organized mob demonstrating at the harbor in Port au Prince. A year later, against prevailing domestic opinion, Clinton took a firmer line and successfully used a combination of negotiation and the threat of airborne invasion (at one point troops were in the air) to cause the military triumvirate to depart. Aristide returned to power, though the American occupation failed (as had prior interventions since 1915) to resolve Haiti's long-term problems.

In Bosnia, Clinton inherited another difficult situation. Bush had left the civil war to the European allies to resolve without success. Some political groups called for American intervention, but broad public opinion remained skeptical. During his first two years, Clinton agonized about the humanitarian situation but was cautious. He sent Secretary of State Warren Christopher to Europe, but the European allies were disappointed that Christopher offered no more leadership than had the Bush administration. The United States urged its allies to lift the UN embargo that prevented the shipment of arms to the besieged Muslim minority, and to allow NATO air strikes against the Serbian forces that were bombarding civilians in Sarajevo. But the Europeans feared that the Serbs would respond by attacking their peacekeeping forces and turn them into hostages. American public opinion remained divided, and it was not until July 1995, after the Serbs executed 8,000 Muslim men and boys who had been under UN protection at Srebrenica, that Clinton authorized NATO air strikes against Serbian forces. That use of military force prepared the way for the Dayton peace negotiations and the positioning of NATO troops to preserve a fragile ceasefire in Bosnia.

Four years later, when Kosovars revolted and demanded independence from Serbia, they were subjected to repressive measures and ethnic cleansing. Secretary of State Madeleine Albright's diplomatic efforts were to no avail, and Russia blocked an effort to get the UN Security Council to authorize the use of force under Chapter 7 of the UN Charter (in contrast to its permissive approach in 1990). Instead, Clinton agreed to a NATO air operation against Serbia, but refused to send ground troops. He argued that the humanitarian intervention had moral legitimacy even if it was questionable in international law. For three months, the Kosovo War looked like a stalemate and strained US–Russian relations before Boris Yeltsin relented and pressed his Serbian ally Slobodan Milosevic to capitulate.

Colin Powell finished his term as Chairman of the Joint Chiefs of Staff under Clinton after serving in the Reagan and Bush administrations where he pronounced the "Powell Doctrine," urging caution in the use of force. Early in the Clinton administration, Madeleine Albright, then Ambassador to the UN, challenged Powell by asking what good it did to have the world's best military if one never used it.[8] While Reagan had used military intervention against the tiny Caribbean island of Grenada, and Bush had used it in Panama, the reluctant Clinton wound up using open military force for humanitarian intervention more than both his predecessors combined. The issue remained contentious at home and abroad. Of Clinton's interventions, Haiti and Bosnia might be considered successes in terms of improving conditions with moderate risk and cost. Kosovo succeeded in humanitarian terms, but realists complain about the burden it placed on relations with Russia. Somalia was a failure, but an inherited problem, and Rwanda was a failure of omission rather than commission.

Clinton never articulated a complete vision for the post–Cold War world, but he "ultimately embraced a strategy very similar to that charted during the Bush years." In September 1993, National Security Advisor Tony Lake declared that the "defining feature of this era is that we are its dominant power" and must "prevent aggressive dictators from menacing the post–Cold War order, and aggressively promote free markets and de- mocracy."⁹ Clinton put his own brand on it with the term "engagement and enlargement."¹⁰ By this he meant engaging former enemies and enlarging the domain of free-market democracies. As one analyst said of Clinton's grand strategy, "The administration wished to support the spread of de- mocracy, but sought to do so using market forces, not military might." Clinton warned, "We cannot police the world."¹¹

Clinton relied heavily on economic change. His prudent fiscal policies and domestic economic initiatives prepared the United States to prosper in a globalizing economy, and he went against public opinion (and many Democratic Party advisors) to pass the North American Free Trade Area legislation that he had inherited from Bush, as well as to complete the Uruguay Round of tariff reductions and to launch the World Trade Organization. His Treasury also supported the liberalization of interna- tional capital markets, though some critics believe that he should have been more cautious in pressing for deregulation.

The Clinton administration worked closely with the International Monetary Fund (IMF) to manage the 1997 Asian financial crisis. Asian policy involved engagement with China, including increased trade and investment, and promoting Chinese membership in the World Trade Organization (WTO). Rather than try to create a Cold War policy of con- tainment of a rising China (which was unlikely to succeed given the attitudes of other countries), Clinton hoped to integrate China into the liberal in- ternational order. Subsequently, critics have charged Clinton with naiveté in believing that trade and growth would change Chinese politics. While Clinton was overoptimistic about the extent that trade and growth would liberalize China, his policy was not as simple as that seems. It started with a realist balance of power strand that reaffirmed and strengthened the US–Japan security treaty as an insurance policy, long before China was invited to join the World Trade Organization. The 1996 Clinton–Hashimoto declaration in Tokyo declared that the security relationship with Japan was not a Cold War relic as some thought, but would provide the basis for stability in the Asia Pacific region, and that proved a good investment. Clinton's Asian policy was a combination of liberal opening and engagement with China, but also a realist alliance with Japan to ensure against China becoming a bully in the region.[12] Clinton's Secretary of Defense William Perry referred to this approach as "shaping the environment" that conditioned the long-term rise of Chinese power.

Clinton also invested major efforts in peacemaking. In 1993, he hosted Israeli Prime Minister Yitzhak Rabin and Palestinian leader Yasir Arafat at the White House, and later traveled to Jordan to encourage an agreement between Jordan and Israel. Had Rabin not been assassinated in November 1995, there might also have been an agreement between Israel and Syria. One of the final acts of Clinton's presidency was a Camp David meeting where he tried unsuccessfully to mediate between Yasir Arafat and Israeli Prime Minister Ehud Barak. Clinton felt he came close, but in the end Arafat told him that compromise with Israel would spell Arafat's death sentence at the hands of radicals in Palestine. Clinton was more successful in his efforts to promote the peace process in Northern Ireland, and his conversations with Pakistan's Nawaz Shariff after the Kargil border incident in 1999 may have helped avert an India–Pakistan war. When North Korea violated its commitments under the Non-Proliferation Treaty in 1994, Clinton successfully combined threats with negotiations to freeze their production of plutonium.

The area of Clinton's foreign policy that is still debated is his handling of Russia. Brzezinski later faulted him for not launching a stronger effort to support Russia's economy and to develop democratic institutions, but Russia was a top priority for Clinton, and he spent a great deal of personal time on it. He made major efforts to develop a relationship with Yeltsin, to provide aid and encourage investment, and to expand the Group of Seven advanced economies to a G-8 with Russian membership.[13] But after

seventy years of Communism, Russia had neither the economic nor political institutions to successfully absorb a Marshall Plan type of aid program, and as corruption grew and Yeltsin became physically and politically
weaker during the decade, he became too frail a foundation to build upon.
By 2000, with political turmoil increasing in Russia, including brutal sup-
pression of a revolt in Chechnya, Yeltsin turned to Putin (a former KGB
officer) to become his successor, protect him, and to restore order.

A different criticism concerns Clinton's initiative to expand NATO to
include former members of the Warsaw Pact. The Pentagon had developed
a modest Partnership for Peace program, which enabled former adversaries
to cooperate closely with NATO without formal membership. However, in
1995 Clinton decided to go further, and in 1999 NATO admitted Poland,
Hungary, and Czechoslovakia to full membership. Some, such as former
NATO Ambassador Robert Hunter, argue that this was "an excellent example of where presidential leadership—at home and abroad—can make
the difference in achieving the nation's larger purposes."[14]

Clinton's defenders believe that this action created a stabilizing framework for a democratic transition in Central Europe that might otherwise
have become an area of insecurity and turmoil. They point to the fact the
Russia was not isolated but was invited to send officers and diplomats
to work with NATO in Brussels. On the other hand, critics like George
Kennan, the father of containment, argued that NATO expansion would
antagonize Russia and play to the paranoia of a country that had just lost
an empire. Putin and other Russians later pointed to NATO expansion as
proof of Western perfidy. But as one White House official later recalled,
"We saw the opportunities of those years differently—a chance to unite
Europe and help make it democratic in the East as well as the West. Through
NATO and EU expansion we were able to liberate and then protect more
than 100 million East Europeans."[15]

The difficult counterfactual is what the world today would look like if
NATO expansion had not stabilized Central Europe. At the end of the Cold
War, some realists like John Mearsheimer predicted that Central Europe
would go "back to the future" and again become a power vacuum and zone
of conflict between the traditional competitors of Russia and Germany.[16]

But this did not happen. And given its domestic political and economic problems, would Russia have wound up in the same place anyway? No one can be sure. William Burns, a former ambassador to Russia, argues that the broken Russian economy "could not be fixed in a single generation, let alone a few years. None of it could be fixed by outsiders," but "NATO expansion was premature at best" and a longer investment in the Partnership for Peace would have made sense.[17]

Another area often criticized as a failure in Clinton's foreign policy was his response to terrorism. The threat from Al Qaeda appeared in 1993 with the first attacks on the New York World Trade Center and grew during the decade, culminating in attacks on American embassies in Kenya and Tanzania, and on American ships in Yemen. In August 1998, Clinton launched missile strikes against Al Qaeda targets in Afghanistan and Sudan, and two submarines were kept on permanent station in the Indian Ocean, able to land cruise missiles on targets in Afghanistan in a matter of hours. (The technology of quick strikes by lingering drones was not yet mature.) Thus it is untrue to say that Clinton ignored the problem, and Al Qaeda was near the top of the list of threats that he warned his successor about. Nonetheless, critics argue that his response was inadequate. As one biographer put it, "A leader's task is to perceive the character of one's times, describe it in vivid terms, and summon people to meet the challenge. As the twin towers burned . . . this aspect of Clinton's leadership could only be judged a failure."[18] At the same time, the press was skeptical of Clinton's 1998 cruise missile strikes, and his successor did not make Al Qaeda a priority until the 9/11 attacks.

How do we summarize the ethics of Clinton's foreign policy? In terms of intentions and a moral vision, Clinton replaced Cold War containment with a view of expanding market economies and encouraging democratic evolution summarized by "engagement and enlargement." In terms of his personal motives, it is not accurate to describe Clinton as succumbing to post–Cold War hubris, though some in his administration overestimated American power. He was prudent in his implementation, relying more on economic change and institutions than on military force. When he did use force for interventions it was prudently applied for humanitarian purposes, though his goals also included democracy promotion. He pursued both peacekeeping and peacemaking as major foreign policy objectives.

In terms of means, Clinton's use of force was proportionate and largely discriminating. If anything, critics argue he should have done more to rescue civilians in Rwanda, and there were a number of options he could have explored short of a major military operation. Some critics feel that he could have used more force against Al Qaeda, or against North Korea, though the prospects for success were far from clear. In terms of liberal means, Clinton was respectful of institutions and human rights. While he quickly moderated his assertive multilateralism after Somalia, he continued to support the UN though he decided to go ahead without a Chapter 7 resolution to legitimize his actions in Kosovo. He strengthened the institutions of the liberal international order by the development of NAFTA and the WTO. When he expanded NATO to three Warsaw Pact countries he also sought to develop a new institutional connection with Russia, and made changes to include Russia in the G-8. He was successful in reaffirming the alliance with Japan, and his general preference for diplomacy led to some success in mediation of disputes like Northern Ireland, India–Pakistan, and the Middle East.

As for consequences, Clinton was a good fiduciary in the promotion of American interests. At the end of his term the American and global economy were strong, alliances with Europe and Japan had been strengthened, relations with the major powers of Russia and China were reasonable, and international institutions had been strengthened. Efforts had begun to deal with climate change and missile proliferation. One exception is whether he responded rapidly enough to the growth of Al Qaeda.

Clinton had a cosmopolitan approach that included concern about damage to others, and this led to successful limited interventions in Haiti and Bosnia, but Clinton was too cautious in the case of the Rwanda genocide. The United States could not solve the problem by sending troops, but it could have done more to support rather than withdraw the UN peacekeeping force in 1994. Where Clinton fell short in terms of consequences was in his educational effects. Not only did he fail to articulate a full vision of the post–Cold War world as Brzezinski charges, but his looseness with the truth in his personal affairs undercut trust in his presidency and was a failure in the broadening of moral discourse. Nonetheless, his overall scorecard is quite good.

Clinton's Ethical Scorecard

Intentions and Motives

Moral vision: attractive values, good motives	good
Prudence: balance of values and risks	good

Means

Force: proportion, discrimination, necessity	good
Liberal: respect for rights and institutions	good

Consequences

Fiduciary: success for long-term US interests	good
Cosmopolitan: minimal damage to others	mixed
Educational: truthful; broad moral discourse	mixed

GEORGE WALKER BUSH

Like Clinton, George W. Bush was born in 1946, and came to the presidency through a Southern governorship. Like Clinton, he avoided service in the Vietnam War. Unlike Clinton, he came from a wealthy family, and graduated from Andover, Yale, and Harvard Business School. He ran for Congress unsuccessfully in 1978 and helped manage his father's campaign in 1988. While he had the folksy twang and mannerisms of Texas, he was not really a Washington outsider. And of course, he was in the rare situation of being the son of a recent president. His father would sometimes jokingly call him "Quincy," in reference to the Adams family precedent early in the republic.

Though he was emotionally close to his father, the younger Bush was keen to differentiate himself from his father and the family's East Coast origins. As he told the House Majority Republican Leader at the beginning of his presidency, "I'm more like Ronald Reagan than my dad."[19] In part this came from growing up in Midland, Texas, instead of Connecticut, but when I once asked Brent Scowcroft why George W. Bush did not heed his father's advice more often, he told me to look for the answer in Freud or Shakespeare. The son revered the father, but considered himself the better politician. He would take greater risks and not play "small ball." In the words of the elder Bush's biographer Jon Meacham, "It would be naïve to think that their story—like the story of most fathers and sons—was not also shaped by emotional complexity. . . . Still the forty-third president protested a bit much on how little he consulted his father."[20]

Never a diligent student like Clinton or Obama, George W. Bush was something of a slacker in his early years. In the words of Fred Greenstein, "For most of the two decades after he graduated from college, he was conspicuous as the underachieving son of a superachieving father. He drank to excess and had a devil-may-care lifestyle that was marked by periodic alcohol-related scrapes."[21] Then in 1986, at the age of forty, Bush gave up alcohol and became a born-again Christian. In his wife's words, "George is pretty impulsive and does pretty much everything to excess. Drinking is not one of the good things to do to excess. . . . Having these two little babies and drinking really didn't fit."[22] So in addition to being impetuous, Bush proved capable of impressive self-discipline when an important personal moral choice was involved.

George W. Bush was often caricatured as unintelligent and not in control during his presidency, but these were politicized myths. Contrary to conventional wisdom, Bush 43 did not lack intelligence, but he rarely explored beyond his area of comfort. As British Prime Minister Tony Blair observed, "George Bush was straightforward and direct. And very smart . . . George had great intuition. But his intuition was less . . . about politics and more about what he thought was right and wrong. This wasn't stated analytically or intellectually. It was just stated."[23] His intellectual curiosity was bounded, but deep on issues that touched him, such as casualties and command during war. He read fourteen Lincoln biographies during his presidency.[24] Bush has been described as having a black-and-white worldview and stubbornly willing to take high risks based on his core moral instincts. In the words of aide Peter Feaver, "If he has thought a matter through and thinks he's doing the right thing, by golly he'll do it no matter what people say." These characteristics helped him to defy the conventional wisdom of his advisors and the Congress and launch the surge policy in Iraq in 2006.[25] Bush was the decision-maker.

Where Bush failed as a leader was in organizing the flow of information in his team. Despite his MBA from Harvard Business School, Bush had major management failures with serious moral consequences. The organization theorist James March once noted that establishing management systems is like an author writing stage directions for a play so that actors know when to enter and exit. Leaders must create and maintain such systems. Their absence can result in the type of chaos that occurred in the Iraq occupation. Military conquest was easy; occupation was difficult and badly managed, with serious consequences. And contrary to rumor, while Vice President Dick Cheney did not control Bush, sometimes he seemed out of control. In the words of George H. W. Bush, "The big mistake was letting Cheney bring in his own State Department. I think they overdid that. But it's not Cheney's fault, it's the president's fault."[26]

In Texas, Bush 43 had prospered as an owner of the Texas Rangers baseball team. In 1994 he ran for governor, and was generally regarded as successful in the job, with good social and political skills, particularly in small settings. He had a reputation for working well across the political aisle. While he was not an inspirational speaker to large audiences, he was genial and personable in smaller groups and with friends. In 2000, Bush ran for president on a platform of "compassionate conservatism." He opposed a globally expansive foreign policy, and criticized Clinton's use of the military for nation-building. He warned against activism and arrogance, famously saying, "If we are a humble nation . . . they'll welcome us." Bush lost the popular vote to Vice President Gore by 1 percent, but won the Electoral College when the Supreme Court awarded Florida's votes to him in December 2000.

The first eight months of Bush's presidency by and large continued his low-key campaign themes and were not marked by hubris. Bush began as a realist and delegated heavily to his experienced foreign policy team of Vice President Richard Cheney, Secretary of Defense Donald Rumsfeld, and Secretary of State Colin Powell. They had worked together (and differed) in previous Republican administrations, and Condoleezza Rice was given the difficult task of trying to coordinate as National Security Advisor. She later described the policy process as "a cycle of distrust and dysfunction."[27] Cheney built a large staff and often had privileged access to the president, and Rumsfeld in turn had special access to Cheney, who had once been his aide in the Nixon administration. During his first eight months in office, Bush assigned a low priority to the Al Qaeda threat even though Clinton had warned him of the problem and he had retained Clinton's anti-terrorist coordinator, Richard Clarke. During this period, while there were a number of unilateral diplomatic actions, a war against Iraq was not on the agenda.

The terrorist attacks on September 11, 2001, transformed Bush and American foreign policy. As summarized by historian Melvyn Leffler, "No account of the Bush administration's foreign policies should underestimate the degree to which fear and anxiety, guilt and responsibility shaped the mentality and psychology undergirding the administration's approach to the Global War on Terrorism."[28] They expected a second attack at any time. Rumors abounded. An attack of letters bearing anthrax[†] accentuated the fear of biological weapons, both among the public and in the administration. After an initial period of shock, Bush delivered successful speeches on September 14, and his approval rating soared in the Gallup Polls from 51 to 90 percent as Americans rallied around the president in a manner typical in such a crisis.[29] Bush declared a "Global War on Terrorism," and his dispatch of troops to Afghanistan to defeat the Taliban government proved popular. His actions were reinforced by successful diplomatic efforts enlisting support at the UN and NATO.

In his January 2002 State of the Union address, Bush announced that he would not wait for the most dangerous regimes to acquire the most destructive weapons, and he identified an "axis of evil" consisting of Iraq, Iran, and North Korea, even though there was no alliance of those states. Later that year he issued a national security strategy that justified pre-emptive action. The evidence connecting those countries to the Al Qaeda attack was scarce, but the faulty intelligence about Iraq's possession of weapons

---

† The attack was later traced to a disaffected American scientist, but that was not known at the time.

of mass destruction was widely believed at the time. Although there were major differences between the State Department and the Pentagon, planning for the invasion of Iraq seems to have begun near the end of 2001, though a decision was not made until the following year.

When diplomacy at the UN failed to produce a second Security Council resolution authorizing the use of force, the United States and Britain nonetheless launched an invasion of Iraq on March 20, 2003. In dismissing further UN diplomacy, Vice President Cheney argued that "the only legitimacy we really need comes on the back of an M1A1 tank."[30] The military campaign was successful, and on May 1, Bush announced the end of major combat operations, but his administration remained bogged down in Iraq for the rest of its days. Hubris was not new to American foreign policy—witness Vietnam—but with the end of bipolarity, the danger increased and the fear and anger that followed 9/11 helped to unleash it. A number of neoconservative supporters of the administration had declared that Iraq would be "a cakewalk." When asked about the dangers of a long, costly, and bloody war, Cheney denied the prospect and declared that "we will be greeted as liberators."[31] Or as Bush explained in 2002, "We're never going to get people all in agreement about force and the use of force. But action—confident action that will yield positive results—provides a slipstream into which reluctant nations and leaders can get behind."[32] Defeating Saddam Hussein's army proved to be relatively easy, but planning for the aftermath had been slipshod. Such imprudent assessments and preparation became culpable negligence.

The invasion of Iraq without a legitimizing UN resolution and the poor preparation for the occupation ranks along with the Vietnam War as a major foreign policy disaster of the era of Pax Americana. In 2016, the Chilcot Inquiry into Britain's allied role concluded that it was "neither right nor necessary" to invade Iraq in 2003 and "on the preparations for what followed, it is hard to exaggerate the sheer awfulness."[33] Some 4,500 American soldiers died and 32,000 were wounded, as well as countless Iraqis. When long-term health and other costs are included, the total costs of the wars in Iraq (and Afghanistan) have been estimated at over $5 trillion, much of it funded by adding to the national debt.[34] Hussein was removed from power, but in the ensuing chaos Al Qaeda and later the Islamic State flourished, Iran's position in the Gulf was strengthened, and America suffered great reputational damage as scenes of torture of prisoners flowed around the world. Moreover, Iraq distracted the Bush administration from serious problems like the deteriorating situation in Afghanistan or North Korea, which tested it first nuclear weapon in 2006.

The historian Melvyn Leffler concludes that "a sense of power impelled US officials to act.... America's power seemed overwhelming; any doubts about US prowess to project power across the world were removed by the swift success of US efforts in Afghanistan." Hubris was a problem, but not originally of the Wilsonian liberal type. "However misguided, the intent was to enhance the nation's security and rid the world of a defiant and portentous foe rather than to promote democracy or remake the Middle East.... Although officials distorted and exaggerated evidence regarding Iraq's WMD [weapons of mass destruction], they genuinely believed that Saddam did possess such weapons." The rhetorical exaggeration of democracy and nation-building came later, after no WMD were found and the problems of occupation grew intractable.[35]

The mixed motives of the different groups in the administration that launched the invasion included a realist fear that Hussein might develop and use nuclear weapons, a realist desire to increase American hegemony in the Middle East, and neoconservative concerns over Hussein's human rights violations and their belief that democratization of the region could destroy the roots of terrorism. As the war became more unpopular among the general public as well as among allies, Bush turned to Wilsonian moral claims for post hoc justification.

Bush's second inaugural address in January 2005 pronounced a freedom agenda for American foreign policy, and it may have helped encourage "color revolutions" in a number of countries. Addressing a West Point graduation in May 2006, he affirmed that the United States "will not rest until the promise of liberty reaches every people in every nation."[36] American opinion was divided about such ambitious goals, and the Republicans lost the Congress in the fall of 2006, and the presidency in 2008. Despite these setbacks, Bush had the personal courage to press for a surge of troops in

2007 that helped to stabilize the military situation, if not end the war. By doing so, against prevailing opinion in Congress and the press, he managed to stave off what would likely have been an even more catastrophic failure. Bush left office with very low popularity ratings, but convinced that history would vindicate him as it had Harry Truman. (He was ranked #33 in the 2017 C-SPAN survey of historians.) Given inevitable historical revisionism and the tendency of many presidential reputations to rise as generations change, Bush's standing is also likely to rise over time. But given the scale of the Iraq debacle, it is unlikely that he will ever near Truman in the top ten.

In judging the morality of Bush's foreign policy, he scores well on expressing a vision with attractive moral values, but his personal motives were complicated by his impatience and his complex relationship with his father. He had no clear vision at the beginning of his administration, but his 2002 National Security Strategy, which came to be called the Bush Doctrine, proclaimed that the United States would "identify and eliminate terrorists wherever they are, together with the regimes that sustain them." America would not wait to act until after it was attacked. In his second term, Bush adjusted his "doctrine" by adding what he called his "freedom agenda" to his strategy.[37] The solution to the roots of the terrorist problem was to spread democracy everywhere, even though it was not within the grasp of American power.

The problem with Bush's vision was not the values, but the failure to balance values and risk. Bush invaded Iraq ostensibly to change the regime and to remove Hussein's capacity to use weapons of mass destruction. While Bush did not do enough to question the intelligence or manage the process, he cannot be blamed for the intelligence failure that attributed such weapons to Hussein, since the estimates were widely shared by many other countries. While no weapons were found, American forces quickly overthrew Hussein's regime. But his removal did not accomplish the mission, and inadequate understanding of the context plus poor planning and management undercut Bush's objectives.

George W. Bush is described as having been obsessed by the idea of being a transformational president, and not a status-quo operator like Bill

Clinton. Problems of emotional intelligence contributed to Bush's inadequate contextual intelligence. Brent Scowcroft observed that in 2003 the
main divisions in foreign policy were not between liberals and conservatives,
but between traditionalists and transformationalists.[38] Despite their shared
genes, the foreign policy of George W. Bush could not have been more different from that of his father. As we saw earlier, Bush 43 was far more like
Woodrow Wilson than like Bush 41.

Both Wilson and George W. Bush were highly religious and moralistic
men who were elected with less than a majority of the popular vote, and initially focused on domestic issues without any vision of foreign policy. Both
tended to portray the world in black-and-white rather than shades of gray.
Both projected self-confidence, responded to a crisis with a bold vision,
and stuck to it. Secretary of State Colin Powell described Bush as knowing
"what he wants to do, and what he wants to hear is how to get it done."[39]

Bush's impatience hindered both his own learning and his ability to teach
the public. In the words of a journalist who spent many hours with him,
"He has a transformational temperament. He likes to shake things up. That
was the key to going into Iraq."[40] That impatient temperament contributed
to the dysfunctional organizational process Bush put in place. Nonetheless,
Bush was capable of learning on the job, and his second term was much
better than the first. "As Bush matured as diplomat and statesman, he became less prone to the overheated and moralistic rhetoric of the first term
on issues from Iraq to North Korea and more focused on the need to rebuild
trust and reassurance with traditional American partners. As the president
gained experience and learned from his own earlier missteps, he became
more willing to demand greater discipline and accountability within the
administration."[41]

Looking at the means of Bush's foreign policy, he used force proportionately and with some discrimination in Afghanistan, but he failed both those
standards in Iraq, where the civilian death toll was very high. Nor was he respectful of liberal institutions and the rights. His early efforts to use the UN
to legitimize his actions in Afghanistan fit these criteria, but in Iraq he failed
to meet the test.[42] Indeed, though elections were held in both countries,
the conditions for meaningful democracy were absent and the exercise of

voting and plebiscitary democracy were not sufficient to meet the liberal standards of legitimacy.

Under conditions of anxiety about a second attack, the use of water-boarding, torture, and rendition can be understood as analogues to the ticking time bomb example that is often used in discussions of the dirty hands dilemmas discussed in chapter 2. But Bush is accused of making insufficient effort to assess the efficacy of the methods the CIA was willing to authorize. In curtailing the enhanced interrogation program "during his second term, Bush himself provided at least implicit support for the critique that he went too far during his first term."[43] Nor were Bush and his officials careful in their assessment of intelligence, but instead exaggerated the information to mobilize public sentiment in favor of war.[44] They told the public that "the smoking gun must not turn into a mushroom cloud." Political opponents accused Bush of lying about the war, but that critique is inaccurate and misses the point. Bush saw and believed the intelligence that Hussein had weapons of mass destruction. His moral flaw was to exaggerate rather than push back on the intelligence because of his inadequate contextual intelligence and personal motives. His flaw was culpable negligence rather than mendacity.[‡]

In judging consequences, Iraq overshadows all other aspects of Bush's foreign policy. In the Iraq case, Bush was not a good fiduciary for American interests. The costs of the war in terms of lives lost, financial implications, and destruction of American reputation and soft power far outweighed any gains. While Bush's rapid response in Afghanistan may have helped prevent a second major terrorist attack on the United States, Iraq became a magnet and breeding ground for terrorism. Pictures of torture at Abu Ghraib undercut American soft power. In 2006, the intelligence community assessed that "the Iraq war has made the overall terrorism problem

---

[‡] I once asked a friend who was an experienced CIA analyst how they got the intelligence wrong. He said it was a question of attention, not lies. He said to imagine that there were two piles of raw intelligence reports: a big one that said Hussein had WMD and a smaller one that said he did not. All the pressure from on high was to explore the big pile; the result was that we failed to properly dig into the small pile.

worse by inflaming anti-Americanism in the Muslim world and bringing a new generation of recruits into the fight."[45]

But Iraq was not the only aspect of Bush's foreign policy. One must also look at his management of relations with other major powers. With China, as expressed in Deputy Secretary of State Robert Zoellick's invitation to become a "responsible stakeholder," Bush continued the general direction of Clinton's engagement policy. At the same time, he also fostered the alliance with Japan and greatly improved relations with India as balancing factors. While differences over Iraq stressed relations with Europe, NATO survived the tension, and Bush improved relations with the allies in his second term. With regard to Russia, Bush's record was less successful. In the initial period after 9/11 relations with Putin were reasonable, but Iraq added to the tensions, and Bush's support for color revolutions and efforts to include Ukraine and Georgia in NATO led to a souring of relations. By 2007, in a speech at the Munich Security Conference, Putin had taken his hard-line position, and after Russia invaded Georgia in 2008, Bush was in a weak position to respond in a significant manner.

In terms of cosmopolitan values, while the loss of lives in Iraq counts against him, in other areas, such as Africa, Bush's health initiatives against AIDS and malaria were not only important for humanitarian purposes, but also for American soft power on the continent. He helped to stabilize the chaotic anarchy in Liberia and tried to mediate in Sudan. The President's Emergency Plan for AIDS Relief (PEPFAR) committed $15 billion, reached nearly 7 million people, and saved many lives in Africa. More broadly, he increased foreign aid and launched a new Millennium Challenge Corporation to improve its quality. These were real accomplishments.

Bush also deserves moral credit for telling the American people only six days after the 9/11 shock that they should not take out their anger on innocent Muslims and warning that those who did "would represent the worst of humankind."[46] In terms of his educational consequences, Bush's personal life in The White House was also a good role model for the nation, but the feeling of deception about Iraq and the fact that his rhetoric so exceeded the grasp of which American power was capable meant that the public lessons learned were often the opposite of what he intended.

Bush 43's Ethical Scorecard

Intentions and Motives

Moral vision: attractive values, good motives	mixed
Prudence: balance of values and risks	poor

Means

Force: proportion, discrimination, necessity	mixed
Liberal: respect for rights and institutions	poor

Consequences

Fiduciary: success for long-term US interests	poor/mixed
Cosmopolitan: minimal damage to others	mixed
Educational: truthful; broad moral discourse	mixed

*****

Unipolarity relaxed the Cold War constraints on American foreign policy. In the words of one foreign service officer who served in both the Clinton and Bush administrations, "I've often thought that we were so powerful during our Unipolar Moment that it did make us arrogant sometimes about our power. There were very few countervailing forces that could limit our options. No real guardrails or checks on our power. That made us too relaxed at times about questioning our assumptions, strategy, tactics."[47] Or in the words of a RAND research report for the Air Force, the United States was the predominant status quo power after 1945, but has "also especially since 1989, arguably been the world's most ardent revisionist. This has been true in areas of norms and values rather than territory. . . . Many other countries see the United States, with its advocacy of liberal values through example and sometimes coercive force, as the most disruptive force in the international system."[48] This was obviously the case for countries with authoritarian political systems, such as Russia and China.

The unipolar moment unleashed the danger of hubris, but it was not just the liberal hubris of Wilsonian democracy about which some realists have complained. Hubris was not new—after all, it occurred well before unipolarity during the Vietnam era, when the Soviet arsenal was growing.

The post–Cold War era was more an example of the problems of power unbalanced and the temptations it creates. The George H. W. Bush administration had set a strategic framework for the unipolar moment that was based on maintaining technological military superiority and heading off the development of new regional hegemons. When this strategy of primacy was made explicit in the draft 1992 Defense Policy Guidelines, Clinton and others criticized it and Bush and Scowcroft drew back from what they saw as its "arrogant" rhetoric. Nonetheless, the strategy remained and "the Clinton Administration would undertake a range of policies that fit squarely within the framework laid down by the Bush Administration."[49] But Bush 41 and Clinton implemented the strategy with a degree of prudence that Bush 43 discarded amidst the security fears after the 9/11 attack. For some neoconservatives like Paul Wolfowitz, the deputy secretary of defense, the security situation spelled an opportunity for crusading democracy promotion, but Cheney and Rumsfeld were hardly liberals and their strategy of preventing the rise of peer rivals went back to Cheney's service as Secretary of Defense in the first Bush presidency.

Clinton's interventions (except for Kosovo) were mostly undertaken reluctantly (or not at all in the case of Rwanda). His strategy of enlargement and engagement placed more emphasis on economic globalization and institutions. In other words, the changes in the bipolar structure do not fully account for the decisions that were taken after the Cold War ended. Nonstate actors such as Al Qaeda did not have the capacity to destroy the sole superpower, but their daring attacks were able to set the agenda for global politics and goaded the superpower into counterproductive actions. And the temperaments of the presidents and their sets of skills exacerbated the actions. Bush was morally brave in the case of the surge, cosmopolitan in his policy toward Africa, and a far-sighted realist in his relations with India, but all this was overwhelmed by his blunder in Iraq. His weak emotional and contextual intelligence undercut his goals, and his use of Wilsonian rhetoric later to justify his action helped to generate a public reaction similar to what Wilson himself had engendered nearly a century earlier. Bush set the scene for Obama and Trump.

8

Twenty-First-Century
Power Shifts

As the twenty-first century began, American power seemed supreme. French Foreign Minister Hubert Vedrine had called the United States a "hyperpower," and George W. Bush's foreign policy reflected the hubris of the unipolar moment. Beneath the surface of international politics, however, two major shifts in the distribution of global power had already begun to take place: a "horizontal" power transition among states and a technologically driven "vertical" power diffusion from states to non-state actors.[1] Power transition from one dominant state to another is a familiar historical process, and in adjusting American foreign policy, all three twenty-first-century presidents—Bush, Obama, Trump—resisted the metaphor of American decline while reacting to the rise of Asian powers such as China and India. Similarly, all three presidents tried to maintain working relations with a declining but assertive Russia.

The other important power transition at the beginning of the new century was power diffusion, a more novel process and one more difficult to manage. As global information technology developed, more things were happening outside the control of even the most powerful states. Nonstate actors ranging from bankers to cybercriminals to terrorists were gaining power, and many transnational networks and issues crossed borders outside the control of governments. The direct effects of the Al Qaeda attack of September 11, 2001, did not have a great economic or military impact on American power, but as we saw in the last chapter, the nonstate attack had a profound psychological and indirect effect on American foreign policy.

The Bush administration tried to squeeze the new nonstate attack into the traditional interstate framework, but it turned out to be a poor fit. Terrorists cannot defeat an organized nation-state, but like the weaker player in jujitsu, they can do grievous damage by turning the strength of the more powerful player against himself. As a matter of statistics, the number of people actually killed by terrorists is trivial, but the public fears of being killed by a terrorist greatly exceed the reality. Terror is a psychological drama in which violence is used by nonstate actors to capture attention, shape the agenda, and shock the stronger players into counterproductive actions. On all three dimensions, Al Qaeda succeeded.

The four-week war in Iraq was a dazzling display of America's hard military power that removed a tyrant, but did not resolve America's vulnerability to terrorism and instead increased it at a cost of nearly five thousand American lives and several trillion dollars.[2] It was also costly in terms of the soft power. Polls showed the attractiveness of the United States declined quite sharply in many countries. Bush's military surge prevented a full defeat by the insurgency in Iraq in 2007, but did not prevent the rise of ISIS. Public opinion in the United States and elsewhere came to view Bush's Iraq War as a serious foreign policy blunder, an opinion that was shared by both Obama and Trump. As Obama put it after leaving office, "The Washington consensus, whatever you want to call it, got a little too comfortable. Particularly after the Cold War, you had this period of great smugness on the part of America and American elites thinking we got this all figured out."[3] In quite different ways, Obama and Trump reacted against

Bush and ushered in a period of retrenchment in American foreign policy. But the retrenchment was more about means than ends. As one of Obama's closest advisors put it, "We're not trying to preside over America's decline. What we're trying to do is to get America another 50 years as leader."[4] And Donald J. Trump famously campaigned on the promise to "Make America Great Again!"

BARACK HUSSEIN OBAMA

Barack Obama, the first president of African American heritage, was born in Hawaii in 1961, and entered office at the age of forty-eight. After his father, a graduate student from Kenya, returned to Africa, Barack was raised by his anthropologist mother, including a period in Indonesia. He attended the private Punahou School in Hawaii, Occidental College in California, Columbia University in New York, and Harvard Law School in Massachusetts, where he was editor of the *Law Review*. He worked as a community organizer and as a law schoolteacher in Chicago, and ran for the presidency during his first term as a senator from Illinois. Though he had lived in many parts of the country, he was not a Washington insider, and was only lightly filtered through the usual political process. His candidacy was greatly helped by the unpopularity of the Iraq War.

When Obama took office, both the American and the world economy were in the midst of the worst financial crisis since the Great Depression. His economic advisors counseled him that unless urgent steps were taken, there was a significant chance of entering a full-scale depression. He also inherited two ongoing wars in Afghanistan and Iraq, nuclear proliferation threats from Iran and North Korea, and the continuing problem of Al Qaeda's terrorism, but Obama's early months in office were absorbed with dealing with the economic crisis. His rescue of the international financial system was a crucial action that staved off a global panic and depression, but saving the banks amidst increasing unemployment increased populist discontent.

Obama had expounded a transformational vision in his campaign, but his crisis responses were those of a pragmatist. Temperamentally, he was noted for his coolness under pressure, a term sometimes summed up by the phrase "no-drama Obama." For example, his reaction to success after the highly risky helicopter raid into Pakistan that killed Bin Laden in 2011 (but could have destroyed his presidency like Carter's) "was self-contained to the extreme: 'we got him,' was all he said."[5] Robert Gates, the veteran Republican whom Obama retained as Secretary of Defense, described Obama as the most deliberative president for whom he worked.[6] Obama was almost always in control of his emotions, and (like Bush) exemplified a stable home life in the White House.

Obama's rhetoric in the 2008 campaign and during the first months of his presidency was inspirational in style and, like John F. Kennedy, set high expectations. As several experts described the campaign, "this image of a new domestic agenda, a new global architecture, and a transformed world was crucial to his ultimate success as a candidate."[7] Obama continued the inspirational rhetoric with a series of speeches in the first year of his presidency, including his inaugural address, a speech in Prague proclaiming the goal of a nuclear-free world, a speech in Cairo promising a new approach to the Muslim world, and his Nobel Peace Prize speech in Oslo that cited Gandhi and Martin Luther King on nonviolence, but also noted that "as a head of state sworn to protect and defend my nation, I cannot be guided by their example alone."

Obama also followed the famous American theologian Reinhold Niebuhr, who had warned against the dangers of American moral self-righteousness and the dangerous temptation of perfectionism.[8] Some critics faulted Obama's approach to human rights as valuing international law and alliances more than the promotion of freedom, but in Obama's words, "I know that engagement with repressive regimes lacks the satisfying purity of indignation, [but] no repressive regime can move down a new path unless it has a choice of an open door."[9]

Obama's objective was to refurbish America's image abroad, especially in the Muslim world; end its involvement in two wars; offer an outstretched hand to adversaries; reset relations with Russia as a step toward ridding the world of nuclear weapons; develop significant cooperation with China on both regional and global issues; and make peace in the Middle East.[10]

His record of achievement on these issues was mixed, and former officials explained that "seemingly intractable circumstances turned him from the would-be architect of a new global order into a leader focused more on repairing relationships and reacting to crises—most notably global economic crisis."[11]

Some observers describe Obama's foreign policy views as going through a cycle: liberalism in the campaign, realism after he entered office, cosmopolitan optimism in 2011 after the rebellions that were called the Arab Spring, and then returning to realism with his refusal to intervene in the Syrian civil war in 2013. James Mann argues that while Obama's "speeches were elegantly phrased and full of idealism," he did not want to sound like a moralist by talking too much about democracy. In Iran, he did not let human rights concerns prevent negotiation with the country's leaders.[12] In 2011, some advisors cautioned him not to be too quick to oust the dictator Hosni Mubarak in Egypt because there was no guarantee that democracy would ensue, and they warned against intervention in Libya, but Obama listened to the cosmopolitan inclinations of other advisors and both situations turned out badly. Subsequently, in declining to intervene in Syria, Obama told one of his young advisors that "you can't stop people from killing each other like that."[13]

It is still too early for a definitive judgment on Obama's foreign policy. The columnist David Brooks described him as "flexible and incremental . . . Following a foreign policy hedgehog, Obama's been a pretty effective fox."[14] Some of the half-empty glasses of unaccomplished goals were the results of intractable events; some were the product of early administration naiveté, such as his initial approaches to Israel and China. But Obama was quick to recover from mistakes in a pragmatic way. James Fallows, a former speechwriter for Jimmy Carter, described Obama's main trait as being adaptable to new realities rather than a prisoner of his rhetoric.[15] At the end of his presidency, *The Economist* summarized that "for all his achievements, his intellect, and his grace, his eight years in office imply that even the most powerful leader in the world—a leader of rare talents, anointed with a nation's dreams—can seem powerless to direct it."[16]

Although Obama never abandoned his rhetorical expressions of transformational goals regarding such issues as climate change or nuclear weapons, in practice, his pragmatism was reminiscent of incremental leaders such as Eisenhower and the first Bush. Despite his relative inexperience in international affairs compared to them, Obama showed a similar skill in reacting to a complex set of foreign policy challenges. He had both emotional intelligence and contextual intelligence as demonstrated by his appointments of experienced advisors, and his management of a relatively orderly White House–centered process. His keen contextual intelligence was honed in part by having an African father, an anthropologist mother, and a childhood spent partly in Asia.[17] Prudence came naturally.

This is not to say that Obama had no transformational effects. He changed the course of an unpopular foreign policy; shifted from labor-intensive counterinsurgency to less costly uses of military power (such as special forces, drones, and cyber); increased American soft power in many parts of the world; and began a slow rebalancing of attention away from the Middle East to Asia, the fastest-growing part of the world economy. His reversal of a half-century of failed policy toward Cuba took courage and careful preparation, but greatly enhanced the US position in Latin America.

The journalist David Sanger described the "Obama Doctrine" as a lighter military footprint combined with a willingness to use force unilaterally when American security interests are directly involved, a reliance on coalitions to deal with global problems that do not directly threaten American security, and "a rebalancing away from the quagmires in the Middle East toward the continent of greatest promise in the future—Asia."[18] Yet scholars James Goldgeier and Jeremi Suri describe Obama's 2015 National Security Strategy as lacking priorities other than to avoid long and costly military conflicts.[19] Obama's aim to avoid mistakes is hardly a strategy, even though "sometimes the best presidential decisions are decisions not to act."[20] As Henry Kissinger put it, Obama was "more concerned with short-term consequences turning into permanent obstacles. Another view of statesmanship might focus to a greater extent on shaping history rather than avoiding getting in its way."[21]

When Obama intervened in Libya in 2011, he sought Arab League and UN resolutions to ensure that the soft power narrative would not be that the United States once again attacks a Muslim country. Obama shared the leadership of the hard power air operation with NATO allies, even though they were not fully up to the task. An incautious comment by a midlevel White House official characterized the Libya policy as "leading from behind," and this became a target for political criticism, but as we saw earlier, Eisenhower was a great exemplar of knowing that sometimes it is most effective to keep a low profile and to lead from behind, particularly if the issue involves secondary interests.

According to Jake Sullivan, one of his aides, Obama thought a lot about what American leadership should look like. He fundamentally saw it as an agenda-setting, catalytic form of leadership, rather than a directive form. In this he resembled Eisenhower. In his ideal world, the US would pull other countries (and nonstate actors) together to figure out solutions to the great shared problems of our time, without telling anyone what to do. He felt that was a sustainable form of leadership that could account for both the vertical and horizontal shifts in power. The Middle East was confounding to him in part because it didn't really fit that model—it was so rooted in traditional old-fashioned power politics. [22] In fact, Obama's problem in Libya was that he wound up too far out front. The original objective in Libya had been to use air power to protect protesters in Benghazi who were threatened by Qaddafi's forces, but over time he allowed the mission to morph into regime change without a viable plan for what happened next.

Some critics argue that Obama was too cautious to take advantage of the revolutionary times, particularly in the Middle East. Obama made a big bet on sending troops for a surge in Afghanistan (which did not pay off) and another on violating Pakistani sovereignty to kill bin Laden (which worked), and another on withdrawing support from Mubarak in Egypt (which did not improve the situation). But given the uncertainties of the revolutions in the region, most of Obama's strategic choices were cautious and hedged. There was nothing akin to the Truman Doctrine and the Marshall Plan or George W. Bush's "Freedom Agenda." This earned him criticism from neoconservatives but plaudits from realists. In the words of one editorialist,

"His stance reflects his own brand of idealism, which values international law and alliances more than the promotion of freedom."[23] While his policies reflected both the democratic and institutional strands of Wilson's liberalism, he placed greater emphasis on the institutional aspect. According to his advisor Ben Rhodes, Obama was concerned about overreach, but he "believed in a competent stabilizing force; the necessity of taking military action against certain terrorist networks, the benefits of globalization in lifting people out of poverty, the indispensability of the United States to international order. He wanted to redirect the ocean liner of American foreign policy, not to sink it."[24]

Obama's first Secretary of State, Hillary Clinton, described the administration approach as "smart power" that combined hard and soft power resources in different ways in different contexts. As Obama said in his inaugural address in 2009, "Our power grows through its prudent use; our security emanates from the justness of our cause, the force of our example, the tempering qualities of humility and restraint." He also expressed American exceptionalism, telling West Point cadets, "The United States is the one indispensable nation. That has been true for the century passed and will likely be true for the century to come."[25] But he worried about overreach, and warned his advisors that "we can't fool ourselves into thinking that we can fix the Middle East."[26] Jeremi Suri and other critics of Obama's international liberalism have argued that, to the contrary, Obama's policy problem was what they saw as its underreach.[27]

In sending additional troops to Afghanistan, his use of air power to create a no-fly zone in Libya, his use of Special Forces to kill Osama bin Laden in Pakistan, and the use of Special Forces and drones against the Islamic State, Obama showed a willingness to use military force with proportion and discrimination. He set guidelines for strikes and signed off personally when there was a risk that a proposed strike in Yemen, Pakistan, and Somalia might exceed the guidelines. According to aides, as a student of the writings on war by Augustine and Aquinas, "he believes that he should take moral responsibility for such actions. And he knows that bad strikes can target America's image and derail diplomacy."[28] Though some disagreed with them, Obama was careful about the means he used.

Ironically, despite his efforts to reduce American involvement in the interminable quagmires of the troubled Middle East and to refocus attention on the rising region of Asia, Obama found that in foreign policy the urgent often drives out the important. According to participants, even after announcing a rebalancing toward Asia, a large portion of the important foreign policy meetings in the White House Situation Room dealt with the Middle East.[29] Obama was unable to persuade Israel to forgo its settlements in the West Bank or to get the Palestinians to engage deeply in a peace process. In line with his campaign promises, instead of pushing hard to keep some American troops in Iraq in 2011, he acquiesced in fully ending the American troop presence, which combined with the policies of the Maliki government in Baghdad created conditions for the Sunni insurgency that gave rise to the Islamic State. Later, Obama had to reverse his position as the role of ISIS strengthened.

Syria became a contentious issue for his foreign policy. Early in the civil war Obama said that Assad must go, and in August 2012 casually declared that the use of chemical weapons would be a "red line" in considering the use of force. But a year later when Assad used chemicals and Obama was unable to obtain allied or Congressional support for an air strike, he worked with Russia on a compromise solution of international removal and inspection of Syrian chemicals. That decision became an oft-cited symbol of weakness that came to haunt his foreign policy, and Obama chafed at the argument that he needed to bomb Syria to maintain his own credibility. In his words, "That's the worst reason to go to war."[30] Some advisors argue that the diplomatic solution removed more chemicals than bombing would have done, but the costs to Obama's credibility extended well beyond Syria.

Obama armed moderate opponents of the Assad regime, but resisted pressures to set up safety or no-fly zones in Syria when it was unclear whether the beneficiary might be the Islamic State. Some realist critics applauded this prudence, but other critics argue that his caution had terrible consequences, including the rise of ISIS, the deaths of hundreds of thousands of Syrian refugees, and a migration crisis that weakened our allies in the European Union. Did Obama have any better options? Some former officials in the administration have argued that the long-term moral repercussions of Obama's act of omission could have been reduced if Obama had modified his objectives about Assad's departure, as well as using a modest degree of American force.[31] William Burns argues that "the mistake we made was that we regularly paired maximalist ends with minimalist means."[32] Like Bill Clinton's choice in Rwanda, all-or-nothing framing eliminated the moral choices that depended on scaling back objectives and adjusting degrees of intervention. In an interview near the end of his presidency Obama denied being too cautious, but the interviewer was struck that even as Secretary of State John Kerry was warning of a "dire Syria-fueled European apocalypse, Obama has not recategorized the country's civil war as a top tier security threat."[33]

Despite his problems in the Middle East, Obama had a number of foreign policy accomplishments on global issues. First was the successful handling of the global economic crisis known as "the Great Recession." If he had not avoided that disaster, all else would have paled. This required not only an economic stimulus package at home but also international coordination, in which the US Federal Reserve provided the crucial public good of being a lender of last resort as a means to restore confidence in the financial system. Obama also made effective use of the Group of 20 in the early days of the crisis. His efforts to negotiate and ratify trade agreements such as the Trans-Pacific Partnership were strategically sound, but encountered Congressional resistance in the face of rising populist pressures at home. Obama's efforts to negotiate an agreement on global climate change led to success with the Paris agreement of December 2015.

Globally, Obama also sought to reframe the issue of nuclear weapons by embracing the long-term goal of a non-nuclear world (although stating that it was unlikely to occur in his lifetime), negotiating a replacement of the Strategic Arms Reduction Treaty that further cut the American and Russian strategic arsenals, and convening summits on nuclear security. He also raised the nonproliferation issue on the agenda of both the UN and the G-20, and developed multilateral support for sanctions on Iran for failing to meet its international obligations under the Non-Proliferation Treaty. In 2015, after patient and painstaking diplomacy, he led a six-power coalition to an agreement that limited Iran's nuclear program, though it was criticized by Israel and domestic opponents for not going further to limit Iran's behavior in the region and was later repudiated by President Trump. And his efforts to denuclearize North Korea proved unsuccessful.

Closely related to these global issues was Obama's handling of relations with China, whose rise is one of the most important foreign policy challenges of the twenty-first century. Obama tried to rebalance foreign policy attention from the Middle East to Asia in a policy that became known as the "pivot" or "rebalancing." He had twenty-four face-to-face meetings with Chinese Presidents Hu Jintao and Xi Jinping, and was able to bridge differences on climate change and cyber norms that had appeared intractable. At the same time, Obama maintained close alliances with Japan, Korea, and Australia, and built on Bush's improvement of relations with India to help maintain the hard power capabilities that shaped the environment for a rising China, particularly in relation to its goals in the East and South China Seas. Some critics complain that he did not push China harder on its trade policies involving subsidies to state-owned enterprises and coerced technology transfer, which later became a focus of Trump's China policy. On the other hand, Obama negotiated a Trans-Pacific Partnership as an overall trade framework that did not include China, though the new Trump Administration immediately jettisoned it upon taking office.[34]

Obama also tried to reset relations with Russia, which had soured after the Bush administration advocacy of NATO membership for Georgia and Ukraine. Obama backed away from those initiatives and developed a good working relationship with Dmitri Medvedev, but had more difficulty when Vladimir Putin returned to the presidency in 2012. Putin saw American support for color revolutions in the former USSR, the revolutions in the Middle East in 2011, and the 2014 revolt in neighboring Ukraine as a threat to his authoritarian regime. His hybrid war in Eastern Ukraine and the seizure of Crimea led to a serious worsening of relations, with the imposition of sanctions by the UN and NATO allies. Putin's use of cyberattacks on Ukraine, and then the interference in the 2016 American presidential elections, brought protests and sanctions from the Obama administration, but not of sufficient strength to serve as an effective deterrent.

How then do we summarize this complexity and judge the ethical standards of Obama's foreign policy? On the first dimension of goals and motives, Obama set forth an ambitious and attractive agenda of values. As one historian put it, his grand strategy "fit squarely within the broad contours of the postwar and post–Cold War eras, as its broadest objective was maintaining US primacy and a liberal international order."[35] Moreover, his motives in pursuing his goals remained principled and were not diluted by conflicting personal or emotional needs. As for balancing values and risks, Obama has sometimes been criticized for being prudent to a fault, but in this he was like the first rather than the second President Bush. William Burns, who served both presidents, sees strong similarities, but unlike Bush 41, Obama "was not moving from a world of bipolarity to rising unipolarity, but from a world of diminishing unipolarity to something far messier . . . For all the agility and imagination of the time, we didn't have the freedom to play our diplomatic cards like Bush 41."[36]

Revolutionary times may produce opportunities, but they can also produce nasty surprises and unintended consequences (as Obama discovered in Libya and feared in Syria). Once again, it is important to remember the importance of nondecisions. Obama once told a group of reporters on Air Force One that they focused too much on escalating conflict, and that Johnson in Vietnam, Carter with the Iran hostage crisis, and Bush in Iraq had seen their tenures defined by mistakes. The Obama doctrine, he declared to chuckles, was "don't do stupid shit."[37] While hardly a grand strategy, it does signify the realist virtue of prudence. But liberal and cosmopolitan critics argue that excessive prudence can also have immoral consequences.

With regard to the second dimension of means, Obama used force proportionately and discriminately in his efforts to develop a light footprint for American power. And he was attentive to the moral details of implementing the new technologies of drone strikes and cyberattacks. But critics charge that by adopting the new technology of precision strikes from afar, he was choosing to kill rather than capture terrorists (including some who had American citizenship). While this policy was regularly reported to the

Congress and was popular with the public, the critics saw it as the revival of the Cold War assassinations policy that had been stopped by Gerald Ford (though loosened by Reagan).[38] But in general, Obama showed respect for liberal values and procedures, and made efforts to use and develop international institutions.

Regarding the moral consequences of Obama's foreign policy, it is difficult to make a definitive judgment until more time has passed, but at this stage he appears to have been a good fiduciary for American interests. Some realists complain that he was not tough enough on Chinese and Russian behavior; others praise his support for NATO and the alliance with Japan, as well as his restraint in the Middle East. Others feel that his excessive prudence contributed to immoral consequences. Neoconservatives argue that he should have taken stronger steps to advance human rights and democracy during the Middle Eastern revolutions. Liberals, on the other hand, praise his use of institutions to preserve the post-1945 international order and update it with agreements on nuclear security and the Paris Climate Accords. His efforts at international cooperation to prevent the 2008 Great Recession from developing into another Great Depression were enormously consequential. Cosmopolitans wanted a more forward posture on human rights, but he made major efforts to minimize damage to other peoples. Initially, with the outbreak of the new Ebola epidemic in West Africa, he did not want the United States to have to take on the lion's share of the effort, but ultimately determined that was the only way to address the epidemic and ended up deploying thousands of troops—producing a genuine success.

As for his educational consequences, Obama respected truth, and broadened moral discourse at home and abroad on major global issues, though some critics argue that he did not do enough to head off populist reactions to globalization. While a Republican Congressman once publicly accused him of lying about his healthcare plans—and all presidents often exaggerate political programs and promises—what was notable about the Obama presidency was the high level of integrity in truthfulness and personal behavior. Though not perfect, his preliminary scorecard looks mostly good.

Obama's Ethical Scorecard	
Intentions and Motives	
Moral vision: attractive values, good motives	good
Prudence: balance of values and risks	good/mixed
Means	
Force: proportion, discrimination, necessity	good
Liberal: respect for rights and institutions	good
Consequences	
Fiduciary: success for long-term US interests	good/mixed
Cosmopolitan: minimal damage to others	good/mixed
Educational: truthful; broad moral discourse	good

DONALD J. TRUMP

Donald Trump is different among American presidents in a number of ways. Not only was he unfiltered by the Washington political process, but the top job was his first political office. At age seventy, he became the oldest person ever to become president. He was also the wealthiest. Trump was born in the New York City borough of Queens in 1946 when Harry Truman was president, Kennedy and Nixon first ran for Congress, and Hawaii was still a territory, where Obama would not be born until fifteen years later.

Son of a real estate developer, who was described as an overbearing father, Trump attended a military prep school before attending Fordham University and then transferring to the University of Pennsylvania's Wharton School of Business. Like Clinton and George W. Bush, he avoided military service in Vietnam. He took charge of his family's real estate business in 1971 and expanded it into Manhattan. The company built skyscrapers, hotels, casinos, and golf courses, and licensed the Trump name for real estate and consumer products. He produced and hosted the reality television show *The Apprentice* from 2003 to 2015. *Forbes* estimated his net worth to be $3.1 billion.

Trump's unique background produced a highly unconventional political style, as well as a new perspective on media and politics. Success in reality television requires keeping the focus of the camera, and that is often accomplished by statements that are more outrageous than true, and by breaking conventional norms of behavior. Trump also learned how to employ the new social media platform of Twitter, which he started using in 2009 (a mere three years after its launch), to dominate the agenda. It allowed him to bypass the press, and he likened it to "owning your own newspaper."[39] When his White House staff tried to curtail his tweets because they did not seem presidential, Trump refused: "This is my megaphone. This is the way that I speak directly to the people without any filter."[40] Trump's innovative skills in political communication were analogous to FDR's fireside chats in the early days of radio and JFK's open press conferences in the early days of television. He was far more original than a normal politician.

Trump put these insights to good use in the 2016 Republican primary, where he debated sixteen opponents on a crowded stage. In addition, he intuited and mobilized a populist discontent about the uneven economic effects of global trade on parts of the country and resentment of immigration and cultural changes, particularly among older, non-college-educated white males. His populist, protectionist, and nationalist statements earned him free media coverage far in excess of the traditional paid political advertisements of his experienced rivals. In a sense, he sucked the oxygen out of their campaigns. Trump went on to a surprise Electoral College victory over the Democratic nominee Hillary Clinton, becoming the fifth person to win the presidency while losing the popular vote.

In the conventional political wisdom of the day, many analysts expected that after the election, Trump would move to the center to broaden his political support as George W. Bush had done after his minority victory in 2000. Instead, Trump continued to play to his loyal base and used that base to threaten primary campaign challenges to those who differed with him, so that Republican Congressional figures feared to express open criticism. Those who openly opposed him tended to lose their primaries, and mainstream Republican foreign policy experts who had signed a "never Trump" letter during the campaign found themselves largely excluded from the new administration.

Conventional analysts also expected a victorious Trump to change his style of using Twitter to make outrageous unstaffed statements and to "become presidential" after his inauguration. Instead he governed as he had campaigned, and became a very unconventional president. Policies were announced and cabinet secretaries were fired on Twitter. The result was an administration with frequent changes in top personnel and often contradictory policy messages that undercut his Secretaries of State and Defense, and other top officials. While this caused problems for Trump with the courts, the press, and among allies, what he lost in organizational coherence he made up for in his virtual complete domination of the agenda.

Unpredictability was one of Trump's political tools. As Reince Priebus, his first chief of staff, described Trump's management style, "Trump is always attentive to narrative. He likes conflict; puts opposites together and lets them fight. He doesn't care about process; he wants to own the decision." In many ways this is more reminiscent of Franklin Roosevelt than of Dwight Eisenhower. And in his bargaining technique, Trump "starts with surprise and extreme positions before turning to bargaining and compromise."[41] As Trump describes in *The Art of the Deal*, this was the management and bargaining style that he used in his New York real estate business.[42]

Trump had little experience of foreign affairs other than his business dealings, and his political views were eclectic rather than traditional Republican. A high-level White House staffer described Trump's initial appointments as a mix of "globalists and nationalists," with Trump shifting between them in an unpredictable manner.[43] His ideological views were not always consistent, but he had long expressed protectionist views on trade and a nationalist feeling that allies took unfair advantage of the United States. In 1987, during the Reagan administration, Trump placed a full-page advertisement in major newspapers accusing allies of growing rich while enjoying military security foolishly provided by America at no charge. He urged, "Let's not let our great country be laughed at any more."[44] He focused on economic issues rather than security or human rights, and described the United States as a victim.

During his political campaign, Trump became the first major candidate to challenge the post-1945 consensus on the liberal international order. He proclaimed NATO obsolete, suggested Japan and Korea might develop their own nuclear weapons to replace their American alliance, criticized NAFTA and other trade arrangements, described the Paris Climate Accords as a Chinese hoax to slow American growth, and refused to criticize autocratic leaders' violations of human rights. When asked about Ronald Reagan and previous Republican presidents, he replied, "I don't think we should be doing nation-building anymore. I think it's proven not to work."[45] All this was under the campaign slogan of "America First" and "Make America Great Again."

While he softened some of his security iconoclasm after becoming president, many of Trump's campaign themes guided his foreign policy. In his inaugural address, he declared that "we've defended other nations' borders while refusing to defend our own and spent trillions and trillions of dollars overseas while America has fallen into disrepair and decay. . . . From this day forward, it's going to be only America first. . . . Protection will lead to great prosperity and strength. . . . We do not seek to impose our way of life on anyone, but rather to let it shine as an example."[46] And Trump's policies followed his promises. In his first two years, he withdrew from the Paris Climate Accords, rejected the Trans-Pacific Partnership trade pact that Obama had negotiated, weakened the World Trade Organization, renegotiated NAFTA, imposed national security tariffs on steel and aluminum imports from allies, launched a broader set of tariffs against China, withdrew from the nuclear agreement that Obama and our allies had negotiated with Iran, criticized NATO and the Group of 7, and praised authoritarian leaders including Vladimir Putin and others who were involved in human rights violations. As two former American ambassadors reported about their interviews with alliance leaders on NATO's seventieth anniversary in April 2019, "nearly all viewed Trump as NATO's most urgent and difficult problem."[47] Europeans felt less confident in the United States and believed that the White House was more interested in dividing than uniting them.

Trump's first National Security Doctrine, issued in December 2017, continued the realist theme about the limits of multilateral institutions and global commerce. It refocused attention on great power rivalry with China and Russia, and in January 2018 Defense Secretary James Mattis proclaimed that "great power competition, not terrorism, is now the primary American focus."[48] George Bush's 2006 National Security Strategy emphasized a growing community of democracies and open markets over protectionism. Obama's 2015 strategy had rebuked Bush for overreach and called for America to act alone only when enduring national interests were at stake, and to lead by example at home. In the view of Britain's *The Economist*, "Trump seems to reject both the Bush and Obama doctrines."[49] Moreover, some administration officials were unsure about the president's commitment to the strategy. As one described the situation in 2019, Trump identified the China challenge, but there is a China trade policy rather than an overall China strategy.[50]

Neoconservative critics, on the other hand, saw more similarity than difference in Trump's and Obama's strategies. In their view, both were misguided responses to domestic demands for retrenchment, though they differed in style. Thomas Donnelly and William Kristol, for example, argued that "the Obama-Trump consensus is leading to a more dangerous world. It is also redefining what it means to be the United States. We are a nation built on expansion—not just territorial and geopolitical expansion, but the expansion of liberty and prosperity. The United States exists not merely to defend what is but to realize what can be."[51] Tod Lindberg described two major differences between the Trump strategy and its two predecessors. "For both Bush and Obama, the United States was part of a larger whole, one (admittedly very powerful) liberal state among a number of liberal states comprising a liberal international order." The second difference was Trump's rejection of his predecessors' notion of an arc of history moving toward universal liberalism. "Again Bush and Obama, so different in so many ways, share a Whig view of history as progress moving towards universal liberalism."[52] In contrast, Lindberg argued, for Trump the relevant standards were Hobbesian realism, a zero-sum perspective, and a narrowly defined national interest. But the neoconservative critique oversimplified the similarities. There were also major differences from Obama's approach that were symbolized by Trump's unilateral withdrawal from the Paris Accords, the Trans-Pacific Partnership, the Iran Agreement, and his criticism of NATO and alliances in general.

The Trump administration also invested less money and rhetoric in developing soft power, and a number of polls (as well as an annual *Soft Power 30* index published in London) showed that American soft power declined considerably after the beginning of the Trump administration.[53] Tweets can help to set the global agenda, but they do not produce soft power if their tone and substance are offensive to foreign publics and leaders. Many of Trump's tweets were far from diplomatic in their language or personal criticism of foreign countries or leaders. Trump's defenders replied that soft power does not matter. Trump's budget director, Mick Mulvaney, proclaimed a "hard power budget" as he slashed funds for the State Department and the US Agency for International Development by 30 percent.[54] Although General Mattis had earlier warned the Congress that if they did not provide funds for the soft power of the State Department they would have to buy him more bullets, this was not the president's approach. Trump increased the defense budget while cutting funding and staff for the State Department. Later, faced with competition from China for political influence, Trump supported some increase in foreign aid.

Similarly, Trump paid less attention to human rights, which was traditionally a source of American soft power. While he used air power to punish Syria for chemical attacks on civilians, and tried to persuade Saudi Arabia to limit its bombing of civilians in the Yemen war, Trump's speeches lacked the embrace of democracy and human rights that had been espoused by every president since Carter and Reagan. He criticized the dictatorial regime in Venezuela and applied sanctions against the Maduro government, but in the words of one critic, "Trump's lionizing of the 'strong leadership' of authoritarian personalities like Putin, Erdogan, Duterte and Sisi—as well as his own attacks on the free press at home—cannot but help to embolden their efforts to crack down on civil society and crush dissent in their own countries."[55] Trump was equivocal in his response to the 2018 murder of the journalist Jamal Khashoggi in the Saudi consulate in Istanbul. Moreover, while prior presidents often claimed that national security should weigh more heavily than our human rights commitments—an argument many Americans would accept—Trump proclaimed that commercial transactions should weigh more heavily, "because the spending produces jobs."[56] As the *Financial Times* columnist Gideon Rachman noted, "Until now, dissidents in Russia, China or other authoritarian regimes could wage a lonely and dangerous fight for the truth, and point to the west to show that a better way existed [but now] the US president is clearly indifferent to the truth."[57] Promotion of democracy and human rights need not involve high degrees of intervention, as we saw in chapter 2. It can also rely on the right words and the city-on-a-hill effect.

Administration supporters made two replies to critics. First, while policy experts, diplomats, and allies were aghast at his iconoclastic changes and style, Trump's base voters were delighted. They voted for change and welcomed the disruption. "This realist worldview is not only legitimate but also resonates with American voters who rightly recognize that the United States is no longer inhabiting the unipolar world it did since the end of the Cold War."[58] Second, some experts argued that the style and disruption would be justified if the consequences were beneficial for American interests, for example a more benign regime in Iran, denuclearization of North Korea, a change of Chinese practices, and a more evenly balanced international trade regime.

Of course it is premature to assess the long-term consequences of Trump's policy changes; it is like predicting the final score in the middle of a game. Nonetheless, Stanford historian Niall Ferguson argued in 2018 that "the key to Trump's presidency is that it is probably the last opportunity America has to stop or at least slow China's ascendency. And while it may not be intellectually satisfying, Trump's approach to the problem, which is to assert US power in unpredictable and disruptive ways, may in fact be the only viable option left. . . . The logic of Trumpism is simply to bully the other empires, exploiting the fact that they are both weaker than the United States, in order to extract concessions and claim victories."[59] Similarly, a former Bush 43 official argued that Trump's greatest success was "smashing the 'responsible stakeholder' consensus that has dominated America's China policy for decades and replacing it with a new paradigm of 'strategic competition' . . . an extraordinarily important conceptual shift in U.S. strategic thought that will almost certainly have profound political, economic, and security ramifications for both the United States and the world."[60]

Another former Republican official argued that "the Trump administration has made an extraordinary contribution to U.S. security by contesting the complacent and dangerous shibboleths regarding the rise of China. . . . On the other hand, Trump's views on climate change will represent crucial challenges for his successors for decades to come."[61] Some supporters of Trump's economic approach compared him to Ronald Reagan, arguing that "his threat of tariffs is a negotiating tactic to get lower trade barriers and 'a level playing field.'"[62] With regard to Russia, the apparent anomaly of Trump's relatively gentle treatment of Putin and his failure to respond more strongly to Russian interference in American elections seemed to be explained by domestic politics and Trump's personal sensitivities to legal challenges, and any questioning of the legitimacy of his 2016 election.

Critics say that even if Trump's iconoclastic style produces some successes, one has to think in terms of a balance sheet that includes costs as well as benefits. They argue the price will be too high in terms of the damage done to international institutions and trust among allies. They point to George Shultz's metaphor of foreign policy as patient gardening and argue that in the competition with China, for example, the United States has sixty allies and few disputes with neighbors while China has few allies and a number of territorial disputes. They fault Trump for not working better with those allies in responding to Chinese behavior. In addition, while rules and institutions can be restraining, the United States has a preponderant role in their formulation and is a major beneficiary. Moreover, the United States has had greater soft power than China. They argue that Trump's character and style undercut these assets.

Take lying, for example. In his first eighteen months in office, Trump made 3,251 false or misleading claims, according to the *Washington Post* Fact Checker's database that analyzed, categorized, and tracked every suspect statement uttered by the president. That's an average of more than 6.5 claims a day, up from 4.9 claims in his first hundred days, and reaching eight per day by May 2018. The numbers continued to mount. Supporters replied that "all politicians lie," and his base believed he was the most honest president because he dared to break conventions and "tell it like it is." As Trump told reporters in November 2018, "When I can, I tell the truth. And sometimes it turns out to be where something happens that's different or there's a change but I always like to be truthful."[63] But as we saw in chapter 2, the amount and type of lying makes a difference. Too much lying debases the currency of trust. Moreover, as we saw with FDR, some lies are self-serving, while others are group-serving. A president may lie to cover his tracks and avoid embarrassment, or to harm a rival, or for convenience. While some of Trump's lies may have been unintended and some were doubtlessly part of his bargaining strategy, a very large proportion were of the self-serving type, and related to his personal behavior.

This issue raises larger questions about the relevance of personal style and character in judging presidents' foreign policy. The August 2016 statement signed by fifty primarily Republican former national security officials stated that "a President must be disciplined, control emotions, and act only after reflection and careful deliberation. . . . Trump has none of these critical qualities. He does not encourage conflicting views. He lacks self-control and acts impetuously. He cannot tolerate personal criticism. He has alarmed our closest allies with his erratic behavior."[64] They and others argued that Trump's personal temperament made him unfit to be president.

As a leader, Trump was clearly smart but his temperament ranks low on the scales of emotional and contextual intelligence that made FDR or George H. W. Bush successful presidents. According to Tony Schwartz, who assisted Trump in writing his book *The Art of the Deal*, "Early on, I recognized that Trump's sense of self-worth is forever at risk. When he feels aggrieved, he reacts impulsively and defensively, constructing a self-justifying story that doesn't depend on facts and always directs the blame to others." Schwartz attributed this to Trump's defense against domination by a father who was "relentlessly demanding, difficult and driven . . . You either dominated or you submitted. You either created fear or you succumbed to it—as he thought his elder brother had. . . . Trump simply didn't traffic in emotions or interest in others. . . . A key part of the story is that facts are whatever Trump deems them to be on any given day."[65] Trump himself described his father as "strong and tough as hell." He wrote that his older brother could not stand up to the father, "but I was never intimidated by my father the way most people were. I stood up to him. . . . Even in elementary school, I was a very assertive, aggressive kid."[66]

Whether Schwartz is correct or not about the causes, Trump's ego and emotional needs often seemed to color his relations with other leaders and his interpretation of events. Journalist Bob Woodward reported that Trump told a friend who acknowledged bad behavior toward women that "real power is fear. . . . You've got to deny, deny, deny and push back on these women. If you admit to anything and any culpability, then you're dead. That was a big mistake you made. You didn't come out guns blazing and just challenge them. You showed weakness. . . . Never admit."[67] His low level of emotional intelligence meant that Trump's personal needs often affected his motives and interfered with his policy objectives. For example, contrary to the public testimony of his intelligence director, Trump declared the North Korean nuclear problem remedied because of his personal relations with the dictator because "I like him a lot and he likes me a lot."[68] When his intelligence chiefs publicly contradicted his views on Iran, North Korea, and the Islamic State in Syria, Trump retorted that they should go back to school.[69]

Trump's temperament also affected his contextual intelligence. His lack of experience in government and international affairs was in contrast to most of his predecessors, but equally striking were his limited efforts to fill in the gaps in his knowledge. He was described by close observers as reading little, insisting that briefing memos be very short, and relying heavily on television news. He was reported to have paid little attention to staff preparations before summits with autocrats like Putin or Kim Jong Un. As a liberal critic put it, "Trump—who can get extensive briefings on any subject, just by saying the word, but prefers to watch 'Fox & Friends' instead—has a picture of world trade in his head that bears as little resemblance to reality as his vision of an America overrun by violent immigrants."[70] Or in the view of conservative columnist Bret Stephens, "We have a 'No Guardrails' presidency, in which Trump's contempt for law, procedure and decorum are a model for the behavior of his minions."[71] If Trump's iconoclastic choice of means were merely a breach of traditional presidential etiquette, one might argue that his critics were being too fastidious, or were trapped in old-fashioned views of diplomacy. But the choice of means is not merely a matter of etiquette; they also affect consequences.

What then is a tentative summary view of the morality of Trump's foreign policy, as can best be ascertained about a work in progress? In terms of the first dimension of intentions, goals, and motives, Trump offers a narrow vision that rejects the liberal institutional order and relies on a zero-sum Hobbesian realism of a narrowly defined American self-interest. As his White House aides explain, America First does not necessarily mean America alone. While pressing for change, he somewhat begrudgingly admits the importance of alliances. And while Trump's rhetoric downplays democracy and human rights, he cites the tradition of being a city on the hill (though critics say his behavior at home weakens the clarity of America's appeal). However, while fair-minded critics could differ about the breadth and attractiveness of the values Trump expresses, an impartial analyst could not excuse the ways in which his personal emotional needs skewed their implementation. Trump's need for personal validation and proclaimed success led to flawed policy that weakens American alliances—for example, after his summit meetings with Putin and Kim in 2018. Declaring the nuclear problem in Korea solved and stating that he believed Putin more than his own intelligence chiefs was not good policy or management. As for prudence in balancing values and risks, Trump's noninterventionism protects him from some sins of commission, but one can question whether his mental maps and contextual intelligence are adequate to understand the risks that the United States faces in the diffusion of power in this century. Unwillingness to confront unwelcome evidence is culpable negligence.

In terms of means, Trump's use of force against ISIS or in response to Syria's use of chemical weapons were proportional and discriminate, and he cited proportionality as a grounds for cancelling a military reprisal after Iran shot down an American drone. On the other hand, questions were raised about the humanitarian costs of his backing of the Saudi bombing of civilians in Yemen. Other critics, including his first Secretary of Defense, objected to his precipitous announcement of withdrawal of all troops from Syria without consultation with allies. As for liberal means, Trump shows little respect for institutions or rights of other peoples.

A full assessment of consequences will have to await the passage of more time. At this early stage, it is not clear whether Trump has been a good custodian of American interests, but some early decisions show an immoral approach to consequences in which personal political convenience prevailed over lives. Trump campaigned on a promise to withdraw from the Paris Climate Accords. When his staff pointed out that reversing Obama's emission goals might cost 4,500 lives per year, and showed him a way he could technically stay in the accord while taking a tougher approach, Trump refused on the grounds that full withdrawal was "the only way I can be true to my base."[72]

As discussed earlier, the costs incurred by Trump's style and his choice of means are already visible and have been considerable, but it is too soon to assess the benefits and thus do a balanced net assessment. As for cosmopolitan concerns, and in educational terms he narrowed rather than broadened moral discourse at home and abroad. Moreover, his lack of respect for institutions and truth produced a loss of soft power, though it remains to be seen if the damage to institutions and reputation will be readily reparable or not. In 2019, Robert Blackwill, an official in prior Republican administration concluded that Trump's realistic approaches to China and the greater Middle East meant that Trump's foreign policies are "better than they seem," but still assigned him a poor grade of D+.[73] In contrast, in April 2018 Trump told Fox News, "I would give myself an A+."[74] However, since the course of Trump's presidency is not finished, his midterm grade must be "incomplete, but needs further work."

Trump's Interim Ethical Scorecard

Intentions and Motives

Moral vision: attractive values, good motives	poor
Prudence: balance of values and risks	mixed

Means

Force: proportion, discrimination, necessity	good
Liberal: respect for rights and institutions	poor

Consequences

Fiduciary: success for long-term US interests	mixed
Cosmopolitan: minimal damage to others	poor
Educational: truthful; moral discourse broadened	poor

*****

Historians warn that the proper appraisal of a presidency requires the passage of time—sometimes decades. Any appraisal of Obama and Trump must be highly tentative. Both were reacting to the excesses of Bush's intervention in Iraq, and both proclaimed a desire to preserve America's place in the world. Neither was an isolationist, but both presided over a period of retrenchment that reflected popular attitudes. Their approaches, however, were very different. Obama tried to preserve the liberal international order that had been established in 1945. He negotiated new nuclear, trade, and climate agreements; worked hard to maintain alliances in Europe and Asia; tried to bring China into the institutional framework; and tried (without much success) to reduce American involvement in the quagmires of the Middle East.

In contrast, Trump rejected the liberal international order, questioned alliances, attacked multilateral institutions, withdrew from Obama's trade and climate agreements, become involved in a trade war with China, and refocused American policy in the Middle East on Saudi Arabia and Iran. He promised to make America great again by a narrow transactional approach and disruptive diplomacy that challenged conventional wisdom.

It is impossible at this point to render a definitive judgment, but the implications of these two radically different approaches will pose important moral choices for Americans. In the final chapter, we turn to the challenges the 46th president will face.

Foreign Policy and Future Choices

M oral choices are an inescapable aspect of foreign policy, even
though cynics pretend otherwise. Humans do not live by the
sword alone. Words are also powerful. Swords are swifter, but words can
change the minds that wield the swords. As Henry Kissinger has argued,
international order depends not only upon the balance of hard power, but
also on perceptions of legitimacy.[1] And legitimacy, of course, depends on
values.

ASSESSING ETHICAL FOREIGN POLICY SINCE 1945

Did morals matter, or were moral arguments just window dressing that
presidents used to justify their personal or national interest—as one friend
put it, "just so much blah, blah, blah" with little causal significance? Interests

bake the cake; morals are just some icing presidents dribbled on to make it look pretty.

What our cases have shown is that such a radically skeptical approach is bad history. Morals did matter. For example, as we saw in chapter 3, a purely realist account of the founding of the postwar order in terms of the bipolar structure of power or an imperial imposition of hegemony does not explain FDR's Wilsonian design or Truman's delay in adapting it after 1945, or the liberal nature of the order that was created after 1947. Kennan suggested a realist policy of containment, but to his chagrin, Truman defined and implemented it in broader liberal terms. Similarly, a good account of the American intervention in Korea in June 1950—in spite of the fact that Secretary of State Acheson had declared earlier in the year that Korea was outside our defense perimeter—would have to include Truman's axiomatic decision to respond to what he saw as immoral aggression. Similarly, in chapter 5, to explain the elevation in the priority of human rights in American foreign policy after the Vietnam era, we must include the moral outlook of Jimmy Carter. And in chapter 6, Ronald Reagan's decision to ignore his advisors and his previous harsh rhetoric about the "evil empire" must be understood in the light of his personal moral commitment to ending the nuclear threat.

Looking back over the seven decades of American primacy, we can see certain patterns in the role of ethics and foreign policy. All presidents expressed formal goals and values that were attractive to Americans. After all, that is how they got elected. All proclaimed a goal of preserving American primacy. While that goal was attractive to the American public, its morality depended on how it was implemented. Imperial swagger and hubris did not pass the test, but provision of global public goods by the largest state had important moral consequences.

The moral problems in the presidents' stated intentions arose more from their personal motives than from their stated formal goals. All too often, personal considerations created a divergence from their formal goals. Johnson and Nixon may have admirably sought the formal goal of protecting South Vietnamese from Communist totalitarianism, but they also expanded and prolonged the war because they did not want to be "the man who lost Vietnam." How does one justify the expenditure of American and other lives if the motive is to avoid domestic political embarrassment? In contrast, Truman allowed his presidency to be politically weakened by the stalemate in Korea rather than follow MacArthur's advice of using nuclear weapons. Morality mattered greatly in both these cases.

In terms of the three-dimensional moral judgments outlined in chapter 2, the founding presidents of the post-1945 world order—FDR, Truman, and Eisenhower—all had moral intentions, both in values and personal motives, and largely moral consequences. Where they sometimes fell short was on the dimension of their means involving the use of force. In contrast, the Vietnam-era presidents, particularly Johnson and Nixon, rated poorly on their motives, means, and consequences. The two post-Vietnam presidents, Ford and Carter, had notably moral foreign policies on all three dimensions but their tenures were brief, and they illustrate that a moral foreign policy is not necessarily the same as an effective one. The two presidents who presided over the end of the Cold War, Reagan and Bush 41, also scored quite well on all three dimensions of morality. The years of unipolarity and then the diffusion of power in the twenty-first century produced mixed results with Clinton and Obama above the average and Bush 43 and Trump falling well below average. Among the fourteen presidents since 1945, in my view the four best at combining morality and effectiveness in foreign policy were FDR, Truman, Eisenhower, and Bush 41. Reagan, Kennedy, Ford, Carter, Clinton, and Obama make up the middle. The four worst were Johnson, Nixon, Bush 43, and (tentatively because of incompletion) Trump. Of course, such judgments can be contested, and my own views have changed over time. Historical revision is inevitable as new facts are uncovered and as each generation re-examines the past in terms of new circumstances and its changing priorities.

Obviously, such judgments reflect the circumstances these presidents faced, and as Arnold Wolfers put it, a moral foreign policy means making the best choices that the circumstances permit. War involves special circumstances. Because wars impose enormous costs on Americans and others, they raise enormous moral issues. Presiding over a major war such as World War II is different from presiding over debatable wars of intervention such as Vietnam and Iraq. Even limited wars often prove very difficult to end.

The importance of prudence as a moral virtue in foreign policy becomes clear when one compares Eisenhower's refusal to send troops to Vietnam with Kennedy's and Johnson's decisions. After losing 241 Marines in a terrorist attack during Lebanon's civil war in 1983, Reagan withdrew the troops rather than double down. Similarly, Obama's and Trump's reluctance to send more than a small number of forces to Syria may look different with time. Bush 41 was criticized for restricting his objectives, terminating the Gulf War after four days' fighting, and not sending American armies to Baghdad in 1991, but his decision seems better when contrasted with the lack of prudence that his son showed in 2003 when members of his administration expected to be greeted as liberators after the invasion of Iraq and failed to prepare adequately for the occupation. In foreign policy as in law, some levels of negligence are culpable.

Realists sometimes dismiss prudence as an instrumental and not a moral value, but we have seen that given the complexity and high prospect of unintended consequences when judging the morality of foreign policy decisions, the distinction between instrumental and intuited values breaks down and prudence becomes a crucial virtue. Three-dimensional ethics means presidents must balance Weber's ethics of conviction with his ethics of responsibility. Moral decisions in foreign policy involve both intuition and reason. Willful ignorance or careless assessment produces immoral consequences. Conversely, not all decisions based on conviction are prudential, as some cases here indicated. Truman's response to North Korea's crossing of the 38th parallel in Korea, for example, was imprudent, though he saw it as a moral imperative. These reasoned and intuited virtues can conflict with each other. Principle and prudence do not always coincide. As we saw in chapter 2, the problem of dirty hands is not a question of right versus wrong, but right versus right.

Prudence was a critical virtue with regard to the dogs that did not bark in our story. In the cases relating to nuclear weapons, the virtues of prudence and moral revulsion against killing innocent civilians began to reinforce each other. Harry Truman used the new atomic weapon to end World War

II without losing sleep over it, but he rejected proposals of nuclear use in 1948 when America had a nuclear monopoly. He again refused to use nuclear weapons to break the Korean stalemate even though the United States had overwhelming nuclear superiority. Prudence about expanding the war and maintaining the support of allies was part of his decision, but he was also appalled at the idea of killing so many children.

Eisenhower threatened to use nuclear weapons as a means of creating deterrence in the Cold War, but at several points he rejected military advice to actually use them. While prudence became an increasingly important part of the mix of virtues after the Soviet Union exploded its first atomic bomb in 1949, privately Eisenhower also invoked moral convictions in explaining his decisions to his advisors in the 1950s. Kennedy's prudence in seeking a compromise to end the Cuban Missile Crisis is a stark moral contrast to Johnson's risky advocacy of an air strike that is revealed by the tapes of conversations during the crisis.* But neither Johnson nor Nixon seriously considered using (as opposed to threatening) nuclear weapons to escape their Vietnam imbroglio. The moral consequences of these "nonevents" were enormous. Had these presidential choices gone the other way, the world would look very different today.

Of course, judgments can differ even when assessing presidents of the same period. Anyone who has engaged in grading student exams, or watched Olympic figure skating or the Westminster Dog Show knows that judging is not a science. Even when there is broad agreement on the facts, different judges may weight them differently. For example, some realists rate Nixon's foreign policy more highly than I did because they focus only on his deft opening to China, and forgive him everything else. They are uninterested in his poor legacy on international economics and inflation, or on human rights. I weigh those factors more highly, and also find it difficult to forgive his spending 21,000 US lives (and countless Vietnamese lives) to create a reputational "decent interval," which in any event turned out to

---

* The US had many more nuclear weapons than the USSR in 1962, and a number of advisors assessed the moral risks and benefits differently than Kennedy did. As one put it in a strangely mixed metaphor, "We had them over a barrel but gave them a piece of cake."

be brief. Similarly, some people might rate LBJ more highly than I did on the grounds that he was dealing with an inherited dilemma and was trying to preserve an innovative domestic record that included more progress on civil rights than any president since Lincoln.[†] And still others might grade JFK more poorly because of what he contributed to the Vietnam dilemma or more highly because of his avoidance of nuclear war during the Cuban Missile Crisis.

I respect my close friends who served in the Bush 43 administration, read my draft chapter, and have told me that I scored him too low. I realize that my scorecards for Carter and Clinton may have been unwittingly affected by my participation in those administrations, and I served as an advisor to the secretaries of State and Defense during the Obama Administration. I tried to be objective, but it is important for readers to be aware of my potential biases. In any event, my personal rankings are less important than the scorecards which readers can alter for themselves. The scorecards are designed to be illustrative rather than definitive. Their value is in exploring the neglected aspects of how to think carefully when assessing morality in foreign policy, because the history shows that even though scoring can be contested, morals did matter.

CONTEXTUAL INTELLIGENCE AND MORAL CHOICES

What moral choices did the circumstances permit? Any net assessment of a president's pluses and minuses must start with the realist insight about the primary value of survival in an anarchic world. The first moral duty of a president is that of a trustee, and that starts with ensuring the survival and security of the democracy that elected him or (in the future) her. That test is pass/fail, and none of our presidents failed. But most of international politics, particularly for a large country like the United States and outside the realm of nuclear war, is not about survival. Realists also appreciate the

---

[†] And of course, my ranking refers only to foreign policy. A 2017 C-SPAN poll of historians ranked LBJ as the 10th best president overall. See Brian Lamb, Susan Swain and C-SPAN, The Presidents: Noted Historians Rank America's Best and Worst Chief Executives. New York, Public Affairs, 2019.

importance of an international order that reduces conflict, and correctly make the moral point that justice presupposes order as Kissinger indicated. There are no rights among the incinerated. So we should start our assessments with realist questions about the degrees of risk and prudence presidents undertook with regard to their fiduciary role, and we find that most presidents did well on this measure.

The morally significant consequential differences among the presidents arose less from their values than from the great differences in their contextual intelligence as they struggled to answer Wolfers's question of what was the most moral decision that the circumstances allowed. Johnson, Bush 43, and Trump were notably deficient on the dimension of contextual intelligence, sometimes teetering on the edge of willful ignorance, reckless assessment, and gross negligence. But how far should we hold a president morally accountable for unforeseen consequences? When George Bush sent humanitarian assistance to Somalia in December 1992, should he have anticipated the tragic denouement ten months later? Probably not. Should his son have foreseen that his 2003 invasion of Iraq might eventually have a price tag of many trillion dollars? Probably yes. No one can predict the future, but a moral foreign policy requires a president to exercise maximum due diligence when there is a reasonable probability of disproportionate unintended consequences. And when one rolls the dice of war, the probability of unintended consequences is always high.

Survival and security, however, are not the only important aspects of world politics, and there are other values that the public wants to see included among the consequences of a president's foreign policy. As we have seen, most Americans also "ascribe substantial importance to achieving justice for people abroad and want the United States to pursue altruistic, humanitarian aims internationally."[2] For these values, it is important to look beyond realism to cosmopolitan and liberal mental maps of the world. For example, many Americans have a general sense of a human community and support a refugee policy based not just on international legal obligations, but upon moral considerations. While foreign aid in general is not popular, public support for international economic and public health assistance was strong enough for presidents to consistently maintain such policies.

For example, George W. Bush's initiatives related to AIDS and malaria in Africa stand out as moral policies that enjoyed such support. The extent of Good Samaritanism may be limited, but contrary to the skeptics' views, helping others is one of the foreign policy objectives for which American presidents have found public support.

Liberal values also enjoy some popular support, and that affected the means that presidents used. Moral crusades do not enjoy broad support, and contrary to conventional wisdom, Wilson did not lead a crusade for democracy. Making the world safe for democracy is not as ambitious as making the world democratic and can be interpreted as defensive rather than aggressive.[†] At the same time, respect for the human rights and institutions of other peoples is part of what John Rawls called "the manner in which decent peoples treat each other." Even where basic democratic values are not shared, normal cooperative relations may be possible when authoritarians are not posing a severe threat. Such Rawlsian liberals do not insist on the export of democracy, but they do react to gross violations of human rights—as Clinton found out in Bosnia and Haiti; Obama encountered in cases like Libya, Egypt, and Syria; and Trump confronted with public reactions to his inadequate response to the Saudi murder of a dissident journalist.

The difficult debates and moral choices over these issues have often been centered on what means to use. As we have seen, the types and degrees of intervention range from a declaratory policy of presidential statements at one end of the spectrum to the large-scale use of military force at the other end. With regard to force, the record is not impressive, with far more failures than successes. As Reagan pithily put it in 1982, "Regimes planted by bayonets do not take root."[3] The success in Germany and Japan came after their total defeat in a prolonged war. Other cases are modest.

[†] The "democratic peace theory" (which can be traced back to Kant and was resurrected by the political scientist Michael Doyle and others in the 1980s) became popular in Washington after the end of the Cold War. It links democracy to security by positing that democratic countries are less likely to go to war with each other. Even if true, however, the path to making all countries democratic is difficult and may involve considerable violence. There is a considerable literature debating this point.

The failure of the humanitarian intervention in Somalia in 1993 affected Clinton's nonintervention in the genocide in Rwanda six months later. The unsuccessful outcome of the use of air strikes in Libya limited Obama's subsequent willingness to use them in Syria. But as one of his aides wrote, Syria became a tragic case of a means-ends gap where hundreds of thousands of civilians were slaughtered and millions became refugees. By setting maximalist ends and declaring that Assad must go, the United States was unable to achieve its objective. "We should have done more to try to achieve less." Pressure on Assad to temper his worst behavior would not have solved the deeper problem of his tyranny, but might have limited the deaths and destabilizing flow of refugees across borders.[4] Ends and means interact in moral judgments. Good ends must be adjusted to fit good means and vice versa. Many of the most difficult moral decisions are not all or nothing. As Michael Walzer points out, the difficult moral choices are in the middle. While it is important to be prudent about the dangers of a slippery slope, moral choices lie in adjusting ends and means to each other.

As for the second aspect of Wilson's liberal legacy, the support of an international order based on institutional cooperation, American presidents were never perfect institutional liberals. They often chafed under restrictions and complained about burden-sharing. Truman extended drilling on the continental shelf; Eisenhower's support of covert action in Iran and Guatemala and Kennedy's in Cuba were hardly consistent with a strict reading of the UN Charter; Nixon broke the Bretton Woods rules and levied tariffs against our allies in 1971; Reagan ignored an International Court of Justice ruling illegal his mining of Nicaraguan harbors; Bush 41 overthrew the Noriega government in Panama; Reagan invaded Grenada; and Clinton bombed Serbia without a Security Council resolution of support.

Nonetheless, prior to 2016, American presidents in most instances supported international institutions and sought their extension, whether it be the Non-Proliferation Treaty under Johnson; arms control agreements under Nixon, Ford, and Carter; the Rio agreement on climate change under Bush 41; the World Trade Organization and the Missile Technology Control Regime under Clinton; or the Paris Climate Accords under

Obama. It was not until Trump that an American administration became broadly critical of multilateral institutions as a matter of policy. In 2018, Secretary of State Mike Pompeo proclaimed that since the end of the Cold War the international order has failed us and he complained that "multilateralism has become viewed as an end unto itself. The more treaties we sign, the safer we supposedly are. The more bureaucrats we have, the better the job gets done."[5] Presidential frustration with international institutions is long-standing, but the Trump administration represented a new narrow transactional approach to institutions.

As we saw in chapter 2, maintenance of international institutions and regimes is part of moral leadership. Institutions are simply regular valued patterns of social behavior. They are more than formal international organizations, which sometimes ossify and need to be reformed or discarded. Institutions include organizations, but even more important is the whole regime of rules, norms, networks, and expectations that create social roles, which entail moral obligations. A family, for example, is not an organization, but a social institution where the role of parent entails moral obligations for the long-term interests of the children. By enhancing the long shadow of the future, international regimes and institutions encourage cooperation with moral consequences that go beyond any single transaction. They often represent codified moral arguments about reciprocity. They can create new circumstances for moral choice. At the same time, institutions can sometimes lose their value and become illegitimate.[6]

The Trump administration worried that the post-1945 institutions had "Gulliverized" the United States, and they had a valid point. The Lilliputians use multilateral institutional threads to limit the bargaining power that the American Gulliver would otherwise bring to bear in any bilateral face-off.[§] The Trump administration used this approach to renegotiate various trade agreements in a manner that damaged the World Trade Organization. The United States can use its exceptional size to break those institutional

---

§   This insight is not new with the Trump administration. In 1968, Stanley Hoffmann titled a book *Gulliver's Troubles: Or the Setting of American Foreign Policy* (New York: McGraw Hill).

gossamer threads and maximize its short-term bargaining power, but as the largest country it can also see such institutions as ways to snare others into support for global public goods that are in the US and others' long-term interests.

Trump's attacks on unfair Chinese trade and technology policies did not involve our allies in the reform of the WTO. Instead, he alienated them with tariffs and focused his efforts on a unilateral attack on China. Trump could claim that this broke the existing inertia in the international trade regime and prevented other countries from diluting the unilateral American pressure on China. Whether the short-term gains will outweigh the institutional loss remains to be seen over time, but it rests on a very different image of exercising power than the long-term patient gardener metaphor.

Finally, among the important long-term moral consequences of a president's foreign policy, one has to consider his effects on truth, trust, and broadening or narrowing of moral discourse at home and abroad. The eighteenth-century founding fathers worried about the effects of a large standing army upon our democratic institutions, and Eisenhower warned against the distortions caused by the development of a military-industrial complex. Excessive secrecy breeds distrust, particularly when actions are eventually unveiled. The secrecy that surrounded his and his successors' covert interventions during the Cold War corrupted open discourse at home and abroad.

As we saw in chapter 2, the American public's loss of trust in government became much worse after the Johnson and Nixon administrations. In the aftermath of Vietnam and Watergate and the revelation of the degree of Cold War CIA covert interventions, there was a severe drop in confidence and trust in government institutions. In the political cycle of action and reaction, Ford and Carter tried to create greater openness and trust, but their era lasted only six years. Reagan's optimism led to some increase in public trust, but the polls dropped again after disclosures of his CIA Director William Casey's covert actions in Central America and Oliver North's illegal Iran–Contra operations organized from the White House. At one point, there was even talk of Reagan's impeachment, and later the House of Representatives impeached Clinton in the aftermath of his lies about his relationship with the intern Monica Lewinsky. The long-term effects of Trump's record number of lies remain to be seen. Independent of Trump, the trends on fake news, weaponization of social media, and manipulation of imagery by artificial intelligence (AI) are not encouraging.

In terms of the attractiveness or soft power of the United States overseas, polls show that the international reactions to Trump's unprecedented number of false statements has created a significant decline in trust of the United States. Unlike authoritarian states, a great deal of American soft power is generated not solely by government actions but by our civil society—everything from Hollywood to universities, foundations, nonprofit organizations, a free press. In the Vietnam era when people around the globe marched through the streets to protest the US government policy in Vietnam, they did not sing the "Internationale" of America's Communist opponents, but the American civil rights anthem "We Shall Overcome." Within a decade, American soft power had recovered. Whether history will repeat itself in the post-Trump era remains to be seen, but in the interim the loss of trust in America is a costly consequence of the administration's short-term transactional rather than a long-term enlightened self-interest approach to foreign policy.

UPS AND DOWNS OF AMERICAN MORAL TRADITIONS

As we saw earlier, Americans have been exceptional in their taste for moralism in foreign policy. This did not make Americans more moral than other peoples, but it affected our self-perception and, at times, American policies. This exceptionalism stemmed from the religious beliefs of the Puritans, the Enlightenment liberalism of the founding fathers, and America's sheer size. As the United States became the world's largest economy and most powerful country in the twentieth century, our options increased. Woodrow Wilson sent two million troops to Europe to make the world safe for democracy, and to create a liberal world order to replace the old balance of power. After a two-decade retreat back to our nineteenth-century tradition of isolationism, FDR, Truman, and Eisenhower founded a liberal international order that remained unchallenged for seven decades, until the election of 2016.

American foreign policy attitudes have always varied by region and party, and they have also oscillated between inward and outward orientations. These cycles of expansion and retrenchment often reflected an era's reaction to its predecessor.[7] Wilson's ambitious moral agenda mobilized the public in 1917, but it also contributed to the strength of the isolationist reaction in the 1930s. Similarly, the disastrous decade of the 1930s contributed to the creation of the liberal order after World War II. Kennedy's inspirational rhetoric, which merged with the domino theory in Vietnam, later contributed to the disillusion and drawback of the 1970s under Ford and Carter. The successful end of the Cold War and unipolarity led to increased military interventions under Bill Clinton and George W. Bush. The invasion of Iraq in 2003 helped create the foreign policy attitudes that prevailed during the Obama and Trump presidencies.

Americans have always been ambivalent about major military interventions; initial enthusiasm often wanes. Even in the case of the existential threat from Hitler in the 1930s, FDR was unable to respond with force until after the Japanese attack on Pearl Harbor. And Truman had to "scare the hell out of the American people" to respond to the threat of Soviet expansion after World War II. He avoided a declaration of war in Korea in 1950 and instead described his response to aggression in Korea in 1950 as a "police action" under a UN flag. Domestic support wore thin after the stalemate.

Kennedy and Johnson gradually escalated American involvement in Vietnam in the context of a bipolar Cold War rivalry, but neither they nor Nixon were successful in developing international support for the war, and by 1968 public opinion at home was deeply divided. Bush 41 was fortunate in gaining Gorbachev's acquiescence for a UN collective security action to expel Iraq from Kuwait in 1991. Bush wisely kept his objective limited, his international coalition intact, and the military campaign brief. After failing to gain legitimacy by the path of UN Security Council resolutions in 1999 and 2003, Bill Clinton and George W. Bush invoked NATO and a "coalition of the willing" to legitimize their use of force in Kosovo and Iraq, but domestic and international support waned over time in both cases.

After 9/11, and later the rise of the Islamic State, the response to terrorism sustained American use of force in Afghanistan and the Middle East, but Trump's 2017 national security doctrine promised that great power competition, not terrorism or nation-building, would be the focus of American policy. Trump intuited that the use of force to protect security is more sustainable in public opinion than the use of force to promote values such as liberal democracy. Americans care about promoting liberal values, but not when it becomes clear that the costs are exceeding the benefits. Nonetheless, in Washington, "American politics pushes military interventionism even as the public is wary." In the view of Obama advisor Ben Rhodes, "Even as the Syria red line episode demonstrated that public opinion was skeptical of war, the political frame for national security debates remained the same: Doing more was tough, anything else was weak."[8]

The issue of American credibility created difficult moral dilemmas for many presidents. Obama was right that going to war just to look tough is the wrong decision, but a reputation for toughness can affect the broader international order that rests on American power. In retrospect, his refusal to bomb Syria was costly for him even though Congress and the public supported his approach at the time and he probably removed more chemical weapons by his diplomatic solution than by bombing. In the aftermath of defeat in Vietnam, Ford felt he needed to be tough in the *Mayaguez* incident, though he had other options. On the other hand, it is never completely clear how tightly issues are coupled. At the height of the Cold War, JFK was correct to see Cuba and Berlin as closely related, but Johnson and Nixon probably overestimated how closely defeat in Vietnam was linked to the bipolar balance of power in a world where a Sino–Soviet split had already begun. Once again, good contextual intelligence is crucial for moral consequences.

Given the limited popular taste for major military intervention, the critical question often becomes how far the United States should go in using non-military means of intervention to promote its values. During the Cold War competition with the Soviet Union, Eisenhower, Kennedy, and others turned often to covert action by intelligence agencies as a solution, but when these activities later became public they proved more costly than expected in terms of relations with other countries and in their damage to trust in the United States. As one careful study concluded, "The vast majority of America's covert and overt regime changes during the Cold War did not work out as their planners intended. . . . There is little reason to believe that they played a decisive role in America's ultimate victory." Former CIA director James Woolsey once cited two covert actions that he thought had a big effect during the Cold War: Radio Free Europe and aid to the Mujahedeen after the Soviet invasion of Afghanistan. Richard Helms, another former CIA director, criticized the Cold War use of covert action as "a political chain saw," and concluded, "at its best, covert action should be used like a well-honed scalpel, infrequently and with discretion lest the blade lose its edge."[9] JFKs covert Operation Mongoose helped set the scene for the enormously dangerous Cuban Missile Crisis. The purported benefits of Cold War covert actions do not seem to have outweighed their moral costs.

As for overt intervention, at the low end of the spectrum of intrusiveness, the soft power of attraction can be promoted by the example of the shining city on the hill, by rhetoric and broadcast, by economic and health assistance, and by support for civil society institutions ranging from universities to nonprofit organizations. There is more contention when verbal or economic support for human rights or sanctions and curtailment of military sales in another country such as Saudi Arabia or the Philippines offends authoritarian leaders and obstructs other aspects of American foreign policy. Such disputes over values are normal and to be expected in a democracy. Americans have a degree of cosmopolitan concern about human rights in China or Myanmar, but human rights and democracy promotion cannot be the sole focus, as Jimmy Carter discovered. Foreign policy involves trade-offs among many objectives, including liberal values. Otherwise, we would have a human rights policy instead of a foreign policy.

CHALLENGES FOR A FUTURE MORAL FOREIGN POLICY

As mentioned earlier, future presidents will confront two global power shifts that will shape the context of American foreign policy in this century, one horizontal and one vertical. The horizontal shift is the rise of Asia, or more accurately, the recovery of Asia. Before the Industrial Revolution boosted the economies of Europe and North America in the nineteenth century, Asia represented more than half the world's people and half the world's economy. By 1900 Asia still had half the population, but its share of the global economy had shrunk to 20 percent. Beginning with the double-digit economic growth of Japan after World War II (which was an objective of US policy), the world has been returning to more normal proportions as Southeast Asia, China, and India followed in Japan's footsteps. Particularly important is the rise of Chinese power and the danger that the world will fall into a "Thucydides trap" in which a devastating war is caused by the fear created in a dominant great power by the rise of a new power.[10] Some think the twenty-first century will be devastated by a war of hegemonic transition similar to what happened in the last century, when Britain was challenged by the rise in the power of Germany.

The other great power shift is vertical and is driven by technology. The information revolution that started in the 1960s with Moore's Law about the doubling of the capacity of computer chips every two years is providing more information to more actors than at any time in history. This second power shift has sometimes been called "the new feudalism," in which sovereigns share authority with a variety of other actors. Technology empowers nonstate actors. They do not replace sovereign states, but they crowd the stage on which governments act, creating new instruments, problems, and potential coalitions.** In addition, technology has increased economic, political, and ecological interdependence and created more transnational linkages and issues that are often outside the control of governments, but affect the relations between them. Such global interdependence has also had redistributive effects within societies, which are in turn altering domestic politics that affect foreign policies.

** At least one European Foreign Ministry, Denmark, has a tech ambassador with offices in Silicon Valley and Beijing. Facebook has a transnational membership larger than the populations of the US and China combined.

Both these power shifts challenge the liberal order of the past seven decades. Respected commentators such as Martin Wolf of the *Financial Times* have argued that "we are at the end of both an economic period— that of Western-led globalization—and a geopolitical one, the post–Cold War 'unipolar moment' of a US-led global order. The question is whether what follows will be an unravelling of the post–Second World War era into a period of deglobalization and conflict much like the first half of the 20th century, or a new period in which non-Western powers, especially China and India, play a larger role in sustaining a co-operative global order."[11] Such a new world poses new challenges for an ethical foreign policy.

The Rise of China

Failure to cope with the rise of China successfully could have disastrous consequences for America and the rest of the world. Robert Blackwill argues that American presidents' misunderstandings of China's long-term objective to become number one in Asia, and in time the world ranks with the Vietnam and Iraq Wars as one of the three most damaging U.S. foreign policy errors since the end of World War II.[12] Moreover, the interaction of an established power and a rising power could lead to miscalculations that could disrupt this century much as the twentieth was devastated in 1914. Many observers believe that the rise of China will spell the end of the American era, but it is equally dangerous to over- or underestimate Chinese power. Underestimation breeds complacency, while overestimation creates fear— either of which can lead to miscalculation. History is replete with misperception about changing power balances.[13] Just since 1945, Nixon and Kissinger interpreted as decline what was really the return to normal of America's artificially high postwar share of world product. They proclaimed multipolarity when what actually transpired over the next two decades was unipolarity. At the same time, opponents of Nixon's détente in the 1970s exaggerated Soviet power, which then collapsed. And subsequently, George W. Bush misunderstood the unipolar reach of American power. It proved far easier for the United States to dominate the global commons of air, sea, and space than to control the domestic politics of social revolutions in urban jungles.[14]

Contrary to current conventional wisdom, China has not yet replaced the United States as the world's largest economy. Measured in purchasing power parity, the Chinese economy became larger than the American economy in 2014, but purchasing power parity is a valid economist's device for comparing estimates of welfare, not for measuring power. For example, oil and jet engines are imported at current exchange rates, and by that measure China is about two-thirds the size of the United States.[15] Moreover, gross domestic product (GDP) is a very crude measure of power. For the first half of its "century of humiliation" that started with the opium wars with Britain in 1839, China had the world's largest GDP (and military).[16] Including per-capita income gives a better index of the sophistication of an economy, and American per-capita income is many times that of China.

Many economists expect China to pass the United States someday as the world's largest economy (measured as GDP in dollars), but the estimated date varies from 2030 to midcentury depending on what one assumes about the rates of Chinese and American growth. By any measure, however, the gravitational pull of China's economy is increasing. Clinton's Secretary of Treasury Lawrence Summers poses the future foreign policy questions: "Can the United States imagine a viable global economic system in 2050 in which its economy is half the size of the world's largest? Could a political leader acknowledge that reality in a way that permits negotiations over what such a world would look like? While it may be unacceptable to the United States to be so greatly surpassed in economic scale, does it have the means to stop it? Can China be held down without inviting conflict?"[17]

Thucydides famously attributed the Peloponnesian War to two causes: the rise of a new power, and the fear that created in an established power. Most people focus on the first half of his statement, but the second is more within our control. Summers properly doubts that US foreign policy can prevent the rise of China's economy, but we can avoid exaggerated fears that could create a new cold or hot war if we use our contextual intelligence well.

Even if China someday passes the United States in total economic size, that is not the only measure of geopolitical power—witness the American experience in the first half of the twentieth century. Economic might is just part of the equation, and China is well behind the United States on military and soft power indices. US military expenditure is several times that of China. While Chinese military capabilities have been increasing in recent years, analysts who look carefully at the military balance conclude that China is not a global peer, and will not be able to exclude the United States from the Western Pacific so long as the United States maintains its alliance and bases in Japan. The RAND Corporation estimated that a non-nuclear war would be costly for both the US and China, but even more so for China.[18] And in soft power, opinion polls as well as a recent index published by Portland, a London consultancy, ranked China in twenty-sixth place while the United States ranked near the top.[19] Mao's Communism had a far greater transnational soft power appeal in the 1960s than "Xi Jinping thought" does today.

On the other hand, China's huge economic scale matters. The United States was once the world's largest trading nation and largest bilateral lender. Today nearly a hundred countries count China as their largest trading partner, compared to fifty-seven that have such a relationship with the United States. China plans to lend more than a trillion dollars for infrastructure projects with its "belt and road" initiative over the next decade, while the United States has cut back aid. China's economic success story enhances its soft power, and government control of access to its large market provides hard power leverage. Moreover, China's authoritarian politics and mercantilist practices make its economic power readily usable by the government. China will gain economic power from the sheer size of its market as well as its overseas investments and development assistance. Of the seven giant global companies in the age of artificial intelligence (Google, Facebook, Amazon, Microsoft, Baidu, Alibaba, and Tencent), nearly half are Chinese.[20] With its large population, the world's largest Internet, and data resources becoming the "new oil" of world politics, China is poised to become the Saudi Arabia of big data. Overall, Chinese power relative to the United States is likely to increase.

China is a country of great strength but also important weaknesses. The United States has some long-term power advantages that will persist regardless of current Chinese actions. One is geography. The United States is surrounded by oceans and neighbors that are likely to remain friendly. China has borders with fourteen countries and has territorial disputes with India, Japan, and Vietnam that set limits on its soft power. Energy is another American advantage. A decade ago, the United States seemed hopelessly dependent on imported energy. Now the shale revolution has transformed it from an energy importer to exporter, and the International Energy Agency projects that North America may be self-sufficient in the coming decade. At the same time, China is becoming more dependent on energy imports, and much of the oil it imports is transported through the Indian Ocean and the South China Sea, where the United States and others maintain a significant naval presence. Eliminating this vulnerability will be difficult.[21]

The United States enjoys financial power derived from its large transnational financial institutions as well as the role of the dollar. Of the foreign reserves held by the world's governments, just 1.1 percent are in yuan, compared with 64 percent for the dollar. While China aspires to a larger role, a credible reserve currency depends on currency convertibility, deep capital markets, honest government, and the rule of law—all lacking in China and not quickly developed. While China could divest its large holdings of dollars, such action would risk damaging its own economy as much as the United States. Although the dollar cannot remain pre-eminent forever, and American overuse of financial sanctions creates incentives for other countries to look for other financial instruments, the yuan is unlikely to displace the dollar in the near term.

The United States also has demographic strengths. It is the only major developed country that is currently projected to hold its place (third) in the demographic ranking of countries. While the rate of American population growth has slowed in recent years, it is not shrinking in population as will happen to Russia, Europe, and Japan. Seven of the world's fifteen largest economies will face a shrinking workforce over the next decade and a half, but the US workforce is likely to increase by 5 percent while China's will decline by 9 percent.[22] China will soon lose its first-place population rank to India, and its working-age population peaked in 2015. Chinese sometimes say they worry about "growing old before growing rich."

America has been at the forefront in the development of key technologies (bio, nano, information) that are central to this century's economic growth, and American research universities dominate higher education. In a 2017 ranking by Shanghai Jiaotong University, sixteen of the top twenty global universities were in the United States; none were in China. At the same time, China is investing heavily in research and development, competes well in some fields now, and has set a goal to be the leader in artificial intelligence by 2030. Some experts believe that with its enormous data resources and lack of privacy restraints on how data is used, and the belief that advances in machine learning will require trained engineers more than cutting-edge scientists, China could achieve its AI goal.[23] Given the importance of machine learning as a general purpose technology that affects many domains, China's gains in AI are of particular significance.

Chinese technological progress is no longer based solely on imitation. While the Trump administration punishes China's cybertheft of intellectual property, coerced intellectual property transfer, and unfair trade practices, a successful American response to China's technological challenge will depend upon improvements at home more than upon external sanctions.[24] However, those who proclaim Pax Sinica and the end of the American era fail to take the full range of power factors into account.†† American complacency is always a danger, but so also is lack of confidence and exaggerated fears that lead to overreaction.

The United States holds high cards in its poker hand, but hysteria could cause failure to play our cards skillfully. Discarding our high cards of alliances and international institutions is a case in point. Another possible mistake would be to try to cut off all immigration. When asked why he did not think China would pass the United States in total power any time soon, former Singapore Prime Minister Lee Kuan Yew cited the ability of America to draw upon the talents of the whole world and recombine them in diversity and creativity that was not possible for China's ethnic Han

†† In the view of John Deutch, former provost of MIT and former CIA Director, if the US attains its potential improvements in innovation potential, "China's great leap forward will likely at best be a few steps toward closing the innovation leadership gap that the United States currently enjoys." But notice the "if" in his statement.

nationalism.[25] If the United States were to discard its high cards of external alliances and domestic openness, Lee could prove wrong.

As China's power grows, many observers worry we are destined for war, but few consider an opposite disruptive danger. Rather than acting like a revolutionary power in the international order, China might decide to be a free rider like the United States was in the 1930s. China may act too weakly rather than too strongly and refuse to contribute to an international order that it did not create. This may overstate the "not invented here" problem. China knows it benefited from the post-1945 international order. In the United Nations Security Council, China is one of the five countries with a veto. China is now the second largest funder of UN peacekeeping forces and participated in UN programs related to Ebola and climate change. China has also benefited greatly from economic institutions like the World Trade Organization and the International Monetary Fund, and China agreed to the 2015 Climate Accords.

On the other hand, China has started its own Asian Infrastructure Investment Bank (AIIB) and a "belt and road" program of international infrastructure projects that some see as an economic offensive. China has not practiced full reciprocity as a market economy, and its rejection of a 2016 Hague tribunal ruling regarding the South China Sea raised questions about whether China would treat its legal obligations a la carte (as the United States has sometimes done).

Thus far, China has not tried to overthrow but rather to increase its influence within the world order from which it benefits, but this could change as Chinese power grows.[26] Appetites sometimes grow with eating. The Trump administration labeled China a revisionist power, but so far it is moderate revisionism. Unlike extreme revisionist powers such as Hitler's Germany, China is not interested in kicking over the card table but in claiming a larger share of the winnings on the table. As a RAND study concludes, "It is not entirely appropriate to speak of China's interaction with 'the' international order—its posture has been highly differentiated depending on the component of the order."[27] At the same time, China's growing economic power will create problems for the United States and the international order, and friction is likely over market access, forced technology transfer, state-directed industrial policies to support national champions, overcapacity, and theft of intellectual property. The American approach to an open international economy will need to be adjusted for greater oversight of Chinese trade and investments that threaten our technological and national security objectives.

As Chinese power grows, the American liberal international order will have to change. China has little interest in liberalism or American domination. Americans would be wise to discard the terms "liberal" and "American" and think in terms of an "open and rules-based" world order. This would mean framing an open international order in terms of Rawls's approach to liberalism as institutional cooperation rather than democracy promotion. That latter part of Wilson's legacy might remain a happy unexpected long-term consequence as the prospects for long-term pluralization would be enhanced by such a situation compared to the alternative of conflict.

As China, India, and other economies grow, the US share of the world economy will be less than it was at the beginning of this century, and the rise of other countries will make it more difficult to organize collective action to promote global public goods. But no other country—including China—is about to replace the United States in terms of overall power resources in the next few decades. Russia is in demographic decline and heavily dependent on energy rather than technology exports; India and Brazil (each with a $2 trillion economy) remain developing countries. Despite their alliance of convenience against the United States, a real alliance of authoritarian countries similar to the Sino-Soviet alliance of the 1950s is unlikely given the underlying mistrust between Russia and China and the difficulty of coordinating competing nationalist ideologies.[28]

Today's axis of authoritarians lacks the soft power appeal of the 1950s Comintern, though steps will need to be taken to counter their covert "sharp power" threat to democratic values.[29] China makes major efforts to promote its soft power by promoting its authoritarian social model through economic inducements as well as manipulation of social media. However, while Maoism used to bring protesters onto the world's streets, it is unlikely that many protesters will march under the banner of "Xi Jinping Thought about Socialism with Chinese Characteristics" (even though that term is now enshrined in the constitution of the Chinese Communist Party). Since Nixon, China and the United States have cooperated despite ideological differences. Now China's use of artificial intelligence applications for domestic surveillance technology and the export of such practices will place new burdens on the relationship, but not prevent all cooperation.

Rapid Asian economic growth has encouraged a horizontal power shift to the region, but Asia has its own internal balance of power. Chinese power is balanced by Japan, India, and Australia, among others. The United States will remain crucial to that Asian balance of power.[30] If the United States maintains those alliances, the prospects are slight that China can drive the United States from the Western Pacific, much less dominate the world. The more relevant question for a moral foreign policy will be whether the United States and China will develop attitudes that allow them to cooperate in producing global public goods, and that is far from clear. Yan Xuetong, a Chinese realist, speculates that with the end of unipolarity and American hegemony, China will carefully avoid war and a "bipolar US–Chinese order will be shaped by fluid issue specific alliances rather than rigid opposing blocs . . . [and] most states will adopt a two-track approach siding with the United States on some issues and China on others."[31] The US–China relationship is a cooperative rivalry where a successful strategy of "smart competition" will require equal attention to both aspects of the description.[32] But such a future will require good contextual intelligence, careful management on both sides, and no major miscalculations.

Technology, Transnational Actors, and Entropy

Presidents will face equally difficult questions arising from the vertical power shift: diffusion away from governments. Power transitions among states are familiar in world politics, but the technology-driven shift of power away from states to nonstate actors brings a new and unfamiliar complexity. Technological change is putting a number of transnational issues like financial stability, climate change, terrorism, cybercrime, and pandemics on the global agenda at the same time that it tends to weaken the ability of governments to respond. The realm of transnational relations that cross borders outside of government control includes actors as diverse as bankers and criminals electronically transferring funds, terrorists transferring weapons and plans, and hackers threatening cybersecurity or using social media to disrupt democratic processes, as well as ecological threats such as pandemics and climate change.

Complexity is growing. Realist mental maps suggest two models for the future—great power conflict or a concert of great powers along the lines of nineteenth-century Europe. However, a third and unexpected model could involve entropy—the inability to get work done. In that world, the answer to the question "Who's next?" is "no one."[33]

While this answer is too simple, it does indicate important trends that will create new foreign policy challenges. Rapid technological change is putting new issues on the agenda and confronting presidents with difficult moral choices. We saw how Truman, Eisenhower, and Kennedy made crucial moral choices regarding the transformational technology of nuclear fission, but nuclear plants and weapons were large, visible, and subject to a degree of governmental control. Many of the new developments in information technology and biotechnology are being developed in the private sector and will have decentralized aspects that empower nonstate actors and will be difficult for governments to monitor or control.[34]

Individuals and private organizations, ranging from Wikileaks to global corporations to NGOs to terrorists to spontaneous societal movements, are all empowered to play direct roles in world politics. The spread of information means that power will be more widely distributed and informal networks will undercut the monopoly of traditional bureaucracy. The speed of the transmission of information on the Internet means that governments will have less control of their agendas and face new vulnerabilities.

Isolation is not an option. America's two oceans are less helpful in guaranteeing security than they once were. When the United States bombed Serbia and Iraq in the 1990s, Slobodan Milosovic and Saddam Hussein could not respond against our homeland. In 1998, Clinton used cruise missiles against Al Qaeda targets in Sudan and Afghanistan, but in 2001 a nonstate actor killed three thousand people in the United States (more than the Japanese attack on Pearl Harbor) by turning our commercial aircraft into giant cruise missiles. Our electrical grids, air traffic control systems, and banks are vulnerable to electrons that can originate anywhere within or outside our borders. Oceans don't help. A cyberattack could come in a matter of seconds from ten miles or ten thousand miles away.‡‡ Leon Panetta, Obama's Secretary of Defense, warned against the dangers of a "cyber Pearl Harbor," but some of the most difficult attacks to deter come in the gray zone of "hybrid warfare" below the threshold of armed conflict.

Not just our infrastructure but our democratic liberties are vulnerable to cyberattack. In 2015, when North Korea objected to a Hollywood comedy that mocked its leader, it launched a successful cyberattack against SONY Films. And in 2016, Russia was able to interfere in the American presidential election by using American social media.[35] Many observers had assumed that because the largest transnational social media corporations such as Facebook, Google, and Twitter originated in the United States they were instruments of American power, but in 2016 Russia was able to turn them into weapons against us.

The 1990s were marked by a libertarian optimism about the decentralizing and democratizing effects of the Internet. President Clinton believed that Chinese Communist Party efforts to control the Internet were like trying to "nail Jell-O to the wall."[36] The Bush and Obama administrations shared this optimism and promoted an Internet Freedom Agenda that included subsidies and technologies to assist dissidents in authoritarian states to communicate. Today, the expected asymmetries seem to have been reversed. Autocracies are able to protect themselves by controlling information flows, while the openness of democracies creates vulnerabilities that autocracies can exploit. Information warfare is not new, but it is far cheaper, quicker, and easier to send electrons across borders than trained spies who might be caught. Along with the Internet, big data and artificial intelligence have made the problem of defending democracy from information warfare far more complicated. And while a successful strategy must

---

‡‡ This does not imply all cyber actors are equal. Preparation for some sophisticated cyberattacks involve long preparation times and large resources associated with intelligence agencies of major states.

include domestic resilience, deterrence, and diplomacy, implementation will raise new questions about moral means in a foreign policy.§§ Private corporations play a larger role than government in identifying fake news and speech. The rule of law, trust, truth, and openness make democracies vulnerable, but those are also the critical values we wish to defend.

Any policy to defend against a cyberinformation war must start with the Hippocratic oath. The temptations for presidents to reply in kind with covert information operations will be great. As one realist friend put it to me, "In a battle, you use any weapon you have." It may make sense to establish an American "political warfare" capability and strategy in an age of hybrid warfare, but presidents will have to monitor a strategy closely.[37] Public diplomacy and broadcasting should be public. It would be a mistake to imitate the authoritarians and use major programs of covert information warfare as we did in the Cold War. Such actions will not stay covert for long and when revealed would undercut our soft power, as we saw in the 1970s when many CIA covert cultural operations were disclosed. Some argue that in the information struggle against authoritarian systems, democracies should use every weapon available and not worry about nice distinctions between soft and hard power. However, the two types of power are difficult to combine successfully in the long term, and some apparent arrows in the quiver of political warfare may turn out to be boomerangs. In the long term, central manipulation of information can make authoritarian states brittle, and openness can make democracies more resilient—but only if we retain that openness.

Governments have only just begun the task of developing norms for cyberspace. It took more than two decades for states to develop institutions to deal with the disruptive new technology of nuclear weapons that burst on the scene in 1945. Kennedy negotiated the Limited Test Ban Treaty in 1963, Johnson signed the Non-Proliferation Treaty in 1968, and Nixon negotiated the first Strategic Arms Limitation Treaty in 1972. Cybersecurity

§§ I outline a strategy for resilience, deterrence, and diplomacy in "Protecting Democracy in an Era of Cyber Information War," Hoover Institution Working Paper, December 2018.

is at a similar stage. In 1996, at the end of Clinton's first term, only 36 million people or about 1 percent of the world population used the Internet. Within two decades, as Trump entered office at the beginning of 2017, 3.7 billion people—or nearly half the world population—used the Internet. As the number of users escalated after the late 1990s, the Internet became a vital substrate for economic, social, and political interactions. This globalization was popular whether populist politicians liked it or not.

Along with rising interdependence came not just economic opportunity, but also vulnerability and insecurity. With big data, machine learning, and the "Internet of things," some experts anticipate that the number of Internet connections may grow to nearly a trillion by 2030. The potential attack surface will expand dramatically and include everything from industrial control systems to heart pacemakers to self-driving cars. The cyber domain will provide opportunities for both private and interstate conflict.[38] Unless a future president thinks he can cut the United States off from the Internet, a moral foreign policy for the cyber age will require not just defense and deterrence, but leadership in the development of norms and institutions.[39] This problem will be further increased by the growing importance of the technologies of artificial intelligence, genomics, and other biotechnologies.

Machine learning and the algorithms of artificial intelligence will create complexity that will be difficult for policymakers to understand and will create difficult new moral choices. Autonomous weapons today are mainly static systems to shoot down incoming threats, and offensive systems like drones have a human "in the loop," who remotely pulls the trigger. But with swarms of drones guided by artificial intelligence instantaneously handing off information about multiple targets over wide areas, it will be difficult to keep a human "on the loop" able to understand enough to step in when necessary.

Obama wrestled with the early stages of this technology when he established restrictive procedures for drone strikes.[40] The problem has implications for targeted strikes and the question of assassination. After the assassination plots of the 1950s and 1960s were revealed in Congressional hearings in the aftermath of Vietnam and Watergate, Gerald Ford issued an executive order excluding assassination as an acceptable means of foreign policy. Ronald Reagan reissued the order, but made it more ambiguous in his reprisal attack on Gaddafi in 1986. Assassination did not exclude targeting leaders under the rules of war, even though the term "state of war" became fuzzy. Obama used this justification for a 2011 drone strike on Anwar Awlaki, an American citizen in Yemen who was involved in the war on terror. But what moral choices will presidents face when autonomous systems range over wide areas for long periods?

Under the influence of the information revolution and globalization, world politics is changing in a way that means that even if the United States remains the largest power, it cannot achieve many of its international goals acting alone. For example, international financial stability is vital to the prosperity of Americans, but the United States needs the cooperation of others to ensure it. Transnational interdependence continues to increase. Regardless of potential setbacks to economic globalization, environmental globalization will increase. Climate change and rising sea levels will affect the quality of life for everyone, but Americans cannot manage the problem alone. And in a world where borders are becoming more porous to everything from drugs to infectious diseases to terrorism, nations must use soft power to develop networks and build regimes and institutions to address shared threats and challenges.

This is why the third aspect of American exceptionalism—size—will become of even greater moral significance. As we have seen, a classic problem with public goods (like clean air, which all can share and from which none can be excluded) is that if the largest consumer does not take the lead, others will free-ride and the public goods will not be produced. The case for the largest country providing leadership in organizing the production of global public goods remains stronger than ever in the "neofeudal" setting. Trump's National Security Strategy focuses on great power competition among states, but says little about these increasingly important transnational threats to national security. As the technology expert Richard Danzig summarizes the problem, "Twenty-first-century technologies are global not just in their distribution, but also in their consequences. Pathogens, AI systems, computer viruses, and radiation that others may accidentally release could become as much our problem as theirs. Agreed reporting systems, shared controls, common contingency plans, norms and treaties must be pursued as a means of moderating our numerous mutual risks."[41] Tariffs and walls cannot solve these problems.

In some areas of military and economic public goods, unilateral American leadership can provide a large part of the answer. For example, the American Navy is crucial in policing the law of the sea and defending freedom of navigation, and in the 2008 financial crisis, the crucial role of lender of last resort was provided by the Federal Reserve Bank.[42] But on the new transnational issues, while American leadership will be important, success will require the cooperation of others. Acting alone, for example, the United States cannot cope with the problem of global climate change. And in confronting geo-economic challenges, the United States will have to work more closely with Europe (an economy larger than China) rather than in the dismissive manner of the Trump administration.

In this sense, power becomes a positive sum game. It will not be enough to think in terms of American power *over* others. One must also think in terms of power *to* accomplish joint goals, which involves power *with* others. On many transnational issues, empowering others can help the United States to accomplish its own goals. The United States benefits if China improves its energy efficiency and emits less carbon dioxide. In this world, networks and connectedness become an important source of relevant power. In a world of growing complexity, the most connected states are the most powerful. Fortunately, the United States comes first in Australia's Lowy Institute ranking of nations by number of embassies, consulates, and missions. Washington also has some sixty treaty allies; China has few.[43]

In the past, the openness of the United States enhanced its capacity to build networks, maintain institutions, and sustain alliances. But will that openness and willingness to engage with the rest of the world prove sustainable in American domestic politics, or will we see a twenty-first-century analogue to the 1930s? Even if the United States continues to possess more military, economic, and soft power resources than any other country, it may not choose to convert those resources into effective power behavior on the global scene. Between the two world wars, it did not. In a view that former

Secretary of State Madeleine Albright expressed in 2018, "I fear a return to the international climate that prevailed in the 1920s and '30s."[44]

If the key to America's future security and prosperity is learning the importance of "power with" as well as "power over," the opening years of the Trump administration are not encouraging. "America First" means every country puts its interests first, but the important question is how broadly or narrowly those interests are defined. Trump has shown an inclination toward short-term, zero-sum transactional interpretations with little attention to institutions and a long shadow of the future. The United States has stepped back from long-term enlightened self-interest. Perhaps the major threat to the future of the American open order is not from without but from within?

Power Conversion and the Threat From Within

The 2016 presidential election was marked by populist reactions to globalization and trade agreements in both political parties. Populism generally signifies a resistance to elites, including the type of institutions and commentators who supported the liberal international order over the past seven decades. As we saw in chapter 1, populism is not new and it is as American as pumpkin pie. Some populist reactions are healthy for democracy (think of Andrew Jackson or the Progressive era at the beginning of the last century), while other nativist populists such the anti-immigrant Know-Nothing Party in the nineteenth century or Senator Joe McCarthy and Governor George Wallace in the twentieth century have emphasized xenophobia and insularity. The recent wave of populism includes both strands.

The roots of populist reactions are both economic and cultural and the subject of important social science research.[45] Voters who lost jobs to foreign competition tended to support Trump, but so did groups like older white males who lost status in the culture wars that date back to the 1970s and involve changing values related to race, gender, and sexual preference. Alan Abramowitz shows that "racial resentment was the single strongest predictor for Trump among Republican primary voters," but the explanations are not mutually exclusive and Trump "explicitly connected these issues by arguing that illegal immigrants were taking jobs from American citizens."[46] Even if there had been no economic globalization or liberal international order, these domestic cultural and demographic changes would have created some degree of populism, as we saw in the 1920s and 1930s. Populism is likely to continue as jobs are lost to robotics as much as to trade, and cultural change continues to be divisive.

The lesson for policy elites who support globalization and an open economy is that they will have to pay more attention to issues of economic inequality as well as adjustment assistance for those disrupted by change, both domestic and foreign.[47] Attitudes toward immigration improve as the economy improves, but it remains an emotional cultural issue. In a Pew survey, in 2015, 51 percent of US adults said immigrants strengthened the country while 41 percent believed they were a burden, compared to 50 percent viewing them as a burden in mid-2010, when the effects of the Great Recession were at their peak.[48] Immigration is a source of America's long-term comparative advantage, but political leaders will have to show that they are able to manage the nation's borders if they wish to fend off nativist attacks, particularly in times and places of economic stress.

However, one should not read too much about long-term trends in American public opinion from the heated rhetoric of the 2016 election or Trump's brilliant use of social media to manipulate the news agenda with cultural wedge issues. While Trump won the Electoral College, he fell three million short in the popular vote, and foreign policy was not the major issue. A September 2016 poll by the Chicago Council on Global Affairs found that 65 percent of Americans said that globalization is mostly good for the United States despite the concern about jobs.[49] While polls are always susceptible to framing by altering the wording and order of questions, the label "isolationism" is not an accurate description of current American attitudes.

Some Americans worry whether the United States can economically afford to sustain an open international order, but the United States currently spends about 3.5 percent of its GDP on defense and foreign affairs. Even if one includes hidden costs related to intelligence or veterans care, as a portion of GDP the United States is spending less than half of what it did at the peak of the Cold War years. In the Eisenhower era, the number exceeded 10 percent. Alliances are not that expensive; Japan pays most of the costs of hosting American troops there. The problem is not guns versus butter, but guns versus butter versus taxes. Unless the budget is expanded by a willingness to raise revenues, defense expenditure is locked in a zero-sum trade-off with important investments such as domestic repair of education, infrastructure, and spending on research and development. Despite political rhetoric, careful analysis shows that the United States remains among the most lightly taxed of all the major developed countries. The OECD average income tax rate in 2012 was 10 percentage points higher than that of the United States.

Another domestic challenge for maintaining an open international order is the age-old issue of intervention. How and in what way should the United States become involved in the internal affairs of other countries? In an age of transnational terrorism and transnational refugee crises and humanitarian crises, some degree of intervention is likely to persist. The Middle East, however, is likely to experience political and religious revolutions for decades, much as Germany experienced in the Thirty Years War of the seventeenth century. These crises will create temptations to intervene, but the United States will need to stay out of the business of invasion and occupation or coercive democracy promotion. In an age of nationalism and socially mobilized populations, even if foreign occupation is initially welcomed, it is bound to breed resentment, as Clinton discovered in Somalia and Bush experienced in Iraq. Periods of maximalist overcommitment have done more damage than retrenchment to the domestic consensus needed to support an open international order. Kennedy's and Johnson's escalation of the war in Vietnam produced an inward-oriented decade in the 1970s, as did Bush's invasion of Iraq in 2003. The hard moral choices will be finding forms of involvement short of large-scale military intervention.

A crucial issue for sustaining domestic support for an open international order is political polarization, and the tendency to use demagogic tactics on foreign policy issues. Such tactics undercut the American ability to bolster institutions, create networks, and establish policies for dealing with the new transnational challenges we face. Nativist demagogy reduces

American soft power. International public opinion polls show a decline in the attractive power of the United States since 2017. Domestic political gridlock often blocks such international leadership. Well before Trump, the US Senate failed to ratify the UN Convention of the Law of the Sea despite pleas from Secretaries of State and Defense. And Nixon, not Trump, was the first president to court domestic votes by unilateral imposition of tariffs on allies and breaking the rules of the Bretton Woods system.[50] In terms of leading on climate change, there is strong domestic resistance to putting a price on carbon emissions. Such attitudes weaken the ability of the United States to take the lead in dealing with global public goods.

Another important aspect of value promotion in foreign policy for future presidents relates to maintaining international order and institutions. As we saw in chapter 1, Wilson's liberal legacy was twofold: promotion of liberal democracy, and creating institutions that would allow states to better cooperate. Institutions are an indirect way to promote values through the creation of global public goods. Order rests on a relatively stable distribution of power as realists describe, but it also benefits from a legitimizing institutional regime to manage security, economic concerns, and ecological interdependence. Institutions help to lengthen the shadow of the future that encourages reciprocity and cooperation.

Alliances like NATO can affect expectations, but security is also enhanced by the existence of institutions like the UN and the Non-Proliferation Treaty and the International Atomic Energy Agency. Open markets and economic globalization can be disruptive, but they also create wealth (albeit often unequally distributed). Maintaining financial stability is crucial to the daily lives of millions of Americans and foreigners alike, even though they may not notice until it is absent. And no matter what nativist political backlash does to economic globalization, ecological globalization will remain. Greenhouse gases and pandemics do not respect sovereign borders. A policy of denial of the science does not reverse physical forces.

States will need a framework to enhance cooperation for uses of the sea, space, coping with climate change, and pandemics. Referring to such a framework as a liberal international order confuses choices by conflating two aspects of Wilson's liberal legacy: direct promotion of liberal democratic values, and creation of an institutional framework for promoting global public goods. The degree of policy intervention a president chooses regarding democracy and human rights promotion can be different from the degree of support for institutions designed to cope with security, economic, and ecological interdependence. The two dimensions of Wilson's liberal legacy can be pursued independently.

In 2019, after two years of the Trump presidency, of the four major strands of the so-called liberal order identified earlier—security, economics, global commons, and values like human rights and democracy—the record was mixed. While the Trump administration weakened American alliances, it had not destroyed them. And the security regimes for restraining proliferation of weapons of mass destruction were challenged, but remained in place. On economic institutions, the damage appeared to be greater to the trade regime than to the monetary order (where the dollar still dominated). On global commons issues, the Trump administration withdrew US participation in the Paris Climate Accords, but market forces and local efforts continued to have some effect.

As for values, in contrast to his predecessors, Trump showed less interest in human rights and often embraced authoritarian leaders. But values are an important part of American soft power. The United States cannot "necessarily outbid China, which has more cash on hand to spend abroad, but it can out-persuade and out-inspire."[51] Some defenders of the administration argue that his unorthodox style and willingness to break institutions will produce major gains on issues like North Korean nuclear weapons or changing Chinese behavior regarding coerced intellectual property transfer. But even so, as the *Economist* argued, the institutional costs of using a wrecking-ball approach may reduce American power to deal with the new transnational issues discussed here.[52] If that proves true, it will prove costly for our national security, prosperity, and way of life.

CONCLUSIONS

The United States will remain the world's leading military power in the decades to come, and military force will remain an important component of power in global politics. In other words, size, the third major source of American exceptionalism, will remain important, and "the distribution of capabilities among states is not shifting nearly as much or as quickly as is commonly believed."[53] China will narrow the gap, but barring unforeseen surprises, the United States is likely to remain the largest country in overall power.

But the Washington conventional wisdom about what the United States should do with its power is undergoing a sea change. The newfound popularity of a grand strategic approach that is alternatively called offshore balancing, retrenchment, disengagement, or restraint reflects shifts in US public opinion after the Cold War. Even before the inauguration of the Trump administration in 2017, some scholars and pundits were questioning the post-1945 order. American foreign policy has always had patterns of oscillation between overreaching and retrenchment.[54] A cycle of retrenchment in reaction to the unipolar illusion had begun well before the election of Donald Trump.

At the same time, a rising China and a declining Russia frighten their neighbors, and American security guarantees in Asia and Europe provide critical reassurance for the stability that underlies prosperity. Yet military force is a blunt instrument. Trying to occupy and control the domestic politics of nationalistic and religious populations in other countries is a recipe for failure that will prove counterproductive. And on many transnational issues like climate change or financial stability or norms to govern the Internet, military force is not the answer. Naval power does not produce cyberpower. Maintaining networks, working with institutions, creating norms and regimes for new areas like cyber and climate change create the soft power needed to complement America's hard power resources. Yet this is the type of power that Trump's unilateralist policies weaken.

The terms "liberal international order" or "Pax Americana" that were used to describe the period after World War II have become obsolete as descriptions of the US place in the world. Nonetheless, the need remains for the largest countries to take the lead in creating public goods or they will not be provided, and Americans, among others, will suffer. An open and rules-based international order covers political-military affairs, economic relations, ecological relations, and human rights. It remains to be seen to what degree these depend on each other and what will remain as the 1945 package is unpacked.

What is clear is that withdrawal from international problems will not be possible, and isolation is not an option. Nationalism versus globalization is a false choice. As we have seen, humans are capable of multiple identities. The issue is not national identity *or* global concern, but a strong national identity *and* global concern. As one historian put it, "Like it or not, humankind faces three common problems that make a mockery of all national borders, and that can be solved only through global cooperation"—nuclear war, climate change, and technological disruption.[55]

The important moral choices for future presidents will be about where and how to be involved. American leadership is not the same as hegemony or domination or military intervention. Even in its heyday, the United States has always needed help from others. There have always been degrees of leadership and degrees of influence during the seven decades of American pre-eminence after 1945. The United States has always relied on networks of multilayered partnerships with others and functioned most effectively when our presidents understood that. Hegemony (in the sense of control) and unipolarity after 1989 were always illusions. Now, with illusions stripped away, the moral choices involved in leadership are more clear.

Foreign partners help when they want to, and that willingness to help is affected not just by our hard military and economic power but also by our soft power of attraction based on an open rather than nativist ethnic culture, our liberal democratic values, and our policies, when they are formulated in ways that are seen as legitimate in the eyes of others. Jeffersonian respect for the opinions of humankind and Wilsonian use of institutions that encourage reciprocity and a long shadow of the future have been crucial to the success of American foreign policy. International order has depended on the ability of a leading state to combine power and legitimacy. Morals matter, when seen in all three dimensions, because they are part of the secret of a successful international order.

Now with less preponderance and a more complex world, the 46th president will face the moral challenge of defining a foreign policy where

America provides global public goods in cooperation with others, and uses not only our hard power but also our soft power to attract their cooperation. We have seen that the success of the era of American primacy after 1945 depended on that formula. We will need to exercise power with as well as power over others. This will not change, but rather will be accentuated by the new transnational problems of the twenty-first century. The future success of American foreign policy may be threatened more by the rise of nativist politics that narrow our moral vision at home than by the rise and decline of other powers abroad.

NOTES

Preface

1. Michael Walzer, *Arguing About War* (New Haven, CT: Yale University Press, 2004), 6.
2. Robert W. McElroy, *Morality and American Foreign Policy: The Role of Ethics in International Affairs* (Princeton, NJ: Princeton University Press, 1992), 3. See also Richard Price, "Moral Limit and Possibility in World Politics," *International Organization* 62 (Spring 2008), 193.
3. George Kennan, *American Diplomacy, 1900–1950* (Chicago: University of Chicago Press, 1951).
4. Richard Haass, *War of Necessity, War of Choice* (New York: Simon & Schuster, 2009).
5. Mark Landler, "Trump Stands With Saudis Over Murder of Khashoggi," *New York Times*, November 21, 2018, A1.
6. "Trump's Crude Realpolitik; His Statement about the Saudis Had No Mention of America's Values," *Wall Street Journal*, November 21, 2018.

Chapter 1

1. Donald J. Trump, Inaugural Address, January 20, 2017.
2. James Chace, *1912: Wilson, Roosevelt, Taft and Debs—the Election that Changed the Country* (New York: Simon and Schuster, 2004), 108.
3. Jake Sullivan, "What Donald Trump and Dick Cheney Got Wrong About America," *The Atlantic*, January/February 2019, https://www.theatlantic.com/magazine/archive/2019/01/yes-america-can-still-lead-the-world/576247/.
4. Ben Rhodes, *The World as It Is: A Memoir of the Obama White House* (New York: Random House, 2018), 41.
5. Stanley Hoffmann, *Chaos and Violence: What Globalization, Failed States, and Terrorism Mean for U.S. Foreign Policy* (Lanham, MD: Rowman & Littlefield, 2006), 115.
6. Morgenthau quoted in Robert W. McElroy, *Morality and American Foreign Policy: The Role of Ethics in International Affairs* (Princeton, NJ: Princeton University Press, 1992), 25.
7. Senator John F. Kennedy, quoted in Jonathan Rauch, "Real Is Not a Four-Letter Word," *National Journal*, June 9, 2006.

8. Daniel Deudney and Jeffrey W. Meiser, "American Exceptionalism," in *US Foreign Policy*, 3rd ed., ed. Michael Cox and Doug Stokes (Oxford: Oxford University Press, 2018), 23.

9. See examples in Constance G. Anthony, "American Democratic Interventionism: Romancing the Iconic Woodrow Wilson," *International Studies Perspectives* 9, no. 3 (August 2008), 249.

10. Deudney and Meiser, "American Exceptionalism," 23.

11. There were also other strands. See Walter A. McDougall, "America's Machiavellian Moment: Origins of the Atlantic Republican Tradition," *Orbis* 82 (Fall 2018), 505.

12. Robert D. Kaplan, *Earning the Rockies: How Geography Shapes America's Role in the World* (New York: Random House, 2017), 142.

13. John Milton Cooper Jr., *Woodrow Wilson: A Biography* (New York: Knopf, 2009).

14. Deudney and Meiser, "American Exceptionalism," 34.

15. Quoted in Arthur Link, "The Higher Realism of Woodrow Wilson," in *Ethics and Statecraft: The Moral Dimension of International Affairs*, 2nd ed., ed. Cathal J. Nolan (Westport, CT: Praeger, 2008), 131.

16. John Mearsheimer, *The Great Delusion: Liberal Dreams and International Realities* (New Haven, CT: Yale University Press, 2018), 218–19.

17. Mearsheimer, *The Great Delusion*, 5.

18. Henry Kissinger, *Diplomacy* (New York: Simon and Schuster, 1994), 54.

19. Henry Kissinger, *World Order* (New York: Penguin, 2014), 268.

20. Stephen Sestanovich, *Maximalist: America in the World from Truman to Obama* (New York: Knopf, 2014).

21. Tony Smith, *Why Wilson Matters: The Origin of American Liberal Internationalism and Its Crisis Today* (Princeton, NJ: Princeton University Press, 2017), 4–5.

22. Andrew J. Bacevich, *Washington Rules: America's Path to Permanent War* (New York: Henry Holt, 2010), 143.

23. Alan I. Abramowitz, *The Great Alignment: Race, Party Transformation, and the Rise of Donald Trump* (New Haven, CT: Yale University Press, 2018), 156.

24. Robert Dallek, *The American Style of Foreign Policy: Cultural Politics and Foreign Affairs* (New York: Knopf, 1983), 110–12.

25. See Jon Meacham, *The Soul of America* (New York: Random House, 2018).

26. Abramowitz, *The Great Alignment*, x.

27. Stephen Walt, *The Hell of Good Intentions: America's Foreign Policy Elite and the Decline of US Primacy* (New York: FSG, 2018).

28. Ivo H. Daalder and James M. Lindsay, *The Empty Throne: America's Abdication of Global Leadership* (New York: Public Affairs, 2018), 35

29. Chicago Council on Global Affairs, *America Engaged: American Public Opinion and US Foreign Policy* (Chicago, 2018). Pew Research Center, "Public Uncertain, Divided Over America's Place in the World," Washington, DC, May 5, 2016.

30. Daniel Drezner, "The Realist Tradition in American Public Opinion," *Perspectives on Politics* 6, no. 1 (March 2008), 63.

31. Benjamin Page with Marshall Bouton, *The Foreign Policy Dis-Connect: What Americans Want From Our Leaders but Don't Get* (Chicago: University of Chicago Press, 2006) 229, 231, 241–42.

32. Walter Russell Mead argues that Trump's supporters were a combination of Jeffersonian isolationists and assertive Jacksonian populists. "Trump Is No Isolationist," *Wall Street Journal*, October 23, 2018, A13.

33. Frances Z. Brown and Thomas Carothers, "Is the New US National Security Strategy a Step Backward on Democracy and Human Rights?," Carnegie Endowment for International Peace, https://carnegieendowment.org/2018/01/30/is-new-u.s.-national-security-strategy-step-backward-on-democracy-and-human-rights-pub-75376

34. John Quincy Adams, quoted in Gary Bass, *Freedom's Battle: The Origins of Humanitarian Intervention* (New York: Random House, 2009), 89.

35. Donald J. Trump, "Remarks by President Trump on the Administration's National Security Strategy," The White House, December 17, 2018, https://www.whitehouse.gov/briefings-statements/remarks-president-trump-administrations-national-security-strategy/.

36. Gary J. Bass, *Freedom's Battle: The Origins of Humanitarian Intervention* (New York: Knopf, 2008), 3.

37. US National Security Strategy, March 2006.

38. Patrick Porter, "A World Imagined: Nostalgia and the Liberal Order," *Policy Analysis* Number 843, Cato Institute, Washington, June 5, 2018. See also Amitav Acharya, *The End of American World Order*, 2nd ed. (Cambridge: Polity Press, 2018).

39. Steven Pinker, *Enlightenment Now: The Case for Reason, Science, Humanism and Progress* (New York: Viking, 2018). The number of electoral democracies tripled; world economic output quadrupled, and the proportion of people in extreme poverty dropped in half. See Francis Fukuyama, "Against Identity Politics," *Foreign Affairs* 97, no. 5 (September/October 2018), 90.

Chapter 2

1. Thucydides, *The Peloponnesian War*, translated by Rex Warner (London: Penguin Classics, 1954).

2. Owen Harries, "Power and Morals," *Prospect*, April 2005, 26.

3. James Q. Wilson, *The Moral Sense* (New York: Free Press, 1997), 15.

4. Jonathan Haidt, *The Righteous Mind: Why Good People Are Divided by Politics and Religion* (New York: Random House, 2012), xx.

5. "Philosophy and Neuroscience: Posing the Right Question," *The Economist*, March 24, 2007, 92.

6. See Kenneth Winston, *Ethics in Public Life: Good Practitioners in a Rising Asia* (London: Palgrave, 2015), chapter 1.

7. Garry Wills, "The Pious Presidency of Jimmy Carter," *New York Times Book Review*, April 26, 2018.

8. Ari Fleisher, "What I Will Miss About President Bush," *New York Times*, November 4, 2008.

9. Joseph Nye Jr., *Soft Power* (New York: Public Affairs, 2004).

10. General James Mattis, "Hearing to Receive Testimony on U.S. Central Command and U.S. Special Operations Command in Review of the Defense Authorization Request for Fiscal Year 2014 and the Future Years Defense Program," March 5, 2013, 16.

11. On the importance and dimensions of contextual intelligence, see Joseph S. Nye Jr., *The Powers to Lead* (New York: Oxford University Press, 2008), chapter 4. See also Anthony J. Mayo and Nitin Nohria, *In Their Time: The Greatest Business Leaders of the Twentieth Century* (Boston: Harvard Business School Press, 2005).

12. Egil Krogh, "The Break-In That History Forgot," *New York Times*, June 30, 2007, 17.

13. Donald J. Trump, "As has been stated by numerous legal scholars, I have the absolute right to PARDON myself, but why would I do that when I have done nothing wrong? In the meantime, the never ending Witch Hunt, led by 13 very Angry and Conflicted Democrats (& others) continues into the mid-terms!" Tweet, June 4, 2018.

14. Interview with Dan Amira, *New York Times Magazine*, April 29, 2018, 54.

15. See Michael Walzer, "Political Action: The Problem of Dirty Hands," *Philosophy & Public Affairs* 2, no. 2 (1973), 160–80. See also Gerald F. Gaus, "Dirty Hands," in *A Companion to Applied Ethics*, ed. R. G. Frey and Christopher Heath Wellman (Malden, MA: Blackwell, 2003), 167–79.

16. Max Weber, "Politics as a Vocation," in *Max Weber: Essays in Sociology*, ed. H. R. Gerth and C. Wright Mills (New York: Oxford University Press, 1958), 126.

17. Alexander Betts and Paul Collier, *Refuge: Rethinking Refugee Policy in a Changing World* (Oxford: Oxford University Press, 2017), 125.

18. Stuart Hampshire, quoted in Joseph L. Badaracco Jr., *Defining Moments: When Managers Must Choose Between Right and Right* (Boston: Harvard Business School Press, 1997), 52.

19. Tom Beauchamp, *Philosophical Ethics: An Introduction to Moral Philosophy* (New York: McGraw Hill, 1982), 179.

20. Walzer, *Arguing About War*, 35–36.

21. With hindsight, historians believe these estimated casualties were too high. J. Samuel Walker, "Recent Literature on Truman's Atomic Bomb Decision: A Search for Middle Ground," *Diplomatic History*, 29, no. 2 (April 2005), 311–34.

22. Nina Tannenwald, *The Nuclear Taboo: The United States and the Non-Use of Nuclear Weapons Since 1945* (Cambridge: Cambridge University Press, 2007), 88. See also, Alex Wellerstein, "Nagasaki: the Last Bomb," *The New Yorker*, August 7, 2015.

23. See Joseph S. Nye Jr., *Nuclear Ethics* (New York: Free Press, 1986), for a fuller description.

24. Charles Guthrie and Michael Quinlan, *Just War: The Just War Tradition: Ethics in Modern Warfare* (New York: Bloomsbury, 2007), 1.

25. Kenneth Winston, "Necessity and Choice in Political Ethics: Varieties of Dirty Hands," in *Political Ethics and Social Responsibility*, ed. Daniel E. Wueste (Lanham, MD: Rowman and Littlefield, 1994), 37–66.

26. Isaiah Berlin, *Liberty: Incorporating Four Essays on Liberty* (New York: Oxford University Press, 2002), 214.

27. Winston Lord, *Kissinger on Kissinger: Reflections on Diplomacy, Grand Strategy and Leadership* (New York: St. Martins Press, 2019), 2.

28. John Rawls, "Distributive Justice," ed. Peter Laslett and W. G. Runciman, *Philosophy, Politics, and Society* (London: Blackwell, 1967), 58–82.

29. Amartya Sen, *The Idea of Justice* (Cambridge, MA: The Belknap Press of Harvard University Press, 2011), 12–13.

30. Robert Axelrod, *The Evolution of Cooperation* (New York: Basic Books, 1984), 128.
31. Graham T. Allison and Lance M. Liebman, "Lying in Office," in *Ethics and Politics: Cases and Comments*, 2nd ed., ed. Amy Gutman and Dennis Thompson (Chicago: Nelson-Hall, 1990), 40–45.
32. Cathal J. Nolan, " 'Bodyguard of Lies': Franklin D. Roosevelt and Defensible Deceit in World War II," in *Ethics and Statecraft: The Moral Dimensions of International Affairs*, 2nd ed., ed. Cathal J. Nolan (Westport, CT: Praeger, 2004), 35–58.
33. John Mearsheimer, *Why Leaders Lie* (Oxford: Oxford University Press, 2011), viii.
34. Tommy Koh, "Can Any Country Afford a Moral Foreign Policy?" in *The Quest for World Order: Perspectives of a Pragmatic Idealist*, edited with an introduction by Amitav Acharya (Singapore: Times Academic Press, 1997), 2. I am indebted to Amitav Acharya for bringing this quote to my attention.
35. Allison and Liebman, "Lying in Office," 40.
36. See the arguments in Sisella Bok, *Lying: Moral Choice in Public and Private Life* (New York: Vintage Books, 1999).
37. Zbigniew Brzezinski, *Second Chance: Three Presidents and the Crisis of American Superpower* (New York: Basic Books, 2007), 45.
38. Niccolo Machiavelli, *The Prince*, 142, cited in Badaracco, *Defining Moments*, 110.
39. Caroline Daniel, "Hard Man Who Sits at the Heart of US Foreign Policy," *Financial Times*, December 19, 2002, 14.
40. Hans J. Morgenthau, *Politics Among Nations* (New York: Knopf, 1955), 9.
41. John Mearsheimer, *The Great Delusion: Liberal Dreams and International Realities* (New Haven, CT: Yale University Press, 2018), 216.
42. Robert D. Kaplan, *The Return of Marco Polo's World* (New York: Random House, 2018), 146.
43. Walzer, *Arguing About War*, 33–34.
44. See Stephen A. Garrett, "Political Leadership and Dirty Hands: Winston Churchill and the City Bombing of Germany," *Ethics and Statecraft*.
45. The White House, "Statement From President Donald J. Trump on Standing With Saudi Arabia," November 20, 2018.
46. Randy Schweller, "Three Cheers for Trump's Foreign Policy," *Foreign Affairs* 97, no. 5 (September/October 2018), 134.
47. David Luban, "The Romance of the Nation State," *Philosophy and Public Affairs* 9 (Summer 1980), 392.
48. Kwame Anthony Appiah, "The Importance of Elsewhere," *Foreign Affairs* 98, no. 2 (March/April 2019), 20.
49. Stanley Hoffmann, *Duties Beyond Borders* (Syracuse, NY: Syracuse University Press, 1981), 155.
50. See Betts and Collier, *Refuge*, chapter 8.
51. Daniel Deudney and G. John Ikenberry, "Liberal World: The Resilient Order," *Foreign Affairs* 97, no. 4 (July/August 2018), 16.
52. Barbara Kellerman, *Bad Leadership* (Boston: Harvard Business School Press, 2004), chapter 9.
53. Michael Walzer, *Just and Unjust Wars* (New York: Basic Books, 1977), 101.

54. Gary J. Bass, *Freedom's Battle: The Origins of Humanitarian Intervention* (New York: Random House, 2008), 4.

55. Daniel Drezner, "The Realist Tradition in American Public Opinion," *Perspectives on Politics* 6 (March 2008), 63.

56. Stephen Walt, *The Hell of Good Intentions: America's Foreign Policy Elite and the Decline of US Primacy* (New York: FSG, 2018).

57. Page and Bouton, *The Foreign Policy Dis-Connect*, 241.

58. See Gautam Makunda, *Indispensable: When Leaders Really Matter* (Boston: Harvard Business School Press, 2012).

59. Daniel Deudney and John Ikenberry, "Realism, Liberalism and the Iraq War," *Survival* 59, no. 4 (August–September 2017), 7–26.

60. Stephen Walt, "What Would a Realist World Have Looked Like?" *Foreign Policy*, January 8, 2016.

61. Quoted in Max Fisher, "Syrian War Magnifies Tension in America's Global Mission," *New York Times*, October 9, 2016, 16. See also Sean Lynn-Jones, "Why the United States Should Spread Democracy," Discussion Paper 98-07, Center for Science and International Affairs, Harvard University, March 1998.

62. Arnold Wolfers, *Discord and Collaboration: Essays on International Politics* (Baltimore: Johns Hopkins University Press, 1962), 47–65.

63. John Rawls, *A Theory of Justice* (Cambridge, MA: Harvard University Press, 1971).

64. John Rawls, *The Law of Peoples* (Cambridge, MA: Harvard University Press, 1999).

65. Brzezinski, *Second Chance*.

66. Anthony J. Mayo and Nitin Nohria, *In Their Time: The Greatest Business Leaders of the Twentieth Century* (Boston: Harvard Business School Press, 2005). See also Nye, *The Powers to Lead*, chapter 4.

67. For a more detailed discussion of emotional intelligence, see Nye, *The Powers to Lead*, 69–71.

68. Derek Chollet, "Altered State: Rice Aims to Put Foggy Bottom Back on the Map," *Washington Post*, April 7, 2005.

69. Henry Kissinger, *World Order* (New York: Penguin, 2014), 367.

Chapter 3

1. FDR quoted in Gideon Rose, "The Fourth Founding," *Foreign Affairs* 98 (January/February 2019), 21.

2. Arne Westad, *The Cold War: A World History* (New York: Basic Books, 2017), 65.

3. On the limits of the concept of American hegemony and why I call it "half-hegemony," see my book *Is the American Century Over?* (Cambridge: Polity, 2015), chapter 1.

4. "On This Day in History: A Memorable Headline from The New York Times. President Insists US-Soviet Amity Is Key to Peace," *New York Times*, November 17, 2018, A2.

5. C-SPAN 2017 Survey of Presidential Leadership, February 14, 2017, https://static.c-span.org/assets/documents/presidentSurvey/2017%20C-SPAN%20Presidential%20Survey%20Scores%20and%20Ranks%20FINAL.PDF.See also, Brian Lamb, Susan Swain, Douglas Brinkley, and Richard Norton Smith, *The*

Presidents: Noted Historians Rank America's Best – and Worst – Chief Executives.
(New York, Public Affairs, 2019).

6. Robert Dallek, *Franklin Roosevelt and American Foreign Policy, 1932–1945* (Oxford: Oxford University Press, 1995), 548.

7. Barbara Farnham, *Roosevelt and the Munich Crisis: A Study of Political Decision-Making* (Princeton, NJ: Princeton University Press, 1997), 49.

8. David K. Adams, "The Concept of Parallel Action: FDR's Internationalism in a Decade of Isolationism," in *From Theodore Roosevelt to FDR: Internationalism and Isolationism in American Foreign Policy* (Staffordshire, UK: Keele University Press, 1995), 115; Steven Casey, *Cautious Crusade: Franklin D. Roosevelt, American Public Opinion, and the War Against Nazi Germany* (New York: Oxford University Press, 2001), 23; Adam J. Berinksy, *In a Time of War* (Chicago: University of Chicago Press, 2009), 46.

9. Quoted in Michael Fullilove, *Rendezvous With Destiny: How Franklin D. Roosevelt and Five Extraordinary Men Took America Into the War and Into the World* (New York: Penguin, 2013), 23.

10. Dallek, *Franklin Roosevelt*, 540.

11. See the discussion in Marc Trachtenberg, *The Craft of International History: A Guide to Method* (Princeton, NJ: Princeton University Press, 2006), chapter 4.

12. Christopher Darnton, "Archives and Inference: Documentary in Evidence in Case Study Research and the Debate Over US Entry Into World War II," *International Security* 42, no. 3 (Winter 2017/2018), 120.

13. Garry Wills, *Certain Trumpets: The Call of Leaders* (New York: Simon & Schuster, 1994), 27–30.

14. Nolan, " 'Bodyguard of Lies,' " 37.

15. Nolan, " 'Bodyguard of Lies,' " 37, 50, 53.

16. See William Taubman, *Stalin's America Policy: From Entente to Detente to Cold War* (New York: Norton, 1982).

17. On this example and the general importance of emotional intelligence, see Nye, *The Powers to Lead*, 69–71.

18. See Philip Roth, *The Plot Against America* (New York: Houghton Mifflin, 2004), for a novelist's counterfactual exploration of the scenario.

19. Benn Steil, *The Marshall Plan: Dawn of the Cold War* (New York: Simon & Schuster, 2018), 3.

20. David McCullough, *Truman* (New York: Simon & Schuster, 1992), 141.

21. George H. Gallup, *The Gallup Poll: Public Opinion 1935–1971* (New York: Random House, 1972), 534–35.

22. Gallup, *The Gallup Poll*, 534.

23. Robert Shapiro, "The Legacy of the Marshall Plan: American Public Support for Foreign Aid," in *The Marshall Plan: Fifty Years After*, ed. Martin A. Schain (New York: Palgrave, 2001), 270.

24. Ernest May, "The Nature of Foreign Policy: The Calculated Versus the Axiomatic," *Daedalus* 91, no. 4 (1962): 653–57.

25. Walter Isaacson and Evan Thomas, *The Wise Men* (New York: Simon & Schuster, 1986), 508.

26. Taubman, *Stalin's America Policy*.
27. Issacson and Thomas, *The Wise Men*, 376.
28. Robert Dallek, *The American Style of Foreign Policy* (New York: Knopf, 1983), 157.
29. Benn Steil, "How to Win a Great Power Competition," *Foreign Affairs* 97 (February 9, 2018).
30. See Alonzo Hamby, "Harry S. Truman: Insecurity and Responsibility," in Fred I. Greenstein, ed., *Leadership in the Modern Presidency* (Cambridge, MA: Harvard University Press, 1988).
31. Issacson and Thomas, *The Wise Men*, 407.
32. See Michael Beschloss, *Presidential Courage* (New York: Simon & Schuster, 2007), 196–234.
33. H. W. Brands, *The General vs. the President: MacArthur and Truman at the Brink of Nuclear War* (New York: Doubleday, 2016).
34. See Hamby, "Harry S. Truman," 35–36. See also John Lewis Gaddis, *Strategies of Containment* (New York: Oxford University Press, 1982).
35. Geir Lundstadt, "Empire by Invitation? The United States and Western Europe, 1945–1952," *Journal of Peace Research* 23, no. 3 (September 1986), 263–77.
36. Martin H. Folly, "Harry S. Truman," in *US Foreign Policy and Democracy Promotion*, ed. Michael Cox, Timothy Lynch, and Nicolas Bouchet (London: Routledge, 2013), 91.
37. Hamby, "Harry S. Truman," 42.
38. "Timeless Leadership: A Conversation With David McCullough," *Harvard Business Review*, March 2008, 3.
39. Hamby, "Harry S. Truman," 64.
40. Issacson and Thomas, *The Wise Men*, 410.
41. Quoted in Anne Pierce, *Woodrow Wilson and Harry Truman: Mission and Power in American Foreign Policy* (Westport, CT: Praeger, 2003), 126.
42. Nina Tannenwald, *The Nuclear Taboo: The United States and the Non-Use of Nuclear Weapons Since 1945* (Cambridge: Cambridge University Press, 2007), 107.
43. Tannenwald, *The Nuclear Taboo*, 110.
44. Raymond Aron, *The Century of Total War* (Garden City, NY: Doubleday, 1954); see also Morton Halperin, *Limited War in the Nuclear Age* (New York: Wiley, 1963).
45. Steil, *The Marshall Plan*, 291.
46. Brands, *The General vs. the President*, chapter 13.
47. Dean Acheson, *Present at the Creation: My Years in the State Department* (New York: Norton, 1969), 526–28.
48. Truman quoted in Jonathan Schell, *The Unconquerable World: Power, Nonviolence, and the Will of the People* (New York: Metropolitan Books, 2003), 47.
49. Alan Axelrod, *Eisenhower on Leadership* (San Francisco: Jossey-Bass, 2006), 283.
50. John Lewis Gaddis, *George F. Kennan: An American Life* (New York: Penguin, 2012), 495.
51. Jean Edward Smith, *Eisenhower: In War and Peace* (New York: Random House, 2012), 701.
52. Ole R. Holsti, *Public Opinion and American Foreign Policy* (Ann Arbor: University of Michigan Press, 1996), 31, 132.

53. Gallup, *The Gallup Poll*, 1262, 1259.
54. William I. Hitchcock, *The Age of Eisenhower: America and the World in the 1950s* (New York: Simon & Schuster, 2018), xv.
55. Fredrik Logevall, *Embers of War: The Fall of an Empire and the Making of America's Vietnam* (New York: Random House, 2012), 508–9.
56. Fredrik Logevall, "We Might Give Them a Few: Did the US Offer to Drop Atom Bombs at Dien Bien Phu?" *Bulletin of the Atomic Scientists*, February 21, 2016. I am also indebted to Marc Trachtenberg on this point.
57. Stephen Ambrose, *Eisenhower: The President*, vol. II (New York: Simon & Schuster, 1984), 11, 17.
58. Fred I. Greenstein, *The Presidential Difference: Leadership Style from FDR to George W. Bush*, 2nd ed. (Princeton, NJ: Princeton University Press, 2004), 57.
59. Stephen Ambrose, *Eisenhower: Soldier and President* (New York: Simon & Schuster, 1991), 547, 542.
60. See Stephen Kinzer, *The Brothers: John Foster Dulles, Allen Dulles, and Their Secret World War* (New York: Henry Holt, 2013).
61. Smith, *Eisenhower*, 614.
62. Hitchcock, *The Age of Eisenhower*, 433.
63. Lindsey A. O'Rourke, *Covert Regime Change: America's Secret Cold War* (Ithaca, NY: Cornell University Press, 2018).
64. Ambrose, *Eisenhower: The President*, 626.
65. Dwight Eisenhower, *Mandate for Change, 1953–1956* (New York: New American Library, 1963), 510.
66. See Kinzer, *The Brothers*.
67. Hitchcock, *The Age of Eisenhower*, 434.
68. Ambrose, *Eisenhower: The President*, 206.
69. Sestanovich, *Maximalist*, 79.
70. Evan Thomas, *Ike's Bluff: President Eisenhower's Secret Battle to Save the World* (New York: Little Brown, 2012), 15.
71. H. W. Brands, "Gambling With the Fate of the World," *National Interest* (November/ December 2012), 88–96.
72. Fred Greenstein, *The Hidden-Hand Presidency* (New York: Basic Books, 1982), 69.
73. Greenstein, *The Hidden-Hand Presidency*.
74. Isaacson and Thomas, *The Wise Men*, 246.
75. Nina Tannenwald, "How Strong Is the Nuclear Taboo Today?" *Washington Quarterly* 41, no. 3 (Fall 2018), 89–109; Scott Sagan and Benjamin Valentino, "Revisiting Hiroshima in Iran: What Americans Really Think About Using Nuclear Weapons and Killing Noncombatants," *International Security* 42, no. 1 (Summer 2017), 41–79; Reid B. C. Pauly, "Would U.S. Leaders Push the Button? Wargames and the Sources of Nuclear Restraint," *International Security* 43, no. 2 (Fall 2018), 151–92.

Chapter 4

1. Sestanovich, *Maximalist*, 88–89.
2. Gordon M. Goldstein, *Lessons in Disaster: McGeorge Bundy and the Path to War in Vietnam* (New York: Henry Holt, 2008), 168.

3. Jill Abramson, "Kennedy, the Elusive President," *International New York Times*, October 26–27, 2013, 20.
4. Macmillan quoted in Alan Brinkley, *John F. Kennedy* (New York: Henry Holt, 2012), 124.
5. Brinkley, *John F. Kennedy*, 3.
6. Andrew Cohen, *Two Days in June: John F. Kennedy and the 48 Hours That Made History* (Toronto: Signal, McClelland & Stewart, 2014), 41.
7. Jon Roper, "John F. Kennedy and Lyndon Johnson," in *US Foreign Policy and Democracy Promotion*, ed. Cox, Lynch, and Bouchet, 111.
8. Sestanovich, *Maximalist*, 88.
9. Robert Dallek, *An Unfinished Life* (New York: Little Brown, 2003), 683.
10. Michael O'Brien, *Rethinking Kennedy: An Interpretive Biography* (Chicago: Ivan Dee, 2009), 168.
11. Michael A. Roberto, *Why Great Leaders Don't Take Yes for an Answer* (Upper Saddle River, NJ: Wharton School Publishing, 2005), 29–33.
12. Sheldon M. Stern, *The Cuban Missile Crisis in American Memory* (Stanford, CA: Stanford University Press, 2012), 149.
13. Cohen, *Two Days in June*, 24.
14. Khrushchev quoted in Brinkley, *John F. Kennedy*, 80.
15. Goldstein, *Lessons in Disaster*, 245, 248.
16. See James Blight, Janet Lang, and David Welch, *Vietnam If Kennedy Had Lived* (Lanham, MD: Rowman & Littlefield, 2009).
17. Logevall, *Embers of War*, 703.
18. Dallek, *An Unfinished Life*, 684; see also Dallek, "What Made Kennedy Great?" *New York Times*, November 22, 2013, 25.
19. Fredrik Logevall, "Kennedy and What Might Have Been," in *The Vietnam War: An Intimate History*, ed. Geoffrey Ward and Ken Burns (New York: Knopf, 2017), 5–6.
20. Dallek, *An Unfinished Life*, 668.
21. Goldstein, *Lessons in Disaster*, 93.
22. Goldstein, *Lessons in Disaster*, 88.
23. Bowles quoted in Brinkley, *John F. Kennedy*, 84.
24. Niall Ferguson, "Kremlin Back Channels Worked Just Fine for JFK," *Sunday Times* (London), July 16, 2017.
25. Larry Berman, "Lyndon B. Johnson: Paths Chosen and Opportunities Lost," in *Leadership in the Modern Presidency*, ed. Greenstein, 145.
26. Robert Caro, *Master of the Senate: The Years of Lyndon Johnson* (New York: Vintage Books, 2003).
27. Greenstein, *The Presidential Difference*, 79.
28. Moyers quoted in Charles Peters, *Lyndon B. Johnson* (New York: Henry Holt, 2010), 140.
29. Robert Caro, *The Path to Power: The Years of Lyndon Johnson, Volume I* (New York: Vintage, 1982), 96, 32.
30. Berman, "Lyndon B. Johnson," 139, 144.
31. Caro, *The Path to Power*, xvii.
32. Peters, *Lyndon B. Johnson*, 8.

33. Quoted in Peters, *Lyndon B. Johnson*, 82.
34. Doris Kearns Goodwin, *Lyndon Johnson and the American Dream* (New York: St. Martin's, 1991), 251–52.
35. Roper, "John F. Kennedy and Lyndon Johnson," 114.
36. Frederik Logevall, "Why Lyndon Johnson Dropped Out," *New York Times*, March 25, 2018, 7.
37. Peters, *Lyndon B. Johnson*, 94.
38. Goodwin, *Lyndon Johnson and the American Dream*, 311.
39. Goodwin, *Lyndon Johnson and the American Dream*, 322.
40. John P. Burke and Fred I. Greenstein, *How Presidents Test Reality: Decisions on Vietnam, 1954 and 1965* (New York: Russell Sage, 1989), 275.
41. Goodwin, *Lyndon Johnson and the American Dream*, 330.
42. Peters, *Lyndon B. Johnson*, 128.
43. Berman, "Lyndon B. Johnson," 147.
44. H. R. McMaster, *Dereliction of Duty: Lyndon Johnson, Robert McNamara, the Joint Chiefs of Staff, and the Lies That Led to Vietnam* (New York: Harper Collins, 1997), 325.
45. Francis M. Bator, *No Good Choices: LBJ and the Vietnam/Great Society Connection* (Cambridge, MA: American Academy of Arts and Sciences, 2007), 16.
46. Michael Beschloss, *Presidents of War*, 503.
47. "Fredrik Logevall Comment on Francis M. Bator's 'No Good Choices: LBJ and the Vietnam/Great Society Connection,'" *Diplomatic History* 32, no. 3 (June 2008), 365.
48. Logevall, "Comment on Francis Bator," 366–67.
49. Goldstein, *Lessons in Disaster*, 3.
50. Goodwin, *Lyndon Johnson and the American Dream*, 392.
51. David Sanger, "US Commander Moved to Place Nuclear Arms in South Vietnam," *New York Times*, October 7, 2018, A1. See also Goldstein, *Lessons in Disaster*, 161.
52. Edwin E. Moise, *Tonkin Gulf and the Escalation of the Vietnam War* (Chapel Hill: University of North Carolina Press, 1996), 253–55.
53. Caro, *The Path to Power*, xvii.
54. Logevall, "Why Lyndon Johnson Dropped Out."
55. Richard Reeves, *President Nixon* (New York: Simon & Schuster, 2001), 12–13. See also the description by Alexander Butterfield in Bob Woodward, *The Last of the President's Men* (New York: Simon & Schuster, 2015), 94.
56. Greenstein, *The Presidential Difference*, 93.
57. Evan Thomas, *Being Nixon: A Man Divided* (New York: Random House, 2015), 529.
58. David Gergen, *Eyewitness to Power: The Essence of Leadership* (New York: Simon & Schuster 2000), 77, 85.
59. Niall Ferguson, *Kissinger: 1923–1968: The Idealist* (New York: Penguin, 2015), 802.
60. See Margaret McMillan, *Nixon and Mao: The Week That Changed the World* (New York: Random House, 2007).
61. Nigel Bowles, *Nixon's Business* (College Station: Texas A&M Press, 2005), 184.
62. Niall Ferguson, "Our Currency, Your Problem," *New York Times*, March 13, 2005.
63. Bowles, *Nixon's Business*, 179.

64. Gary J. Bass, "Nixon and Kissinger's Forgotten Shame," *New York Times*, September 30, 2013. See also his book *The Blood Telegram: Nixon, Kissinger, and a Forgotten Genocide* (New York: Knopf, 2013), 6–7.

65. John A. Farrell, "Tricky Dick's Treachery," *New York Times*, January 1, 2017. See also Peter Baker, "Nixon Sought 'Monkey Wrench' in Vietnam Talks," *New York Times*, January 3, 2017, 1.

66. Richard Sobel, *The Impact of Public Opinion on U.S. Foreign Policy Since Vietnam* (New York: Oxford University Press, 2001), 37, 81.

67. Thomas, *Being Nixon*, 218–19.

68. Thomas, *Being Nixon*, 429.

69. Ken Hughes, *Chasing Shadows: The Nixon Tapes, the Chennault Affair, and the Origins of Watergate* (Charlottesville: University of Virginia Press, 2014), 102.

70. I am indebted to private communication with Niall Ferguson for this number and his stimulating criticism.

71. Gergen, *Eyewitness to Power*, 61–62.

72. Henry Kissinger, *Diplomacy* (New York: Simon & Schuster, 1994), chapter 2.

73. Gergen, *Eyewitness to Power*, 61.

74. Joseph Nye, Philip Zelikow, and David King, eds., *Why People Don't Trust Government* (Cambridge, MA: Harvard University Press, 1997), 80.

75. Goldstein, *Lessons in Disaster*, 231, 238, 239.

Chapter 5

1. Sestanovich, *Maximalist*, chapter 8.

2. Stuart E. Eizenstat, *President Carter: The White House Years* (New York: St. Martin's Press, 2018), 5.

3. Greenstein, *The Presidential Difference*, 112.

4. Gergen, *Eyewitness to Power*, 140.

5. Gergen, *Eyewitness to Power*, 147.

6. Roger B. Porter, "Gerald R. Ford: A Healing Presidency," in *Leadership in the Modern Presidency*, ed. Greenstein, 199–227.

7. Jan Lodal, "Brezhnev's Secret Pledge to 'Do Everything We Can' to Reelect Gerald Ford," *The Atlantic*, July 26, 2017.

8. Gerald R. Ford, *A Time to Heal* (New York: Harper and Row, 1979), 274–75.

9. Ford, *A Time to Heal*, xvii.

10. Peter Rodman, *Presidential Command: Power, Leadership and the Making of Foreign Policy from Richard Nixon to George W. Bush* (New York: Knopf, 2009), 107–8.

11. I am indebted to my colleague Roger Porter for this insight.

12. Douglas Brinkley, "The Rising Stock of Jimmy Carter," *Diplomatic History* 20, no. 4 (Fall 1996), 526.

13. Greenstein, *The Presidential Difference*, 141.

14. Eizenstat, *President Carter*, 2.

15. Julian E. Zelizer, *Jimmy Carter* (New York: Henry Holt, 2010), 147.

16. Eizenstat, *President Carter*, 2. See also Lamb, *The Presidents*, where the 2017 C-SPAN poll ranked him #26.

17. Erwin Hargrove, "Jimmy Carter: The Politics of Public Goods," in *Leadership in the Modern Presidency*, ed. Greenstein, 233.

18. Jimmy Carter, *Keeping Faith* (New York: Bantam Books, 1982), 65.

19. Betty Glad, *An Outsider in the White House: Jimmy Carter, His Advisors, and the Making of American Foreign Policy* (Ithaca, NY: Cornell University Press, 2009), 285–86.

20. Hendrik Hertzberg, "Jimmy Carter," in *Character Above All*, ed. Robert A. Wilson (New York: Simon & Schuster, 1995), 189.

21. Robert D. Kaplan, "The Statesman: In Defense of Henry Kissinger," *The Atlantic*, May 2013, 78.

22. Eizenstat, *President Carter*, 555–74.

23. Carter, *Keeping Faith*, 245.

24. Joseph S. Nye, "Maintaining a Nonproliferation Regime," *International Organization* 35, no. 1 (Winter 1981), 15–38.

25. Eizenstat, *President Carter*, 587–88.

26. Hargrove, "Jimmy Carter," 235, 249.

27. Brinkley, "The Rising Stock of Jimmy Carter," 522.

28. Robert A. Pastor, "Review of Betty Glad," *H-Diplo Roundtable Review* XII, no. 6 (2011), 20.

29. Zbigniew Brzezinski, *Power and Principle: Memoirs of the National Security Advisor, 1977–81* (New York: FSG, 1983), 321.

30. Walter Russell Mead, "The Carter Syndrome," *Foreign Policy*, January–February 2010.

31. Justin Vaisse, "Thank You, Jimmy Carter: Restoring the Reputation of America's Most Underrated Foreign-Policy President," *Foreign Policy*, July 2018, 17.

32. Brzezinski, *Power and Principle*, 522, 397.

33. Cyrus Vance, *Hard Choices: Critical Years in America's Foreign Policy* (New York: Simon & Schuster, 1982), 346.

34. Brzezinski, *Power and Principle*, 473.

35. Erwin C. Hargrove, *Jimmy Carter as President: Leadership and the Politics of the Public Good* (Baton Rouge: Louisiana State University Press, 1988), 181.

36. Hargrove, *Jimmy Carter as President*, 245.

37. Bernard Williams, *Moral Luck* (Cambridge: Cambridge University Press, 1981).

38. Strong, "Review of Betty Glad," *H-Diplo*, 24.

Chapter 6

1. Quoted in Stephen Sestanovich, "Gorbachev's Foreign Policy: A Diplomacy of Decline," *Problems of Communism* (January–February 1988), 2.

2. Paul Kennedy, *The Rise and Fall of the Great Powers: Economic Change and Military Conflict from 1500 to 2000* (New York: Random House, 1987), 515.

3. Greenstein, *The Presidential Difference*, 149.

4. "The Man Who Beat Communism" and "The Reagan Legacy," *The Economist*, June 24, 2004, 13, 24, 25.

5. Gergen, *Eyewitness to Power*, 153.

6. Quoted in Henry Nau, "Ronald Reagan," in *U.S. Foreign Policy and Democracy Promotion*, ed. Cox, Lynch, and Bouchet, 140.

7. Gergen, *Eyewitness to Power*, 208.

8. "The Reagan Legacy."

9. Gergen, *Eyewitness to Power*, 187.

10. As his notes and correspondence show, Reagan was not bereft of foreign policy ideas, but various participants in his administration have confirmed that he was often weak on their operational implications. See Kiron Skinner, Annelise Anders, and Martin Anderson, eds., *Reagan: A Life in Letters* (New York: Free Press, 2003).

11. David Abshire, *Saving the Reagan Presidency: Trust Is the Coin of the Realm* (College Station: Texas A&M Press, 2005).

12. Jack Matlock, *Reagan and Gorbachev: How the Cold War Ended* (New York: Random House, 2004), 5.

13. Gergen, *Eyewitness to Power*, 204–5.

14. Melvyn P. Leffler, "Ronald Reagan and the Cold War: What Mattered Most?" *Texas National Security Review,* May 2018, 85.

15. Leffler, "Ronald Reagan and the Cold War," 88.

16. Scott Sagan, *The Limits of Safety: Organizations, Accidents, and Nuclear Weapons* (Princeton, NJ: Princeton University Press, 1993).

17. Jon Meacham, *Destiny and Power: The American Odyssey of George Herbert Walker Bush* (New York: Random House, 2015), 392.

18. Mary E. Sarotte, "A Broken Promise?" *Foreign Affairs* 93 (September/October 2014).

19. Mary E. Sarotte, "In Victory, Magnanimity: US Foreign Policy, 1989–91, and the Legacy of Prefabricated Multilateralism," *International Politics* 48, no. 4/5 (2011), 494. See also her book *1989: The Struggle to Create Post–Cold War Europe* (Princeton, NJ: Princeton University Press, 2009).

20. Zbigniew Brzezinski, *Second Chance: Three Presidents and the Crisis of American Superpower* (New York: Basic Books, 2007).

21. Philip Zelikow and Condoleezza Rice, *Germany Unified and Europe Transformed: A Study in Statecraft* (Cambridge, MA: Harvard University Press, 1997), 21.

22. Nicholas Burns, "Our Best Foreign Policy President," *Boston Globe*, December 9, 2011.

23. George Bush and Brent Scowcroft, *A World Transformed* (New York: Vintage Books, 1998), xiii–xiv.

24. Zelikow and Rice, *Germany Unified and Europe Transformed*, 29.

25. Zelikow and Rice, *Germany Unified and Europe Transformed*, 95, 105.

26. Hal Brands, "Choosing Primacy: US Strategy and Global Order at the Dawn of the Post–Cold War Era," *Texas National Security Review* 1, no. 2 (March 2018), 8–33.

27. Meacham, *Destiny and Power*, 529.

Chapter 7

1. Charles Krauthammer, "The Unipolar Moment," *Washington Post*, July 20, 1990.

2. Mearsheimer, *The Great Delusion*, 6.

3. Quoted in Greenstein, *The Presidential Difference*, 175.

4. Greenstein, *The Presidential Difference*, 174.

5. Gergen, *Eyewitness to Power*, 251.

6. Susan Page, "The Clinton Tapes: Revealing History," *USA Today*, September 21, 2009, 1.

7. Kellerman, *Bad Leadership*, chapter 9.

8. Colin Powell, *My American Journey* (New York: Ballantine Books, 1996), 576.

9. Hal Brands, "Choosing Primacy: US Strategy and Global Order at the Dawn of the Post–Cold War Era," *Texas National Security Review* 1 (March 2018), 29.

10. The White House, "A National Security Strategy of Engagement and Enlargement," Washington, DC, February 1995. The personalities and politics behind this strategy are described well in George Packer, *Our Man: Richard Holbrooke and the End of the American Century.*(New York: PenguinRandom House, 2019).

11. James D. Boys, *Clinton's Grand Strategy* (London: Bloomsbury, 2015), 252.

12. Michael Green, *By More than Providence: Grand Strategy and American Power in the Asia Pacific Since 1783* (New York: Columbia University Press, 2017), 468–73.

13. Brzezinski, *Second Chance*, chapter 4. See also James Goldgeier, "Bill and Boris: A Window Into a Most Important Post–Cold War Relationship," *Texas National Security Review*, 1, no. 4 (August 2018), 43–54.

14. Robert Hunter, "Presidential Leadership: Bill Clinton and NATO Enlargement," in *Triumphs and Tragedies of the Modern Presidency: Seventy-Six Case Studies in Presidential Leadership*, ed. David Abshire (Westport, CT: Praeger, 2001).

15. Personal communication with former White House official, January 2019.

16. John Mearsheimer, "Back to the Future: Instability in Europe After the Cold War," *International Security* 15, no. 1 (Summer 1990), 5–56.

17. William Burns, *The Back Channel: A Memoir of American Diplomacy and the Case for Its Renewal* (New York: Random House, 2019), 110–11.

18. John Harris, *The Survivor: Bill Clinton in the White House* (New York: Random House, 2005), 402.

19. Robert Draper, *Dead Certain: The Presidency of George W. Bush* (New York: Free Press, 2007), 110.

20. Jon Meacham, *Destiny and Power: The American Odyssey of George Herbert Walker Bush* (New York: Random House, 2015), 567–68.

21. Greenstein, *The Presidential Difference,* 196.

22. Draper, *Dead Certain,* 39.

23. Blair quoted in Stephen F. Knott, *Rush to Judgment: George W. Bush, The War on Terror, and His Critics* (Lawrence: University of Kansas Press, 2012), 164.

24. George W. Bush, *Decision Points* (New York: Crown, 2010), 368.

25. Stephen Benedict Dyson, "George W. Bush, the Surge, and Presidential Leadership," *Political Science Quarterly* 125, no. 4 (2010–11), 559.

26. Meacham, *Destiny and Power,* 589.

27. Condoleezza Rice, *No Higher Honor: A Memoir of My Years in Washington* (New York: Crown, 2012), 22.

28. Melvyn P. Leffler, "The Foreign Policies of the George W. Bush Administration: Memoirs, History, Legacy," *Diplomatic History* 37 (June 2013), 24, 25.

29. Greenstein, *The Presidential Difference,* 203.

30. James Mann, "The Dick Cheney of 'Vice' Just Craves Power. The Reality Is Worse," *Washington Post,* January 2, 2019.

31. William Burns, *The Back Channel,* 172.

32. Bush quoted in Bob Woodward, *Bush at War* (New York: Simon & Schuster, 2002), 341.

33. "Iraq's Grim Lessons," *The Economist*, July 9, 2016, 48.
34. Linda Bilmes, "The Ghost Budget," *Boston Globe*, October 11, 2018, A10.
35. Leffler, "The Foreign Policies of the George W. Bush Administration," 24, 19.
36. Guy Dinmore, "US Right Questions Wisdom of Bush's Democracy Policy," *Financial Times*, May 30, 2006, 8.
37. Bush, *Decision Points*, 397.
38. Brent Scowcroft, personal conversation, May 2003 (MD: & .
39. David Rothkopf, *Running the World: The Inside Story of the National Security Council and the Architects of American Power* (New York: Public Affairs, 2005), 33.
40. Personal conversation with Bob Woodward, August 2005.
41. Hal Brands and Peter Feaver, "The Case for Bush Revisionism: Reevaluating the Legacy of America's 43rd President," *Journal of Strategic Studies* (July 2017), 30.
42. Richard Haass, *War of Necessity, War of Choice: A Memoir of Two Iraq Wars* (New York: Simon & Schuster, 2009).
43. Brands and Feaver, "The Case for Bush Revisionism," 14.
44. Leffler, "The Foreign Policies of the George W. Bush Administration," 11, 14.
45. Brands and Feaver, "The Case for Bush Revisionism," 14.
46. Brands and Feaver, "The Case for Bush Revisionism," 13.
47. Personal communication, former Foreign Service officer, January 2019.
48. Michael Mazarr et al., *Understanding the Emerging Era of International Competition* (Santa Monica, CA: RAND Corporation, 2018), 18.
49. Brands, "Choosing Primacy," 30.

Chapter 8

1. For a detailed description, see J. S. Nye, *The Future of Power* (New York: Public Affairs, 2011).
2. Linda Bilmes and Joseph Stiglitz, *The Three Trillion Dollar War: The True Cost of the Iraq Conflict* (New York: Norton, 2008), ix.
3. Peter Baker, "From Two Formers, a Shared Lament for a Lost Consensus," *New York Times*, November 29, 2018.
4. Michiko Kakutani, "For the White House's New Generation, It's a Different World," *New York Times*, July 10, 2012.
5. David E. Sanger, *Confront and Conceal: Obama's Secret Wars and Surprising Use of American Power* (New York: Crown, 2012), 101.
6. Robert M. Gates, *Duty: Memoirs of a Secretary at War* (New York: Knopf, 2014), 298.
7. Martin S. Indyk, Kenneth G. Lieberthal, and Michael E. O'Hanlon, *Bending History: Barack Obama's Foreign Policy* (Washington: Brookings Institution Press, 2012), 6.
8. Rhodes, *The World as It Is*, 81.
9. See Fred Hiatt, "Why Freedom Is Low on Obama's Agenda," *Washington Post*, April 9, 2012. Obama quoted in Jeremi Suri, "Liberal Internationalism, Law, and the First African American President," in *The Presidency of Barack Obama*, ed. Jullian E. Zelizner (Princeton, NJ: Princeton University Press, 2018), 196.
10. Indyk et at., *Bending History*, 1.
11. Indyk et al., *Bending History*, 21.

12. James Mann quoted in Kakutani, "For the White House's New Generation."
13. Joe Klein, "Deep Inside the White House," *New York Times Book Review*, June 24, 2018, 9.
14. "Gaffes and Choices," *The Economist*, August 4, 2012, 11; David Brooks, "Where Obama Shines," *New York Times*, July 29, 2012.
15. James Fallows, "Obama, Explained," *The Atlantic*, March 2012.
16. "Barack Obama," *The Economist*, December 24, 2016, 60.
17. This is the argument of James Mann in *The Obamians: The Struggle Inside the White House to Redefine American Power* (New York: Viking, 2012).
18. Sanger, *Confront and Conceal*, 421.
19. James Goldgeier and Jeremi Suri, "Revitalizing the National Security Strategy," *Washington Quarterly* (Winter 2016), 38.
20. Gideon Rachman, "Staying Out of Syria Is the Bolder Call for Obama," *Financial Times*, May 14, 2013.
21. Jeffrey Goldberg, "The Lessons of Henry Kissinger," *The Atlantic*, December 2016, 53.
22. I am indebted to Jake Sullivan for this description.
23. Hiatt, "Why Freedom Is Low on Obama's Agenda."
24. Rhodes, *The World as It Is*, 49.
25. Carol E. Lee, "Obama Resets Military Policy," *Wall Street Journal*, May 29, 2014, 8.
26. Rhodes, *The World as It Is*, 200.
27. Suri, "Liberal Internationalism, Law, and the First African American President," 209.
28. Jo Becker and Scott Shane, "Secret 'Kill List' Proves a Test of President's Principles and Will," *New York Times International*, May 29, 2012, A11. Also based on conversations with administration officials in 2019. On Afghanistan and Obama's rejection of the Vietnam analogy, see George Packer, *Our Man*.
29. "A Dangerous Modesty," *The Economist*, June 6, 2015, 16. I am indebted to Susan Rice for help on this point.
30. Rhodes, *The World as It Is*, 339.
31. Personal discussions with former officials, Autumn 2018.
32. Burns, *The Back Channel*, 335.
33. Jeffrey Goldberg, "The Obama Doctrine," *The Atlantic*, April 2016, 89.
34. See Kurt Campbell and Ely Ratner, "The China Reckoning: How Beijing Defied American Expectations," *Foreign Affairs* 97 (March/April 2018).
35. Hal Brands, "Barack Obama and the Dilemmas of American Grand Strategy," *Washington Quarterly* 39, no. 4 (Winter 2017), 101.
36. Burns, *The Back Channel*, 292.
37. Rhodes, *The World as It Is*, 277–78.
38. Kathryn Olmsted, "Terror Tuesdays: How Obama Refined Bush's Counterterrorism Policies," in Julian Zelizer, ed., *The Presidency of Barack Obama: A First Historical Assessment* (Princeton, NJ: Princeton University Press, 2018), 212–26.
39. P. W. Singer and Emerson Brooking, *Like War: The Weaponization of Social Media* (New York: Houghton Mifflin Harcourt, 2018), 49.
40. Bob Woodward, *Fear: Trump in the White House* (New York: Simon & Schuster, 2018), 205.

41. Personal conversation, March 24, 2018, Singapore.
42. Donald J. Trump with Tony Schwartz, *The Art of the Deal* (New York: Ballantine, 1987).
43. Personal conversation with White House official, November 2018.
44. *The Economist*, December 23, 2017, 12.
45. Dan Balz, "Trump's Foreign Policy Views: A Sharp Departure From GOP Orthodoxy," *Washington Post*, March 21, 2016.
46. Trump's Inaugural Address, *New York Times*, January 21, 2017, A16.
47. Douglas Lute and Nicholas Burns, "NATO's Biggest Problem Is President Trump," *Washington Post*, April 2, 2019.
48. David Sanger and William Broad, "A Russian Threat on Two Fronts Meets a US Strategic Void," *New York Times*, March 6, 2018, A10.
49. "Defending America, Donald Trump's Way," *The Economist*, December 23, 2017, 12.
50. Personal conversation, Washington, DC, April 2019.
51. Thomas Donnelly and William Kristol, "The Obama-Trump Foreign Policy," *The Weekly Standard*, February 19, 2018, 24.
52. Tod Lindberg, "The Gap Between Tweet and Action," *Weekly Standard*, January 1, 2018, 17.
53. Portland Consultancy, *The Soft Power 30: A Global Ranking of Soft Power* (London: Portland Consultancy, 2018).
54. Glenn Thrush, "China's Weight Fuels Reversal by Trump on Foreign Aid," *New York Times*, October 15, 2018.
55. Stewart Patrick, quoted in Declan Walsh, "In US Embrace, Autocrats Steamroll Their Opposition," *New York Times*, February 2, 2018, A1.
56. Tamara Cofman Wittes quoted in Peter Baker, "Bottom Line Steers Trump With Saudis," *New York Times*, October 15, 2018.
57. Gideon Rachman, "Truth, Lies and the Trump Administration," *Financial Times*, January 24, 2017.
58. Randall Schweller, "Three Cheers for Trump's Foreign Policy," *Foreign Affairs* 97 (September/October 2018), 135.
59. Niall Ferguson, "We'd Better Get Used to Emperor Donaldus Trump," *Sunday Times*, June 10, 2018, 23.
60. John Hannah, "Trump's Foreign Policy Is a Work in Progress," *Foreign Policy*, February 14, 2019.
61. Robert Blackwill, *Trump's Foreign Policies Are Better Than They Seem* (New York: Council on Foreign Relations Special Report No. 84, April 2019), 67.
62. Stephen Moore, Arthur B. Laffer, and Steve Forbes, "How Trump Could Be Like Reagan," *New York Times*, August 1, 2018.
63. "Trump Says He Tries to Tell the Truth Whenever Possible," *Boston Globe*, November 2, 2018, A6. See also Glenn Kessler , Salvador Rizzo and Meg Kelly, "President Trump has made more than 10,000 false or misleading claims," *Washington Post*, April 29, 2019.
64. "Statement by Former National Security Officials," letter in the *Washington Post*, August 8, 2016.
65. Tony Schwartz, "I Wrote 'The Art of the Deal' With Trump. His Self-Sabotage Is Rooted in His Past," *Washington Post*, May 16, 2017.

66. Trump, *The Art of the Deal*, 70–71.
67. Bob Woodward, *Fear*, 175.
68. Peter Baker, "Was Obama Set to Bomb North Korea? Never, Allies Say," *New York Times*, February 17, 2019, A20.
69. Robert Blackwill, *Trump's Foreign Policies Are Better Than They Seem*, 65.
70. Paul Krugman, "A Ranting Old Guy With Nukes," *New York Times*, March 6, 2018, A25.
71. Bret Stephens, "The Trump Presidency: No Guardrails," *New York Times*, July 29, 2017, A25.
72. Woodward, *Fear*, 193.
73. Blackwill, *Trump's Foreign Policies*, 67.
74. Daalder and Lindsay, *Empty Throne*, 160.

Chapter 9

1. Henry Kissinger, *World Order* (New York: Penguin, 2014).
2. Page and Bouton, *The Foreign Policy Disconnect*.
3. Michael McFaul, *Advancing Democracy Abroad: Why We Should and How We Can* (Stanford, CA: Hoover Institution, 2010), 160.
4. Sullivan, "What Donald Trump and Dick Cheney Got Wrong About America."
5. Gardiner Harris, " Pompeo Questions the Value of International Groups Like UN and EU," *New York Times*, December 4, 2018.
6. Allen Buchanan and Robert O. Keohane, "The Legitimacy of Global Governance Institutions," 405.
7. Sestanovich, *Maximalist*.
8. Rhodes, *The World as It Is*, 276.
9. Lindsey A. O'Rourke, *Covert Regime Change: America's Secret Cold War* (Ithaca, NY: Cornell University Press, 2018), 225, 226, 236.
10. Graham Allison, *Destined for War*. Michael Beckley challenges this analysis and argues that power transition theory is littered with false positives and false negatives. "The Power of Nations: Measuring What Matters," *International Security* 43, no. 2 (Fall 2018), 42–43. Kori Schake argues that there has been only one successful peaceful transition. *Safe Passage: The Transition from British to American Hegemony*. Cambridge, MA: Harvard University Press, 2017.
11. Martin Wolfe, "The Long and Painful Journey to World Disorder," *Financial Times*, January 5, 2017. See also, Fareed Zakaria, "The Self-Destruction of American Power," *Foreign Affairs* 92 (July/August) 2019, 10-16.
12. Robert Blackwill, *Trump's Foreign Policies Are Better Than They Seem*, 9–10.
13. See Joshua Shifrinson, *Rising Titans: Falling Giants* (Ithaca, NY: Cornell University Press, 2018).
14. Barry Posen, "Command of the Commons," *International Security* 28, no. 1 (Summer 2003), 5–46.
15. "World GDP Ranking 2016," *Knoema*, April 10, 2017, ranks China first if purchasing power parity is used.
16. Beckley, 22.
17. Lawrence H. Summers, "Can Anything Hold Back China's Economy?" *Financial Times*, December 3, 2018.

18. Terrence Kelly, David Gompert, and Duncan Long, *Smarter Power, Stronger Partners, Vol. I: Exploiting US Advantages to Prevent Aggression* (Santa Monica, CA: RAND Corporation, 2016).

19. Portland Consultancy, *The Soft Power 30*.

20. Kai-Fu Lee, *AI Superpowers: China, Silicon Valley, and the New World Order* (Boston: Houghton Mifflin, 2018), 83.

21. Meghan O'Sullivan, *Windfall: How the New Energy Abundance Upends Global Politics and Strengthens America's Power* (New York: Simon & Schuster, 2017).

22. Adele Hayutin, *Global Workforce Change: Demographics Behind the Headlines* (Stanford, CA: Hoover Institution, 2018). See also Nicholas Eberstadt, "With Great Demographics Comes Great Power," *Foreign Affairs* 98 (July/August) 2019, 149.

23. Lee, *AI Superpowers.*

24. John Deutch, "Assessing and Responding to China's Innovation Initiative," in *Maintaining America's Edge*, ed. Leah Bitounis and Jonathon Price (Washington: Aspen Institute, 2019), 163.

25. Conversation with Lee Kuan Yew, Singapore, September 22, 2012. See also Nye, *Is the American Century Over?*, 77.

26. Ceri Parker, "China's Xi Jinping Defends Globalization From the Davos Stage," *World Economic Forum,* January 27, 2017; "Statement by Wang Yi," filmed February 17, 2017, Munich Security Conference, 23:41. See also G. John Ikenberry and Shiping Tang, "Roundtable: Rising Powers and the International Order," *Ethics and International Affairs,* 32 (Spring 2018) ,15-44.

27. Michael Mazarr, Timothy Heath, and Astrid Cevallos, *China and the International Order* (Santa Monica, CA: RAND Corporation, 2018), 4.

28. See Bobo Lo, *A Wary Embrace: What the Russia–China Relationship Means for the World* (Docklands, VIC: Penguin Random House Australia, 2017).

29. Larry Diamond and Orville Schell, *Chinese Influence and American Interests: Promoting Constructive Vigilance* (Stanford, CA: Hoover Institution Press, 2018).

30. Bill Emmott, *Rivals: How the Power Struggle Between China, India and Japan Will Shape Our Next Decade* (New York: Houghton Mifflin Harcourt, 2008).

31. Yan Xuetong, "The Age of Uneasy Peace," *Foreign Affairs* 98 (January/February 2019), 46.

32. Orville Schell and Susan L. Shirk, chairs, *Course Correction: Toward an Effective and Sustainable China Policy* (New York, Asia Society Task Force, February 2019).

33. Randall Schweller, "Entropy and the Trajectory of World Politics: Why Polarity Has Become Less Meaningful," *Cambridge Review of International Affairs* 23, no. 1 (March 2010).

34. For more detail, see my "Nuclear Lessons for Cyber Security," *Strategic Studies Quarterly* 5 (Winter 2011), 18.

35. See David Sanger, *The Perfect Weapon: War, Sabotage and Fear in the Cyber Age* (New York: Penguin Random House, 2018). See also P. W. Singer and Emerson Brooking, *Like War: The Weaponization of Social Media* (Boston: Houghton Mifflin, 2018).

36. William J. Clinton, "Remarks at the Paul H. Nitze School," The American Presidency Project, March 8, 2000, http://www.presidency.ucsb.edu/ws/index.php?pid=87714.

37. See Charles Cleveland, Ryan Crocker, Daniel Egel, Andrew Liepman, and David Maxwell, "An American Way of Political Warfare: A Proposal," in Perspective (Santa Monica, CA: RAND Corporation, 2018).

38. Joseph Nye, "Normative Restraints on Cyber Conflict," Cyber Security: A Peer-Reviewed Journal 1, no. 4 (2018), 331–42.

39. See Nye, "Normative Restraints on Cyber Conflict."

40. Peter Baker, "In Shift on Terror Policy, Obama Took a Long Path," New York Times, May 28, 2013, A1.

41. Richard Danzig, "Technology Roulette," in Bitounis and Price, Maintaining America's Edge, 2019.

42. Adam Tooze, "The Forgotten History of the Financial Crisis," Foreign Affairs 97 (September/October 2018), 208.

43. Nye, Is the American Century Over?.

44. Madeleine Albright, Fascism: A Warning (New York: HarperCollins, 2018), 223.

45. Ronald Inglehart and Pippa Norris, "Trump, Brexit, and the Rise of Populism: Economic Have-Nots and Cultural Backlash," Harvard Kennedy School, Faculty Research Working Paper Series, 2016.

46. Alan I. Abramowitz, The Great Alignment (New Haven, CT: Yale University Press, 2018), 153.

47. Jeff Colgan and Robert Keohane, "The Liberal Order Is Rigged," Foreign Affairs 96 (May/June 2017); Dani Rodrik, Straight Talk on Trade: Ideas for a Sane World Economy (Princeton, NJ: Princeton University Press, 2018).

48. "U.S. Public Has Mixed Views of Immigrants and Immigration," Pew Research Center, September 28, 2015, chapter 4; "Most Say Illegal Immigrants Should Be Allowed to Stay, But Citizenship Is More Divisive," Pew Research Center, March 28, 2013.

49. Dina Smeltz, Craig Kafura, and Lily Wojtowicz, "Actually, Americans Like Free Trade," Chicago Council on Global Affairs, September 7, 2016.

50. Bowles, Nixon's Business, 179.

51. Sullivan, "What Donald Trump and Dick Cheney Got Wrong About America."

52. "Present at the Destruction," The Economist, June 9, 2018, 21.

53. Stephen Brooks and William Wohlforth, America Abroad: The United States' Global Role in the 21st Century (Oxford: Oxford University Press, 2016), ix.

54. Sestanovich, Maximalist.

55. Yuval Noah Harari, "Moving Beyond Nationalism," The Economist, The World in 2019, 92.

INDEX

For the benefit of digital users, indexed terms that span two pages (e.g., 52–53) may, on occasion, appear on only one of those pages.

Note: Tables are indicated by *t* following the page number